MANAGEMENT ACCOUNTING: DECISION AND CONTROL

STUDY TEXT

Qualifications and Credit Framework

AQ2016

The material in this book may support study for the following AAT qualifications:

AAT Professional Diploma in Accounting – Level 4

AAT Diploma in Business Skills

AAT Professional Diploma in Accounting at SCQF – Level 8

British Library Cataloguing-in-Publication Data

A catalogue record for this book is available from the British Library.

Published by
Kaplan Publishing UK
Unit 2, The Business Centre
Molly Millars Lane
Wokingham
Berkshire
RG41 2QZ

ISBN: 978-1-78740-272-0

CONTENTS

Page number

Introduction	P.5
Unit guide	P.7
The assessment	P.20
Unit link to the synoptic assessment	P.21
Study skills	P.22

STUDY TEXT

Chapter

1	Standard costing	1
2	Collection of cost information	13
3	Accounting for overheads	49
4	Breakeven analysis	101
5	Decision making techniques	125
6	Life cycle costing	149
7	Target costing	183
8	Trend analysis	191
9	Linear regression	213
10	Index numbers	219
11	Cost variance analysis	233
12	Fixed overhead variances	273
13	Operating statements and backwards variances	299
14	Nature of variances	315
15	Interpreting variances	321
16	Performance indicators	367
17	Ethics	485
Mock Assessment Questions		499
Mock Assessment Answers		513
Glossary		523
Index		I.1

INTRODUCTION

HOW TO USE THESE MATERIALS

These Kaplan Publishing learning materials have been carefully designed to make your learning experience as easy as possible and to give you the best chance of success in your AAT assessments.

They contain a number of features to help you in the study process.

The sections on the Unit Guide, the Assessment and Study Skills should be read before you commence your studies.

They are designed to familiarise you with the nature and content of the assessment and to give you tips on how best to approach your studies.

STUDY TEXT

This study text has been specially prepared for the revised AAT qualification introduced in September 2016.

It is written in a practical and interactive style:

- key terms and concepts are clearly defined

- all topics are illustrated with practical examples with clearly worked solutions based on sample tasks provided by the AAT in the new examining style

- frequent activities throughout the chapters ensure that what you have learnt is regularly reinforced

- 'pitfalls' and 'examination tips' help you avoid commonly made mistakes and help you focus on what is required to perform well in your examination

- 'Test your understanding' activities are included within each chapter to apply your learning and develop your understanding.

ICONS

The study chapters include the following icons throughout.

They are designed to assist you in your studies by identifying key definitions and the points at which you can test yourself on the knowledge gained.

 Definition

These sections explain important areas of knowledge which must be understood and reproduced in an assessment.

 Example

The illustrative examples can be used to help develop an understanding of topics before attempting the activity exercises.

 Test your understanding

These are exercises which give the opportunity to assess your understanding of all the assessment areas.

Quality and accuracy are of the utmost importance to us so if you spot an error in any of our products, please send an email to mykaplanreporting@kaplan.com with full details.

Our Quality Co-ordinator will work with our technical team to verify the error and take action to ensure it is corrected in future editions.

UNIT GUIDE

Introduction

This unit is one of the mandatory Professional level units. It takes students from Advanced level costing principles and prepares them to be valuable members of a management accounting finance team. This unit was formerly known as Financial Performance.

A student who has successfully completed this unit, together with the Professional level unit, Management Accounting: Budgeting, should be a useful member of a management accounting team. Working with little supervision, the student could be expected to liaise with key business unit managers and/or budget holders in order to: prepare a basic budget and/or standard cost budget; create budgetary reports, control reports and standard costing control reports; and prepare key performance indicators and workings to aid management decision making.

This unit teaches students management accounting principles and concepts. Students will understand the nature and importance of different concepts such as cost behaviour, cost analysis, standard costing and contribution theory. They will know when each technique should be used to aid the planning and decision making of an organisation and the subsequent analysis for control purposes.

They will learn the key performance indicators that should be used to aid the performance monitoring of an organisation and the techniques for assessing changes to an organisation (what-if analysis). The student will build a toolbox of techniques, understand the nature of these techniques and know when each technique should be used.

Management Accounting: Decision and Control is a mandatory unit and builds on the fundamental concepts and techniques introduced in Foundation level Elements of Costing and Advanced level Management Accounting: Costing.

Learning outcomes

On completion of this unit the learner will be able to

- Analyse a range of costing techniques to support the management accounting function of an organisation

- Calculate and use standard costing to improve performance

- Demonstrate a range of statistical techniques to analyse business information

- Use appropriate financial and non-financial performance techniques to aid decision making

- Evaluate a range of cost management techniques to enhance value and aid decision making.

Scope of content

To perform this unit effectively you will need to know and understand the following:

Chapter

1   **Analyse a range of costing techniques to support the management accounting function of an organisation**

1.1   **Distinguish between different cost classifications and evaluate their use in a management accounting function**

Students need to know:

- product costing and the elements of direct and indirect costs, cost classification into materials, labour and production overhead

- cost classification by behaviour (fixed, variable, stepped fixed and semi-variable) and the relevant range for fixed costs   2

- prime cost, full production cost and marginal cost

- the differences between cost centres, profit centres and investment centres

- the High-Low method of cost estimation.

Students for semi-variable costs need to be able to:

- use the high-low method to extract the fixed and variable elements, including making adjustments for a step up in cost or a quantity discount.

Chapter

1.2   Discriminate between and use marginal costing and absorption costing techniques

Students need to know:

- the difference between marginal costing and absorption costing, and how to critically evaluate the differences between the two methodologies   3

- how to reconcile a marginal costing profit with an absorption costing profit for changes in inventory to demonstrate the differences in the two methodologies.

1.3   Recognise and calculate measures of profitability and contribution

Students need to know:

- the difference between contribution and profit   3
- the contribution per unit and per £ of turnover   4
- when to use contribution analysis as a decision-making tool   4
- the break-even point and margin of safety   4
- the optimal production mix when labour, materials or machine hours are restricted and opportunity costs of limited resources   5
- the outcomes of the various decision-making tools to aid the decision-making process.   5

KAPLAN PUBLISHING

Chapter

2   Calculate and use standard costing to improve performance

2.1   Discuss how standard costing can aid the planning and control of an organisation

Students need to know:

- how standard costs can be established and revised   1

- the different types of standard (ideal, target, normal and basic)   1

- how the type of standard can affect behaviour and variances   1

- how the type of standard can impact on variance   15

- flexible budgeting and how the calculation of the standard cost budget is affected by changes in output.   2

2.2   Calculate standard costing information

Student need to be able to:

- prepare standard cost card from given information   1

- extract information contained in a budgetary control report.   2

2.3   Calculate standard costing information

Students need to be able to calculate:

- raw material variances (total raw material, price and usage)   11

- labour variances (total, rate, idle time and efficiency)   11

- the variable overhead variances (total, rate and efficiency)   11

- the fixed production variances (total, expenditure, volume, capacity and efficiency)   12

- actual and standard costs derived from variances (backward variances).   13

Chapter

2.4 Prepare and reconcile standard costing operating statements

Students need to be able to:

• prepare a standard costing operating statement reconciling budgeted cost with actual cost of actual production	13
• explain the differences between marginal costing and absorption costing operating statements	13
• reconcile the difference between the operating statement under marginal costing and absorption costing.	13

2.5 Analyse and present effectively a report to management based on standard costing information

Students need to know

• how variances may interrelate.	11/12/15

Students need to be able to:

• identify the nature of variances	14
• identify what causes standard costing variances such as wastage, economies of scale, learning effect, inflation and skills mix	11/12/15
• identify possible action that can be taken to reduce adverse variances and increase favourable variances	15
• identify elements of a variance that are controllable and non-controllable	14
• effectively communicate what the standard costing variance means in report format.	15

Chapter

3	**Demonstrate a range of statistical techniques to analyse business information**	
3.1	**Calculate key statistical indicators**	
	Students need to be able to:	
	• calculate	
	– index numbers	10
	– Time series analysis – moving averages, seasonal variations and trend information	8
	• use the regression equation	9
	• calculate the outputs from various statistical calculations.	8/9/10
3.2	**Use and appraise key statistical indicators**	
	Students need to know:	
	• the key statistical indicators to forecast income and costs and recommend actions	8/9/10
	• the reasons for their recommendations	8/9/10
	• the key variations (seasonal, cyclical and random).	8
4	**Use appropriate financial and non-financial performance techniques to aid decision making**	
4.1	**Identify and calculate key financial and non-financial performance indicators**	
	Students need to be able to:	
	• identify a range of and select key performance indicators	16
	• calculate a range of key performance indicators and manipulate them.	

Chapter

4.2 Evaluate key financial and non-financial performance indicators

Students need to know:

• what the performance indicator means	16
• how the various elements of the indicator affect its calculation	16
• the impact of various factors on performance indicators including learning effect and economies of scale	16
• how some performance indicators interrelate with each other	16
• how proposed actions may affect the indicator	16
• what actions could be taken to improve the indicator	16
• how lack of goal congruence can affect the overall business objectives when managers are attempting to maximise a given indicator	16
• how ethical and commercial considerations can affect the behaviour of managers aiming to achieve a target indicator.	17

The following is a list of the type of performance indicators students might be asked to calculate   16

- Financial (profitability, liquidity, efficiency and gearing)

- Gross profit margin, = gross profit/sales revenue × 100%

- Profit margin = profit/sales revenue × 100%

- Administration costs as a percentage of revenue, any cost as a percentage of revenue = cost/sales revenue × 100%

- Current ratio = current assets/current liabilities

- This can be expressed as a number only or as a number: 1, for example if current assets are £10,000 and current liabilities are £8,000 the ratio is 1.25 or 1.25:1. In questions students should just use 1.25 as their answer

- Quick ratio = (current assets less inventory)/ current liabilities and again should be expressed as a single number in assessments

- Trade cycles (receivable days = receivables/ revenue × 365, inventory days = inventory/cost of sales × 365, payable days = payables/cost of sales × 365)

- Gearing ratio can be calculated as either total debt/(total debt plus equity) × 100% or total debt/total equity × 100%. Total debt must include both long term and short term debt. Both computer marked and human marked tasks will allow both calculations

- Value added = revenue less the cost of materials used and bought in services.

Indicators to measure efficiency and productivity   16

- Measures of efficiency include ROCE or RONA, profit margin and efficiency ratio for labour ROCE = Net income/capital employed; in tasks return will be equal to the profit in the statement of profit or loss (income statement). This ratio is always expressed as a percentage

- RONA = Net income/net assets, net income will be equal to the net profit in the statement of profit or loss (income statement). This ratio is always expressed as a percentage   16

- Productivity measures are likely to be measured in units of output, or related to output in some way. Examples include number of, say, vehicles manufactured per week, operations undertaken per day, passengers transported per month, units produced per worker per day, rooms cleaned per hour or meals served per sitting.

Indicators to measure quality of service and cost of quality

- The number of defects/units returned/warranty claims/customer complaints, the cost of inspection/ repairs/re-working

- Prevention costs, appraisal costs, internal failure costs, external failure costs.

Tasks may require the calculation of specific performance indicators. If this is the case the calculation of the indicator will either be obvious or the formula for the indicator will be provided. For example, if the task is based on a hotel, the occupancy rate calculation should be obvious given the number of rooms sold in the month divided by the total number of room nights available in the month. If the indicator is more complicated the formula will be given.

4.3 Make recommendations using decision-making technique

Students need to know:

- the optimal production mix when resources are limited and opportunity costs of limited resources — 5

- the break-even point and margin of safety — 4

- the way to analyse decisions about: make or buy, closure of a business segment, automation — 5

- the use of relevant and non-relevant costing information to aid decision making. — 5

4.4 Make recommendations and effectively communicate to management based on analysis

Students need to know:

- how analysis and calculations lead to recommendations. — 5

Students need to be able to

- use the analysis to make reasoned recommendations and communicate them effectively — 5

- identify the risks associated with a particular decision. — 5

Chapter

5 Evaluate a range of cost management techniques to enhance value and aid decision making

5.1 Use life cycle cost to aid decision making

Students need to be able to:

- identify the components of the life cycle cost of a product

- calculate the discounted and non-discounted life cycle cost of a product, machine, business unit

6

- interpret the results of calculations of life cycle costs.

5.2 Use target costing to aid decision making

Students need to know:

- analyse and evaluate target costs

- identify the components of a target cost.

7

Students need to be able to

- the concepts behind target costing, including value analysis and value engineering.

5.3 Calculate activity based costing (ABC) information

Students need to be able to:

- calculate product costs using ABC

- recognise that ABC is a refinement on absorption costing, where production costs are analysed into cost pools affected by cost drivers other than simple production volumes.

3

Students need to know:

- why products with short production runs may have a higher production overhead absorbed into each unit.

Chapter

5.4   Evaluate the commercial factors that underpin the life cycle of a product

Students need to know:

- the stages of the product life cycle

- how costs change throughout the product life cycle   6

- concepts of economies of scale, mechanisation and learning effect and how costs can switch between variable and fixed through the stages of the product life cycle.

5.5   Take account of ethical considerations throughout the decision-making process

Students need to know:

- how ethical considerations can be included throughout the life of a product

- how ethical considerations can be included in the value analysis/engineering of a product in order to promote good corporate citizenship.   17

Delivering this unit

Unit name	Content links	Suggested order of delivery
Management Accounting: Budgeting Cash and Treasury Management	To deliver this unit effectively, tutors need to have a solid understanding of the topics that make up Management Accounting: Decision and Control (formerly known as Financial Performance). This unit brings together many fundamental techniques –mathematical and management accounting.	Students may find it useful to study Management Accounting: Decision and Control and Management Accounting: Budgeting concurrently, as there are many overlapping concepts.

THE ASSESSMENT

Test specification for this unit assessment

Assessment type	Marking type	Duration of exam
Computer based unit assessment	Partially computer/ partially human marked	2 hours 30 minutes

The sample assessment for this unit consists of 8 compulsory, independent, tasks.

The competency level for AAT assessment is 70%.

Learning outcomes		Weighting
1	Analyse a range of costing techniques to support the management accounting function of an organisation	10%
2	Calculate and use standard costing to improve performance	40%
3	Demonstrate a range of statistical techniques to analyse business information	10%
4	Use appropriate financial and non-financial performance techniques to aid decision making	30%
5	Evaluate a range of cost management techniques to enhance value and aid decision making	10%
Total		**100%**

KAPLAN PUBLISHING

UNIT LINK TO SYNOPTIC ASSESSMENT

AAT AQ16 introduced a Synoptic Assessment, which students must complete if they are to achieve the appropriate qualification upon completion of a qualification. In the case of the Professional Diploma in Accounting, students must pass all of the mandatory assessments and the Synoptic Assessment to achieve the qualification.

As a Synoptic Assessment is attempted following completion of individual units, it draws upon knowledge and understanding from those units. It may be appropriate for students to retain their study materials for individual units until they have successfully completed the Synoptic Assessment for that qualification.

With specific reference to this unit, the following learning objectives are also relevant to the Professional Diploma in Accounting Synoptic Assessment.

LO1 Analyse a range of costing techniques to support the management accounting function of an organisation

LO2 Calculate and use standard costing to improve performance

LO4 Use appropriate financial and non-financial performance techniques to aid decision making

LO5 Evaluate a range of cost management techniques to enhance value and aid decision making

STUDY SKILLS

Preparing to study

Devise a study plan

Determine which times of the week you will study.

Split these times into sessions of at least one hour for study of new material. Any shorter periods could be used for revision or practice.

Put the times you plan to study onto a study plan for the weeks from now until the assessment and set yourself targets for each period of study – in your sessions make sure you cover the whole course, activities and the associated questions in the workbook at the back of the manual.

If you are studying more than one unit at a time, try to vary your subjects as this can help to keep you interested and to see the relationships between subjects.

When working through your course, compare your progress with your plan and, if necessary, re-plan your work (perhaps including extra sessions) or, if you are ahead, do some extra revision/practice questions.

Effective studying

Active reading

You are not expected to learn the text by rote, rather, you must understand what you are reading and be able to use it to pass the assessment and develop good practice.

A good technique is to use SQ3Rs – Survey, Question, Read, Recall, Review.

1   **Survey the chapter**

    Look at the headings and read the introduction, knowledge, skills and content, so as to get an overview of what the chapter deals with.

2   **Question**

    Whilst undertaking the survey ask yourself the questions you hope the chapter will answer for you.

KAPLAN PUBLISHING

3 Read

Read through the chapter thoroughly working through the activities and, at the end, making sure that you can meet the learning objectives highlighted on the first page.

4 Recall

At the end of each section and at the end of the chapter, try to recall the main ideas of the section/chapter without referring to the text. This is best done after short break of a couple of minutes after the reading stage.

5 Review

Check that your recall notes are correct.

You may also find it helpful to reread the chapter to try and see the topic(s) it deals with as a whole.

Note taking

Taking notes is a useful way of learning, but do not simply copy out the text. The notes must

- be in your own words
- be concise
- cover the key points
- well organised
- be modified as you study further chapters in this text or in related ones.

Trying to summarise a chapter without referring to the text can be a useful way of determining which areas you know and which you don't.

Three ways of taking notes

1 Summarise the key points of a chapter

2 Make linear notes

A list of headings, subdivided with sub-headings listing the key points.

If you use linear notes, you can use different colours to highlight key points and keep topic areas together.

Use plenty of space to make your notes easy to use.

3   Try a diagrammatic form

The most common of which is a mind map.

To make a mind map, put the main heading in the centre of the paper and put a circle around it.

Draw lines radiating from this to the main sub-headings which again have circles around them.

Continue the process from the sub-headings to sub-sub-headings.

Annotating the text

You may find it useful to underline or highlight key points in your study text – but do be selective.

You may also wish to make notes in the margins.

Revision phase

Kaplan has produced material specifically designed for your final examination preparation for this unit.

These include pocket revision notes and a bank of revision questions specifically in the style of the new syllabus.

Further guidance on how to approach the final stage of your studies is given in these materials.

Further reading

In addition to this text, you should also read the 'Student section' of the 'Accounting Technician' magazine every month to keep abreast of any guidance from the examiners.

TERMINOLOGY

There are different terms used to mean the same thing – you will need to be aware of both sets of terminology.

UK GAAP IAS

UK GAAP	IAS
Profit and loss	Income statement
Sales	Revenue
Balance sheet	Statement of financial position
Fixed assets	Non-current assets
Stock	Inventory
Trade debtors	Trade receivables
Trade creditors	Trade payables
Capital	Equity
Profit	Retained earnings

KAPLAN PUBLISHING

Standard costing

1

Introduction

In this chapter, we examine how standard costs are set for the various inputs that go into production. This is called 'standard costing'. In later chapters we examine how and why the actual results may vary from the standard.

ASSESSMENT CRITERIA	CONTENTS
How standard costs can be established (2.1)	1 Standard costing
The different types of standard (ideal, target, normal and basic) (2.1)	2 Methods of developing standards
How the type of standard can affect behaviour (2.1)	3 Setting standards
Prepare standard cost cards from given information (2.2)	4 Standard cost card – absorption costing
	5 Types of standard
	6 Advantages and disadvantages of standard costing

1 Standard costing

1.1 Introduction

Standard costing provides detailed information to management as to why actual performance differs from expected performance.

Standard costing systems are widely used because they provide cost data which can be used for many different purposes, including the following:

(a)   To assist in budget setting and evaluating performance.

(b)   To act as a control device by highlighting those activities that do not conform to plan and thus alerting managers to those situations which may be 'out of control' and hence in need of corrective action.

(c)   To provide a prediction of future costs to be used in decision-making.

(d)   To simplify the task of tracing costs to products for inventory valuation.

(e)   To provide a challenging target that individuals are motivated to achieve.

An effective standard costing system relies on standard cost reports, with variances clearly identified, presented in an intelligible form to management as part of the overall cost reporting cycle.

🔍 Definitions

A **standard cost** is a predetermined cost which is calculated from management's standards of efficient operation and the relevant necessary expenditure. It may be used as a basis for fixing selling prices, for valuing inventory and work in progress, and to provide control over actual costs through the process of variance analysis.

Standard costing is the preparation and use of standard costs, their comparison with actual costs, and the analysis of variances to their causes.

---

2 Methods of developing standards

2.1 The nature of standards

Whenever identical operations are performed, or identical products are manufactured time and time again, it should be possible to decide in advance not only what they are likely to cost but also what they ought to cost. In other words, it is possible to set a standard cost for each operation or product unit, taking account of:

(a) technical standards for the quantities of material to be used and the working time required

(b) cost standards for the material prices and hourly rates that should be paid.

2.2 Standards from past records

Past data can be used to predict future costs if operating conditions are fairly constant between past and future time periods. This method may not be appropriate for newly introduced operations.

The main disadvantage with this method is that past data may contain inefficiencies which would then be built into the standards.

2.3 Engineering standards

This involves engineers developing standards for materials, direct labour and variable overheads by studying the product and the production process, possibly with the help of time and motion studies. This method is particularly useful when managers are evaluating new products.

The main disadvantage is that engineering standards may be too tight as they may not allow for the behaviour of the workers.

3 Setting standards

3.1 Standard material usage

In setting material usage standards, the first stage is to define what quantity of material input is theoretically required to achieve one unit of measured output.

In most manufacturing operations the quantity or volume of product emerging will be less than the quantity of materials introduced. This type of waste is normal to most operations and the usage figure would be increased by an allowance for this normal waste.

3.2 Standard time allowed

The standard or allowed time for an operation is a realistic estimate of the amount of productive time required to perform that operation based on work study methods. It is normally expressed in standard hours.

Various allowances may be added to the theoretical operating time, to take account of operator fatigue and personal needs, and periodic activities such as machine setting, clearing up, regrinding tools and on-line quality inspection. An allowance may also be made for spoilt work, or for rectification of defects appearing in the course of processing.

3.3 Basic approach to price standards

When setting cost standards, there are two basic approaches:

(a) **To use the prices or rates which are current at the time the standards are set.**

This has the advantage that each standard is a clearly known fact. On the other hand, if prices are likely to change then the standards based on these prices will have limited value for planning purposes.

The standards would have to be revised in detail from time to time to ensure that they are up to date. If this is not done, then any differences between standard and actual costs are likely to be largely due to invalid standards.

(b) **To use a forecast of average prices or rates over the period for which the standard is to be used.**

This can postpone the need for revision, but has the disadvantages that the standard may never correspond with observed fact (so there will be a price variance on all transactions) and the forecast may be subject to significant error.

3.4 Material price standards

In setting material price standards, a particular item of material may be purchased from several suppliers at slightly different prices; which price shall be adopted as standard? There are three possible approaches:

(a) **To identify the major supplier and to use their price as the standard**

This is particularly appropriate where there is no intention of buying large quantities from the alternative suppliers, but merely to use them as a means of ensuring continuity of supply should there be any delay or failure by the principal supplier.

(b) **To use the lowest quoted price as the standard**

This method can be used if it is desirable to put pressure on the buyer to obtain price reductions from other suppliers.

(c) **To forecast the proportion of supplies to be bought from each supplier and to calculate a weighted average price as the costing standard**

This is the most satisfactory method for control purposes if the required forecast can be made with reasonable accuracy.

Another question in relation to material price standards is whether to include the cost of carriage inwards and other costs such as non-returnable packing and transit insurance.

The objective always will be to price incoming goods at their total delivered cost, so these costs should be included in the standards.

3.5 Standard labour rates

When setting standard labour rates, one can either use basic pay rates only, or incorporate overtime premiums as well. The nature of the overtime work and the approach to cost control adopted by management will decide this issue.

(a) If a normal level of overtime work can be identified and is accepted as necessary, or if overtime is planned for the company's convenience, then the relative overtime premium payments will normally be included in the standard labour rate.

(b) If it is a management objective to reduce or eliminate overtime working, the standard rate may be restricted to basic pay.

4 Standard cost card – absorption costing

A standard cost card is built up using the appropriate standards for one unit.

A simple standard cost card is as follows:

Standard cost card – absorption costing	
For one unit of output:	£
Direct material: 1.5 sq m @ £28 per sq m	42.00
Direct labour: 4 hours @ £5.25 per hour	21.00
Variable overheads: 4 hours @ £3 per hour	12.00
Fixed overheads: 4 hours @ £7 per hour	28.00
	———
Total standard cost	103.00
	———

You can see that:

(a) Standard direct material cost

  = Standard quantity of material × standard material price.

(b) Standard direct labour cost

  = Standard direct labour hours × standard labour rate.

(c) Standard variable overhead cost

  = Standard direct labour hours × standard variable overhead rate.

(d) Standard fixed overhead cost

  = Standard direct labour hours × standard fixed overhead rate.

Test your understanding 1

North manufactures a single product which has the following specification:

- Raw materials – 1 tonne @ £75 per tonne
- Direct labour – 3 hours @ £10 per hour
- Variable overheads – 3 hours @ £5 per hour
- Fixed overheads – 3 hours @ £2 per hour

Complete the standard cost card using absorption costing principles.

	Workings:	£
Raw material		
Labour		
Variable overhead		
Fixed overhead		
Standard cost for one unit		

Test your understanding 2

South manufactures a single product which has the following specification:

- Raw materials – 5 kg @ £7.50 per kg
- Direct labour – 2 hours @ £7.50 per hour
- Variable overheads – 2 hours @ £2 per hour
- Fixed overheads – 2 hours @ £5 per hour
- Complete the standard cost card using absorption costing principles.

	Workings:	£
Raw material		
Labour		
Variable overhead		
Fixed overhead		
Standard cost for one unit		

5 Types of standard

5.1 Introduction

The way in which control is exercised, and the interpretation and use of variances from standards, will depend on which type of standard is used.

5.2 Basic standards

A basic standard is one which, having been fixed, is not revised with changing conditions, but remains in force for a long period of time. It may be set originally having regard to either ideal or expected conditions. Under circumstances of rapid technological change or of significant price changes, basic standards are of limited value in relation to the achievement of the benefits outlined above since they will be out of date.

5.3 Normal standards

Normal standards are those which give consideration to the usual level of activity managed by the company. They are more recent than the basic standard and are usually based on what the company manages to achieve on a regular basis.

5.4 Target standards

In other cases the standards set will be those which give consideration to the state of efficiency which can be achieved from the existing facilities. The target set will be 'stretching' and a positive effort will made to achieve a high level of efficiency, but there is no question of going beyond what is attainable.

The aim should be to set the standard cost which is likely to be the most realistic for the business concerned. It should be remembered that standards are the yardstick against which efficiency is measured and therefore, if they are unrealistic then any variances calculated will be of little meaning. Management and staff are usually motivated using this method.

5.5 Ideal standards

In some cases standards are established on the assumption that machines and employees will work with optimal efficiency at all times, and that there will be no stoppages and no losses of material or services. Such standards would represent an ideal state of affairs and therefore the objectives they set are never achieved.

Managers who are responsible for the costs can hardly approve of targets which they can never reach and which, therefore, result in large adverse variances from the standards. This is demotivating for managers (and their staff), particularly if there is an element of performance-related pay in their remuneration. Managers and staff have often been found to 'give up' when faced with these standards.

Test your understanding 3

The setting of ideal standards is motivational to employees.

True ☐

False ☐

---

6 Advantages and disadvantages of standard costing

6.1 Advantages

The advantages of standard costing fall into two broad categories: planning and control.

Planning

Predetermined standards make the preparation of forecasts and budgets much easier. If the standards are to be used for these operational decisions then they must obviously be as accurate as possible. This again means that standards should be revised on a frequent basis.

Control

Control is primarily exercised through the comparison of standard and actual results, and the isolation of variances. This is done by breaking down the simple variance identified in a budgetary control system into components based upon an expected outcome. This will highlight areas of apparent efficiency and inefficiency, and as necessary investigations as to the causes of the variance can be made. If these investigations discover the causes of the variances, then corrective action can be taken to improve efficiency in the future or alter the standards if necessary.

In addition to the above, there are subsidiary advantages such as:

(a)   if the standards are perceived to be attainable, then they will serve to motivate the employees concerned

(b)   a standard costing bookkeeping system can be set up that will fulfil all requirements, for both internal and external reporting

(c)   recording of stock issues is simplified, as it is done at the standard price.

6.2   Disadvantages

A standard costing system is costly to set up and maintain, and standards must be revised on a regular basis to maintain effectiveness. It is for this reason that standard costing is most effective for well-established and repetitive processes, so that the revisions of standards are kept to a minimum.

7   Summary

In this chapter we have looked at the various ways of establishing standard costs within a standard cost reporting system.

Test your understanding answers

Test your understanding 1

	Workings:	£
Raw material	1 tonne × £75 per tonne	75.00
Labour	3 hours × £10 per hour	30.00
Variable overhead	3 hours × £5 per hour	15.00
Fixed overhead	3 hours × £2 per hour	6.00
		———
Standard cost for one unit		126.00
		———

Test your understanding 2

	Workings:	£
Raw material	5 kg × £7.50 per kg	37.50
Labour	2 hours × £7.50 per hour	15.00
Variable overhead	2 hours × £2 per hour	4.00
Fixed overhead	2 hours × £5 per hour	10.00
		———
Standard cost for one unit		66.50
		———

Test your understanding 3

False. It is impossible to be 100% certain, since different managers will react in different ways, but generally ideal standards will demotivate since adverse variances will continually be reported.

Collection of cost information

Introduction

This chapter is concerned with the classification of costs by behaviour. Much of the information here has been met in Elements of Costing and Management Accounting: Costing so should be considered to be revision of relevant areas.

Some costs change when activity levels change, whilst others do not. The ability to isolate cost elements by behaviour is essential to management who are concerned with predicting future costs as part of the planning and decision making processes. It will also be necessary to enable a marginal costing approach to be taken, as covered in the next chapter.

ASSESSMENT CRITERIA
The differences between cost centre, profit centre and investment centre (1.1)
Cost classification by behaviour (fixed, variable, semi-variable and stepped costs) and the relevant range (1.1)
Product costing and the elements of direct and indirect costs, cost classification into materials, labour and production overhead (1.1)
Prime cost, full production cost and marginal cost (1.1)
High-Low method of cost estimation, including making adjustments for a step up in cost or a quantity discount (1.1)
Flexible budgeting and how the calculation of the standard cost budget is affected by changes in output (2.1)
Extract information contained in a budgetary report (2.2)

CONTENTS

1   Cost accounting

2   The cost accounting department

3   Cost units

4   Cost centres

5   Cost classification

6   Cost behaviour

7   Cost estimation

8   The high/low method

9   Flexed/flexible budgets

1 Cost accounting

1.1 The need for cost accounting

Historically, financial accounts have reflected the transactions of a business entity in its relationships with the outside world: customers, suppliers, employees, shareholders and other investors. To this end, financial accounting has been geared up to the preparation of annual and other periodic accounts, with the emphasis upon statutory requirements.

A typical income statement has the following general layout.

🔅 Example

Income statement for the period ended...

	£
Revenue	500,000
Cost of sales	(370,000)
Gross profit	130,000
Expenses	(80,000)
Operating profit	50,000

Typically the income statement will include a subjective analysis of expenses according to category either by function (distribution/administrative) or by nature (materials/staff costs/depreciation). Despite some recent changes, financial accounts do not readily disclose

(a) profit performance by individual products, services or activity; but more importantly

(b) the responsibility of individual managers for performance.

Thus financial accounts can only provide 'scorekeeping', statistical information, rather than information that will form the basis of decision-making or control. The provision of this additional detail is one of the functions of cost accounting: cost-finding.

Definition

Cost-finding means taking the transactions which make up the financial accounts and analysing them to turn data into information which will be more helpful to the managers of the business. This will be an 'objective' analysis, matching the expenses to the purposes for which they were incurred. This analysis may be done on a purely memorandum basis, the results being reconciled with the financial records, or it may be sometimes incorporated into the general bookkeeping system of the company.

Whichever approach is adopted, cost accounting has two important effects on business documentation.

(a) Additional internal documents will be needed to identify which products or departments are affected by various transactions.

(b) Additional data regarding transactions will be needed to assist accurate classification and analysis.

 Example

Assume that the income statement illustrated above related to a company marketing four different products during a particular month. For management a more detailed analysis is required.

From his analysis of the source documents (purchase invoices, payrolls, petty cash vouchers and so on), the cost accountant is able to provide the following detailed report.

	Product A	Product B	Product C	Product D	Total
Revenue					
Quantity	315,000	32,500	80,500	28,100	–
Price per unit	£0.50	£2.50	£1.50	£5.00	–
Amount	£157,500	£81,250	£120,750	£140,500	£500,000
	£	£	£	£	£
Costs					
Materials	50,000	40,000	75,000	85,000	250,000
Wages	40,000	30,000	20,000	30,000	120,000
Expenses	22,000	25,500	17,500	15,000	80,000
Total	112,000	95,500	112,500	130,000	450,000
Operating profit/(loss)	45,500	(14,250)	8,250	10,500	50,000

From this 'product income statement', the managers of the business can see that the total profit of £50,000 resulted from profits on products A, C and D, offset by a loss on product B, and that product A alone yielded 91% of the company total.

We do not know at this stage whether the information will lead them to take any decision to change things for the future, because we do not know whether the above result is in accordance with a deliberate plan or not. Nor can we be sure without further information whether it would be a good thing to discontinue product B since such a decision might involve some further analysis of the costs incurred, and some forecasts of future developments.

Both comparisons against plan and the preparation of special analyses for decision purposes fall within the scope of the cost accounting function.

2 The cost accounting department

2.1 Data required for reports

A company's requirements for historical information include three main types of data.

(a) Data from the financial accounts of the business: the statement of financial position and profit and income statement with their supporting notes and schedules, and the statement of cash flows.

(b) Data obtained by analysing the accounts of the business, identifying items with cost units and cost centres: in other words the work of the cost accounting department (details of stockholdings would come from this source).

Sources of information for some costs might include the following.

Materials – Invoices received from suppliers in previous months and quotes received for future orders.

Labour – The Human Resources or Payroll department should have all the required information on salary levels and deductions so that wage rates can be established for costing purposes.

Overheads – Again, invoices received from suppliers of gas, electricity, telephone, rent, etc. should enable a manager to forecast these future costs with reasonable accuracy. Other information, such as a communication from the landlord stating a rent increase of a certain percentage should also be borne in mind and included in the forecast.

(c)   Data derived immediately from source documents without evaluation, such as statistics on labour efficiency, material usage, sickness, absenteeism and machine breakdowns.

In addition, most reports will include comparisons with budgets, standards, targets or estimates, and the explanation of variances based on detailed investigation and knowledge of the data used in budget preparation.

2.2   Organisation

The accounts department, therefore, comprises a financial accounting segment, a costing segment and a budgetary control segment. The extent to which these are separate departments within the organisation depends on the number and diversity of the transactions to be handled and on the management organisation of the business, including the extent of divisional autonomy. All these factors affect the required number of accounting staff and the consequent need for specialisation of effort.

2.3   Cost recording

The cost accounting department is responsible for maintaining the cost accounting records. To be effective these records should

(a)   analyse production, administration and marketing costs to facilitate cost and profit computations, inventory valuations, forecast and budget data and decision-making data

(b)   enable the production of periodic performance statements which are necessary for management control purposes

(c)   permit analysis of

(i)   past costs for profit measurement and inventory valuation

(ii)   present costs for control purposes

(iii)   future costs – forecasts, targets and budgets.

2.4   Cost accountant and other managers

The cost accountant's job is to interpret physical facts into money values, the position provides an excellent opportunity to ensure that all accounting reports are integrated and are prepared on a consistent basis. Although other departments will wish to report on their own activities, the cost accountant should maintain close liaison, and build a good relationship, with them so that

(a)   the information provided can assist them in interpreting the results of their own activities

(b)   there is no conflict on questions of fact between reports prepared by, for example, the sales manager or the production manager and the information emerging from the costing system.

2.5 Cost accounting and computers

Whilst records can be maintained manually, computer-based data concerning sales and production quantities, inventory levels and costs, will assist the cost accounting function in the following ways

(a) Reports and cost accounts can be prepared quickly

(b) Information for decision-making will be more plentiful and be available more speedily than would be the case with manual data

(c) Large volumes of data can be stored and manipulated with ease.

2.6 The benefits of cost accounting

The benefits of cost accounting can be identified as

(a) disclosure of profitable and non-profitable activities (as might appear in the product profit and loss account already illustrated). This data could also be modified to identify locations which are unprofitable

(b) identification of waste and inefficiency, particularly in relation to usage of materials and labour

(c) analysis of movements in profit

(d) assistance in the determination of selling prices

(e) valuation of inventory (there are auditing and taxation implications here)

(f) development of planning and control information

(g) evaluation of the cost effect of policy decisions.

3 Cost units

3.1 Cost units

Definition

A cost unit is a quantitative unit of product or service in relation to which costs are ascertained.

Example

Have a look at the costing income statement illustrated earlier. This showed the sales quantity of various products (A–D) and the total cost of those sales under the headings materials, wages and expenses.

Further additional calculations could be made from that example.

Solution

Calculation of cost per unit for the month ended … 20X0

	Product A	Product B	Product C	Product D
	£	£	£	£
Materials	0.16	1.23	0.93	3.02
Wages	0.13	0.92	0.25	1.07
Expenses	0.07	0.78	0.22	0.53
Total cost per unit	0.36	2.93	1.40	4.62

We have taken the total costs attributable to each product in a month (any other period could have been used) and arrived at the average cost per unit of each product, rounded to the nearest penny, by dividing the totals by the numbers of units involved. The 'cost unit' in this instance is the unit of product sold.

The cost unit might have been a piece, a pack, a kilogram, a litre or any other measure appropriate to what was being produced.

3.2   Average unit costs

In practice the business would probably have produced more or less units than it sold in the period, the unsold quantity being taken into (or out of) inventory. In such a case, the costs of production would have been collected and divided by the number of units produced to give the average unit cost. This would then have been applied to the number of units sold to give the cost of sales, and to the number of units remaining to give the costs of the residual inventory.

This average unit cost approach is used whenever production is continuous and leads to uniform product units, as in the case of many chemical plants, food processors or extractive operations such as mining and quarrying.

3.3 Job costs

Some businesses, however, undertake special jobs for their customers. A workshop making tools and jigs does this; and so on a much larger scale does the contractor building a bridge or putting up a factory. In such cases, costs are first analysed between the various jobs or contracts, and then the costs of the jobs invoiced will be gathered together into the periodic summary income statement. For such businesses, in other words, the 'cost unit' is the job or contract.

3.4 Batch costs

In the manufacture of, for example, mechanical or electrical components, such products are customarily made in batches of say 1,000 or 10,000 items, according to the circumstances of the case. In this type of business, the cost of each batch is determined and the batch is the primary 'cost unit'. Thereafter it is possible, if desired, to calculate the average cost per item in the batch.

3.5 Non-manufacturing cost units

The above examples have concentrated on cost units for production or manufacturing processes. Examples of cost units for service industries, or non-manufacturing activities within a business are as follows.

Service industry/activity	Cost unit
Accountants	Chargeable hour
College	Student enrolled
Hotel	Bed-night
Hospital	Patient-day
Transport department	kg-mile
Credit control department	Customer account
Selling	Calls made
Maintenance department	Man-hours

Note that some of these are in fact composite cost units, where a cost is considered to be dependent upon two main factors. For example, if the manager of a chain of hotels wanted to compare costs between two of the hotels, calculating costs per bed would not take account of the differing levels of occupation of the beds of the two hotels. Thus the cost can be calculated per bed-night (i.e. the cost of one bed per night of occupation).

A cost unit is a quantitative unit of product or service in relation to which costs are ascertained; the purpose of product costing is to arrive at the cost of whatever cost unit is appropriate to the business concerned.

4 Cost centres

 Definition

A cost centre is a location, function or item(s) of equipment in respect of which costs may be accumulated and related to cost units for control purposes.

A cost centre is used as an initial collection point for costs; once the total cost of operating the cost centre for a period has been ascertained, it can be related to the cost units that have passed through the cost centre during that period.

The location, function or item of equipment can be directly related to a production department, to a service department or to a business.

4.1 Examples of cost centres

Production department	Assembly line Packing machine
Service department	Stores Canteen Quality control
Service	Tax department (accountants) Ward (hospital) Faculty (college)

4.2 Responsibility for cost centres

Control can only be exercised by people, and for every cost somebody must be responsible. They will be responsible for that cost centre.

4.3 Profit centres

 Definition

A profit centre is a location, function or item(s) of equipment in respect of which costs and revenues may be ascertained for the purposes of control of the resulting profit.

While the paint shop in a factory might be treated as a cost centre (to monitor the costs incurred there), a large company might treat its French operation as a profit centre (since it generates both costs and revenues).

4.4 Investment centres

 Definition

An investment centre is a location, function or item(s) of equipment in respect of which costs and revenues and investments may be ascertained for the purposes of control of the resulting profit.

A large company might treat one of its divisions as an investment centre since it generates both costs and revenues, and has the ability to make investments in assets, such as buying a fleet of sales vehicles or a new photocopier.

 Test your understanding 1

A location or function for which costs and revenues are ascertained for the purpose of controlling the resultant profit is a:

A   Cost centre

B   Revenue centre

C   Profit centre

D   Investment centre

5 Cost classification

5.1 Types of cost classification

Costs can be classified (collected into logical groups) in many ways. The particular classification selected will depend upon the purpose for which the resulting analysed data will be used.

Purpose	Classification
Cost control	By nature – materials/labour/overheads.
Cost accounts	By relationship to cost units – direct/indirect costs.
Budgeting, contribution analysis	By behaviour – fixed/variable costs.
Decision-making	Relevant/non-relevant costs.
Responsibility accounting	Controllable/uncontrollable costs.

You will come across these classifications in more detail as you work through this study text. At this stage, we will revise the basic classification terms used in cost accounting.

5.2 Classification of costs

For cost accounting purposes, the costs of the business will be classified in quite a different way from the analysis required by a financial accountant for the income statement in published accounts.

The basic classification of costs in cost accounting may be illustrated as follows.

Example

	£	£
Direct costs		
Direct materials		250,000
Direct labour		120,000
Direct expenses		10,000
Prime cost (= total of direct costs)		380,000
Indirect production costs		25,000
Production cost		405,000
Indirect non-production costs		
Administration overhead	20,000	
Selling and distribution overhead	25,000	
		45,000
Total cost		450,000

5.3 Direct costs

Definition

Direct costs are costs which can be related directly to one cost unit. Direct costs comprise direct materials, direct labour and direct expenses. The total direct cost of a unit is also called the **prime cost**.

For example, considering a cost unit of a chair, direct costs will include the cost of wood and screws used (direct material cost) and the cost of manufacturing labour hours per chair (direct labour cost). Direct expenses might include the hiring of a particular piece of equipment required to manufacture the chair.

In a service context, the direct costs relating to, say, a student enrolled at a college would include the costs of books provided, individual tuition and marking costs.

5.4 Indirect costs

 Definition

Indirect costs cannot be identified directly with a cost unit and are often referred to as *overheads*.

For inventory valuation purposes a distinction needs to be made between overheads incurred in the production process (factory costs, e.g. factory rent and rates, power etc.) and non-production costs.

Non-production costs are indirect costs involved in converting finished goods into revenue, comprising:

(a) administrative overhead costs (e.g. executive salaries and office costs); and

(b) marketing, selling and distribution overhead costs.

Non-production costs are not included in inventory valuation since they are not costs of making a product, but costs of selling it. Inventory on hand at the end of a period is valued at total production cost only, including production overheads (in a total absorption costing system). We shall return to this point in the next chapter.

Considering the cost unit of a chair, the salaries of the sales representatives who promote and sell the chairs to retail outlets would be a selling overhead.

Indirect costs associated with a college would include premises running costs, lecturers' salaries and administrative staff costs.

Overhead costs can always be identified with cost centres; and because cost centres are the responsibility of particular functional managers one will find overheads classified according to the main functional divisions of the business.

5.5 Full production cost

Full production cost is the total of all costs (direct and indirect) that were incurred in the production of a unit. This means that selling costs are excluded. In the previous example, the full production cost was £405,000.

5.6 Marginal cost

The marginal cost of a product is the total of all variable costs. (Often the words marginal and variable are substituted for each other because they mean the same thing.)

Test your understanding 2

The total of all direct costs is:

A   Marginal cost

B   Absorption cost

C   Prime cost

D   Standard cost

 6 Cost behaviour

6.1   The nature of costs

We mentioned earlier the need for cost classification by behaviour for budgeting purposes. In order to make predictions of future cost levels, we must determine the basis of the charge.

As an example, consider the cost of direct materials expected next month. The charge would depend on the amount used and the cost per unit. The amount used would depend, in turn, on the production anticipated for the period.

In order to derive this cost therefore we must make an estimate such as the following:

(a)	Production levels	10,000 units
(b)	Usage of materials per unit:	
	Material A	2 kg
	Material B	1 kg
	Material C	0.2 kg
(c)	Costs of materials:	
	Material A	30 pence per kg
	Material B	25 pence per kg
	Material C	50 pence per kg

Estimate of next month's material cost

		£
Material A	20,000 kg @ 30p/kg	6,000
Material B	10,000 kg @ 25p/kg	2,500
Material C	2,000 kg @ 50p/kg	1,000
Total estimated material cost		9,500

6.2   Variable costs

We could set up a simple mathematical model which would, for any level of production, usage and cost of materials, enable the total level of material cost in a future period to be predicted.

Direct labour costs tend to vary due to changes in productivity in addition to grade of labour and rate of payment. A certain amount of estimation will be required; if payment is on a production related basis we would expect a cost which, like materials, will vary in line with the volume of production.

At this stage, therefore, we have come to the assumption that direct material, labour and expenses will probably vary roughly in line with anticipated production levels or the level of activity. We call such costs **variable** costs.

6.3   Fixed costs

Not all costs vary in line with productivity levels. If we take the cost of rent and rates, for example, the charge is not determined on the basis of the intensity of usage of the premises but rather on the basis of time. Costs that are unaffected by the volume of production are called **fixed costs**. Rent and rates are an example. Labour paid on a time basis would also fall under this heading. How then can we predict the cost of such expenses for next month? Well, there is no difficulty in doing this as all we have to do is consult our rental agreement and the rates notice and we can forecast with complete certainty what these costs will be for the month.

6.4   Classification of costs by behaviour

The above example illustrates the need for cost behaviour classification. For cost prediction purposes, we must make a distinction between costs which vary with production or activity levels (variable costs) and those which do not (fixed costs). There also exists a type of cost which moves in sympathy with production levels but contains an element which does not, such as an electricity charge which contains a minimum standing charge plus an element which relates to the usage of the period. Such a cost would be described as semi-variable or mixed.

 Definition

Variable costs are those that vary (usually assumed in direct proportion) with changes in level of activity of the cost centre to which they relate (e.g. output volume), for example the raw material used in a product. It should be noted that the variable cost per unit may not remain constant over a wide range. It may be possible, for example, to obtain discounts for large purchases of material, reducing the cost per unit.

Fixed costs are those that accrue with the passage of time and are not affected by changes in activity level; they are therefore also known as period costs, for example rent of premises.

Stepped costs are fixed over a range of output and then suddenly increase in one big jump, for example a staffing level of up to 20 people may only require one supervisor but, if the staff level is more than 20, an extra supervisor will be needed.

Semi-variable (mixed) costs contain both a fixed and a variable element. When output is nil, the fixed element is incurred, but they also increase, like variable costs, as output increases. An example is telephone charges where there is a fixed rental to which is added the charge for calls made. These are also sometimes known as semi-fixed costs.

6.5   Graphical illustrations

Various cost behaviour patterns are illustrated in the graphs below.

(a)   **Variable cost:** direct materials, the purchase price per unit being constant.

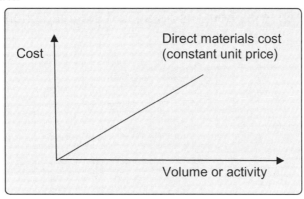

(b)   **Fixed cost:** rent of factory payable under a long-term lease.

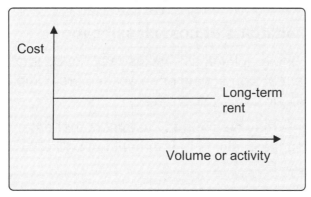

(c)   **Stepped costs**

   (i)   Canteen cost where additional assistants are required as increases in activity result in larger numbers of factory personnel.

   (ii)   Rent of premises, additional accommodation eventually being required.

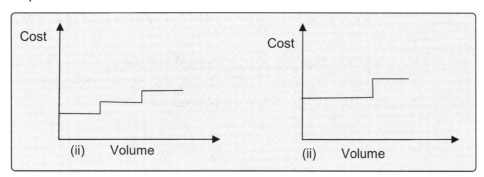

(d) **Semi-variable costs**

    (i)   Direct materials cost (trade discount at higher levels of activity)

    (ii)   Salesmen's remuneration with added commission from a certain level of activity

    (iii) Electricity charges comprising a fixed standing charge and variable unit charge.

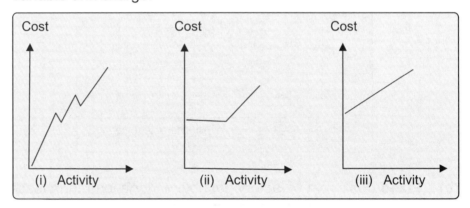

6.6 Practical limitations of cost classification

As you can see from the graphs above, costs may not be totally fixed or totally variable. In the real world costs often act in more complex ways than we have seen so far.

For example, discounts may be given to customers that order goods in large volumes causing the cost line to fragment not unlike the graph above for semi-variable costs (i).

Similarly, whilst labour is usually considered to be a variable cost, if activity levels increase then overtime may be incurred, and this will mean that the cost is no longer a straight-forward variable cost.

Production in large quantities can bring economies of scale to a business whereby the cost graph may not be a linear variable cost but a curved one that becomes less steep at higher volumes.

The common approach that we take in order to keep it simple is as follows

(a)   treat as variable those costs which change roughly in line with the activity level

(b)   treat as fixed those costs which only change at wide intervals of activity; this recognises that review will be required if there is a permanent change in the normal level of activity.

Test your understanding 3

Required:

(a) Electricity charges are an example of:

   A   Fixed costs

   B   Semi-variable costs

   C   Variable costs

   D   Stepped costs

(b) Rents paid are an example of:

   A   Fixed costs

   B   Semi-variable costs

   C   Variable costs

   D   Stepped costs

(c) Material costs are an example of:

   A   Fixed costs

   B   Semi-variable costs

   C   Variable costs

   D   Stepped costs

(d) Labour costs are an example of:

   A   Fixed costs

   B   Semi-variable costs

   C   Variable costs

   D   Stepped costs

(e) Supervisors' salaries that increase occasionally due to increases in volume are best described as:

   A   Fixed costs

   B   Semi-variable costs

   C   Variable costs

   D   Stepped costs

Test your understanding 4

The rent of premises where at certain levels of activity extra premises will have to be rented is an example of a:

A   Fixed cost

B   Variable cost

C   Stepped cost

D   Mixed cost

7   Cost estimation

7.1   Introduction

As we have seen, some costs may have both fixed and variable elements. These will need to be identified for budgeting purposes.

If it is not easy to do this directly (as it is in the case of the telephone cost, where the bill clearly shows the fixed charge and rate per unit), then an analysis of past cost and volume data will need to be carried out.

7.2   Methods of cost estimation

It is assumed that there is a linear relationship, i.e.:

Total cost = Fixed cost + (Variable cost per unit × Units produced)

and that the total fixed cost and the variable cost per unit are constant at all levels of production unless told otherwise.

Possible techniques to identify this relationship include the high/low method and linear regression.

8   The high/low method

8.1   Introduction

This is a simple method of estimating future costs from past results. It takes the costs for the highest and lowest activity levels, and assumes that a linear relationship covers the range in between.

Example

Widgets are produced by a process that incurs both fixed and variable costs.

Total costs have been recorded for the process for each of the last six months as follows.

Month	Output (units)	Total cost £
1	4,500	33,750
2	3,500	30,500
3	5,100	34,130
4	6,200	38,600
5	5,700	38,000
6	4,100	31,900

(a) What is the estimated fixed cost element and estimated variable cost per unit?

(b) What would be the estimated total cost at the budgeted activity level for month 7 of 6,000 units?

Solution

Select the months with the highest and lowest output levels as follows.

	Output (units)	Total cost £
Lowest output	3,500	30,500
Highest output	6,200	38,600
Increase	2,700	8,100

For an increase of 2,700 units, cost has increased by £8,100. If we assume that the fixed cost element remains constant, this cost increase must represent a change in variable costs only.

Assuming a straight-line relationship, then the variable cost per unit =

$$\frac{£8,100}{2,700} = £3 \text{ per unit}$$

Note that the factors determining which values to choose are the total cost at the highest output level and the total cost at the lowest output level. These are not necessarily the highest and lowest costs. The high/low observations are always based on the independent variable (in this case, output).

We can now substitute back into either of the two output levels to obtain the fixed cost.

At the 3,500 units level:

	£
Total cost	30,500
Variable cost (3,500 × £3)	(10,500)
Fixed costs	20,000

As a check on the accuracy of the calculations, at the 6,200 units level:

	£
Total costs	38,600
Variable cost (6,200 × £3)	(18,600)
Fixed costs	20,000

(a) Therefore the estimated fixed cost element is £20,000 and the estimated variable cost is £3 per unit.

(b) At an output level of 6,000 units the total estimated cost would be:

	£
Variable cost (6,000 × £3)	18,000
Fixed cost	20,000
Total cost	38,000

8.2 High/low method with stepped fixed costs

Sometimes fixed costs are only fixed within certain levels of activity (stepped fixed costs). The high/low method can still be used to estimate fixed and variable costs.

Choose the two activity levels where the fixed costs remain unchanged and calculate the variable cost per unit and the total fixed cost using the high/low technique.

Adjustments may need to be made to the fixed costs when calculating the total cost for a new activity level.

Example

An organisation has the following total costs at three activity levels:

Activity level (units)	4,000	6,000	7,500
Total cost	£40,800	£50,000	£54,800

Variable cost per unit is constant within this activity range and there is a step up of 10% in the total fixed costs when the activity level exceeds 5,500 units.

Required:

What is the total cost at an activity level of 5,000 units?

Solution

Calculate the variable cost per unit by comparing two output levels where fixed costs will be the same:

Variable cost per unit = [(54,800 − 50,000) ÷ (7,500 − 6,000)] = £3.20

Total fixed cost above 5,500 units = [54,800 − (7,500 × 3.20)] = £30,800

Total fixed cost below 5,500 units = 30,800/110 × 100 = £28,000

Total cost for 5,000 units = [(5,000 × 3.20) + 28,000] = £44,000

Or the information could be presented like the next example, when an adjustment to the change in cost can be made.

 Example

A company has achieved the following output levels and total costs:

Volume of production (units)	190	240
Total cost	£150,000	£210,000

Total cost includes a fixed element which steps up by £25,000 at an activity level of 200 units.

The variable cost per unit is constant.

Required:

Calculate the variable cost per unit.

Solution

£210,000 – £150,000 = £60,000 of which £25,000 is the step up. Therefore only £35,000 is the total variable cost.

Change in output = 240 – 190 = 50 units.

Variable cost per unit = £35,000/50 units = £700

8.3 High/low method with changes in the variable cost per unit

Sometimes there may be changes in the variable cost per unit, and the high/low method can still be used to determine the fixed and variable elements of semi-variable costs. As with the stepped fixed costs, it is best to choose activity levels where the variable costs per unit remain unchanged.

 Example

A company has achieved the following output levels and total costs:

Output (units)	Total cost (£)
200	7,000
300	8,000
400	8,600

For output volumes above 350 units the variable cost per unit falls by 10%.

(Note: this fall applies to all units – not just the excess above 350).

Required:

Estimate the cost of producing 450 units of Product LL in 20X9.

Solution

Variable cost per unit (<350) = (£8,000 – £7,000)/(300 – 200)

= £1,000/100 = £10 per unit

Total cost at 300 unit = £8,000

Total variable cost = 300 × £10 = £3,000

Therefore fixed cost = £5,000

If output is 450 units:

Variable cost per unit = £10 × 0.9 = £9

Variable cost = 450 units × £9 = £4,050

Fixed cost = £5,000

Total cost = £9,050

 Test your understanding 5

The total costs incurred in 20X3 at various output levels in a factory have been measured as follows:

Output (units)	Total cost (£)
26	6,566
30	6,510
33	6,800
44	6,985
48	7,380
50	7,310

When output is 80 units or more, another factory unit must be rented and fixed costs therefore increase by 100%.

Variable cost per unit is forecast to rise by 10% in 20X4.

Required:

Calculate the estimated total costs of producing 100 units in 20X4.

8.4 Advantages of the high/low method

- Simple to operate.
- Easy to understand.

8.5 Disadvantages of the high/low method

The problem with the high-low method is that it could give a completely inaccurate result. This is because we are only considering two sets of data, and ignoring all of the others. It is possible that the points we have chosen are completely unrepresentative of the rest of the data. This is a distinct possibility since we have chosen the two points at the extreme ends of the activity range. At these levels it is more likely that operating conditions will be atypical compared with more normal output.

One way around this problem is to choose the 'next to highest' and 'next to lowest' figures, but this destroys some of the simplicity of the model.

 Test your understanding 6

Production

Given below are the production quantities and production overhead costs for each of the last six months:

Month	Production quantity (units)	Production overheads £
January	10,000	58,000
February	9,000	50,000
March	12,000	65,000
April	11,000	62,000
May	8,000	45,000
June	9,500	52,000

Production in July is anticipated to be 10,500 units.

Task

What should be the cost of the budgeted production overhead for July?

Solution

Using the high/low method:

	Production quantity (units)	Production overheads £
Highest	12,000	
Lowest	8,000	
Increase in activity and overheads		

Variable cost = $\dfrac{£}{\text{units}}$

= £ [   ] per unit

Therefore at 12,000 unit level:

	£
Total cost	65,000
Variable cost 12,000 × £	
Fixed cost	

At a production level of 10,500 units:

	£
Variable cost 10,500 × £	
Fixed cost	
Total cost	

 Test your understanding 7

A company has achieved the following output levels and total costs:

Volume of production (units)	100,000	140,000
Total cost	£110,000	£135,000

Total cost includes a fixed element which steps up by £5,000 at an activity level of 120,000 units.

The variable cost per unit is constant.

The variable cost per unit is £ [   ]

Test your understanding 8

You work as an accounting technician for Eastoft Feeds and Fertilisers Ltd.

You use a computer model for forecasting the quarterly costs on your various product lines. The software builds a simple linear cost model. After inputting data for product 'EF 3', values for the quarterly fixed cost and variable cost per unit are determined and the cost model is y = 25,000 + 35x, where x is the quarterly production volume (in tonnes) and y is the total quarterly cost (in £).

The following is the estimated volume of output for the quarters ended March, June, September and December.

Product 'EF3'

Quarter ended	Volume (tonnes)
March	15,000
June	12,000
September	16,000
December	14,000

Task

Estimate the fixed cost, variable cost and total cost for each quarter and complete the table below.

Product 'EF3'

Quarter ended	Volume tonnes	Fixed cost £	Variable cost £	Total cost £
March				
June				
September				
December				

9 Flexed/flexible budgeting

9.1 Flexed budgets

A flexible budget is a budget which recognises different cost behaviour patterns and is designed to change as the volume of activity changes. When preparing flexed budgets it will be necessary to identify the cost behaviour of the different items in the original budget. In some cases you may have to use the high-low method in order to determine the fixed and variable elements of semi-variable costs.

Example

	Budget	Actual	Variance
Sales units	1,000	1,200	
Production units	1,300	1,250	
	£	£	£
Sales revenue	10,000	11,500	1,500 Fav
Labour costs	2,600	2,125	475 Fav
Material costs	1,300	1,040	260 Fav
Overhead costs	1,950	2,200	250 Adv
Profit	4,150	6,135	1,985 Fav

The fixed budget shown above is not particularly useful because we are not really comparing like with like. For example, the budgeted sales were 1,000 units but the actual sales volume was 1,200 units.

The overall sales variance is favourable, but from the report shown we don't know how much of this variance is due to the fact that actual sales were 200 units higher than budgeted sales (or whether there was an increase in the sales price).

Similarly, actual production volume was 50 units less than the budgeted production volume, so we are not really making a very useful comparison. It is more useful to compare actual results with a budget that reflects the actual activity level. Such a budget is known as a flexed budget.

It may be necessary to identify the cost behaviour from the flexible budget and identify what the standard or revised flexed budget maybe.

 Example

Wye Ltd manufactures one product and when operating at 100% capacity can produce 5,000 units per period, but for the last few periods has been operating below capacity. Below is the flexible budget prepared at the start of last period, for three levels of activity at below capacity:

	Level of activity		
	3,500 units	4,000 units	4,500 units
	£	£	£
Direct material	7,000	8,000	9,000
Direct labour	28,000	32,000	36,000
Production overhead	34,000	36,000	38,000
Administration and distribution overhead	15,000	15,000	15,000
Total cost	84,000	91,000	98,000

The last period turned out to be worse than expected, with production of only 2,500 units.

Required

Prepare a flexed budget for 2,500 units.

Solution

	2,500 units
	£
Direct material (W1)	5,000
Direct labour (W2)	20,000
Production overhead (W3)	30,000
Administration and distribution overhead (W4)	15,000
Total cost	70,000

1   **Material is a variable cost**

Variable material cost = £7,000/3,500 units = £2 per unit

2,500 × £2 = £5,000

2   **Labour is a variable cost**

Variable labour cost = £28,000/3,500 = £8 per unit

2,500 × £8 = £20,000

3   **Production overheads are a semi-variable cost**

Using the high-low method:

Variable cost = (£34,000 − £38,000)/(4,500 − 3,500) = £4

Fixed cost = £34,000 − (£4 × 3,500) = £20,000

£20,000 + (£4 × 2,500) = £30,000

4   Administration and distribution overhead are a fixed cost and do not change with the stated levels of activity.

10 Summary

Much of cost accounting is about gathering information about current costs and using it to make predictions about future costs. Some costs, direct costs, can be allocated directly to a cost unit whereas other costs, indirect costs/overheads, are allocated initially to a cost centre.

Costs can also be usefully classified according to their behaviour. This is particularly useful when budgeting costs for future periods or for making decisions about activity levels. Costs can be classified as variable, fixed, stepped or semi-variable.

For semi-variable costs the fixed element and the variable element will need to be identified for forecasting purposes. This can be done using the high/low method. The high/low method can also be used to identify the fixed and variable cost elements of total cost.

Test your understanding answers

Test your understanding 1

C   A profit centre is a location or function for which costs and revenues are ascertained for the purpose of controlling the resultant profit.

Test your understanding 2

C   Prime cost is the total of all direct costs.

Test your understanding 3

(a) B   Electricity costs usually have a standing charge (fixed cost) and the usage (variable cost).

(b) A   (Rent is usually a fixed cost unless there is mention of having to rent further space when it becomes a stepped cost.)

(c) C   Materials are usually a variable cost.

(d) C   Labour is usually a variable cost.

(e) D   Supervisors' salaries can be a fixed cost but there is mention here of extra supervisors being required therefore it will actually be a stepped cost.

Test your understanding 4

C   An example of a stepped cost is the rent of premises where at certain levels of activity extra premises will have to be rented.

Test your understanding 5

Variable cost per unit (20X3) = (£7,310 – £6,566)/(50 – 26)

= £744/24 = £31 per unit

Substituting as high activity level:

Total cost = £7,310

Total variable cost = 50 × £31 = £1,550

Therefore fixed cost (in 20X3) = £5,760

Estimated costs of producing 100 units in 20X4:

Variable cost = 100 × £31 × 1.1 = £3,410

Fixed cost = £5,760 × 2 = £11,520

Total cost = £14,930

Test your understanding 6

Production

Use the high/low method.

	Production quantity (units)	Production overheads £
Highest	12,000	65,000
Lowest	8,000	45,000
Increase in activity	4,000	20,000

$$\text{Variable cost} = \frac{£20,000}{4,000 \text{ units}}$$

$$= £5 \text{ per unit}$$

Therefore at 12,000 unit level:

	£
Total cost	65,000
Variable cost 12,000 × £5	60,000
Fixed cost	5,000

At a production level of 10,500 units:

	£
Variable cost 10,500 × £5	52,500
Fixed cost	5,000
Total cost	57,500

 Test your understanding 7

£135,000 – £110,000 = £25,000 of which £5,000 is the step up. Therefore only £20,000 is the total variable cost.

Change in output = 140,000 – 100,000 = 40,000 units.

Variable cost per unit = £20,000/40,000 units = £0.50

Test your understanding 8

Quarter ended	Volume tonnes	Fixed cost £	Variable cost £	Total cost £
March	15,000	25,000	525,000	550,000
June	12,000	25,000	420,000	445,000
September	16,000	25,000	560,000	585,000
December	14,000	25,000	490,000	515,000

Accounting for overheads

Introduction

Overhead is the general term used to describe costs which are not direct costs of production. They are also known as indirect costs and they may be indirect production costs or indirect non-production costs. When a management accountant is trying to ascertain the cost of a product or service, there are two approaches for dealing with overheads.

Firstly, apportionment and allocation of all production overheads may be used to arrive at a 'full' cost per unit. This is known as absorption costing. Remember that as well as the indirect production cost there are indirect non-production costs. These non-production costs are never included in the cost of the product, or inventory or cost of sales.

Alternatively, one can use only direct costs to arrive at the cost per unit and leave indirect costs as a general overhead not related to units of output. This approach is generally known as marginal costing.

ASSESSMENT CRITERIA	CONTENTS
The difference between marginal costing and absorption costing, and how to critically evaluate the differences between the two methodologies (1.2)	1 Allocation, apportionment and absorption of overheads
How to reconcile a marginal costing profit with an absorption costing profit for changes in inventory to demonstrate the differences in the two methodologies (1.2)	2 Activity-based costing (ABC)
The difference between contribution and profit (1.3)	3 Absorption costing and marginal costing
Calculate product costs using ABC (5.3)	4 Contribution
Why products with short productions runs may have a higher production overhead absorbed into each unit (5.3)	5 Implications for pricing
Recognise ABC as a refinement on absorption costing where production costs are analysed into cost pools affected by cost drivers other than simple production volumes (5.3)	

1 Allocation, apportionment and absorption of overheads

1.1 Introduction

We have already identified two types of costs that make up the full production cost of a unit:

(a) Direct costs are those that can be uniquely identified with an individual cost unit (e.g. direct materials, direct labour, direct expenses).

(b) Indirect costs (overheads) are costs incurred in production but not easily 'traced' to individual units, e.g. machine power (variable), factory rent (fixed), telephone (semi-variable).

The problem we are considering here is how to divide indirect production costs between cost units, in order to calculate a total cost per unit for budgeting, inventory valuation and pricing purposes.

The method used to divide production overheads between production units is made up of three processes: allocation, apportionment and absorption.

Step 1 **Identify the indirect cost with a cost centre**

This can be done in two ways depending on the nature of the cost.

(a) **Allocation**

Definition

Where the indirect cost is borne entirely by one cost centre, the entire cost is allocated to that cost centre.

(b) **Apportionment**

Definition

Where the indirect cost is shared by more than one cost centre, the cost is apportioned or shared between the cost centres.

Step 2   Attribute the indirect costs of the cost centre calculated in Step 1 to the cost units produced by that centre.

This is called absorption.

 Definition

Absorption is the technique of attributing a cost centre's indirect costs to the units produced by the cost centre.

We shall now look at each of these in more detail.

1.2   Cost allocation

Certain cost items will be incurred entirely by one cost centre. Allocation deals with this type of cost and simply allots it to the cost centre which has incurred the cost.

Cost centre	Allocated cost
Canteen	Spaghetti
	Tea bags
	Chef's wages
Packing department	Cardboard
	String

1.3   Cost apportionment (primary)

More frequently the benefit of an item of cost will be shared by a number of cost centres. The overhead will be split or apportioned between the relevant cost centres on an 'equitable' basis.

The rent of buildings, for example, can relate to the total floor space occupied by a number of different departments and it is usual to allot the rental charge to those departments in proportion to the floor space they occupy.

Nature of cost	Possible bases of apportionment
Rent and rates	Floor area occupied by various departments
Lighting and heating	Cubic capacity of locations or metered usage
Insurance of inventory	Value of inventory in various locations

Example

A general cost in a manufacturing company is factory rental. Annual rental costs are £80,000. How should this cost be apportioned between production departments and service departments?

Rental costs are usually apportioned between departments on the basis of the floor space taken up by each department. For example, suppose that three departments have floor space of 10,000 square metres, 15,000 square metres and 25,000 square metres. If we apportion rental costs between the departments on the basis of their floor space, the apportionment would be as follows.

Annual rental	£80,000
Total floor space (10,000 + 15,000 + 25,000)	50,000 square metres
Apportionment rate (£80,000/50,000)	£1.60/square metre

	£
Apportion to department with 10,000 square metres	16,000
Apportion to department with 15,000 square metres	24,000
Apportion to department with 25,000 square metres	40,000
	———
	80,000
	———

 Example

The costs of heating and lighting might also be apportioned on the basis of floor space. Alternatively, since heating relates to volume rather than floor space, it could be argued that the costs should be apportioned on the volume of space taken up by each department. Yet another view is that electricity costs relate more to the consumption of electrical power by machines, therefore the apportionment of these costs should be on the basis of the number and power of the machines in each department.

A reasonable argument could be made for any of these bases of apportionment.

KAPLAN PUBLISHING

1.4   Cost apportionment (secondary)

After completing the allocation and primary apportionment stages, you should have assigned all costs to cost centres.

Some cost centres, however, will not have production units passing through them; these cost centres are called service departments (e.g. quality control department, works canteen). Before the final stage of absorption into cost units can be carried out, it is necessary to perform a further type of apportionment whereby the total costs of the service cost centres are reassigned to production cost centres. This is known as secondary apportionment. This should be done on a fair basis to reflect the benefit derived from the service centre.

The following example is an illustration of primary and secondary apportionment.

Example

Overhead Analysis Sheet — Period Ending...................

	Total £	Production Assembly £	Production Finishing £	Service Stores £	Service Canteen £
Overheads allocated directly to cost centres	133,000	49,000	36,000	27,000	21,000
Overheads to be apportioned					
Rent (Apportionment basis: ....)	76,000	26,000	24,000	15,000	11,000
Equipment depreciation (Apportionment basis: ....)	15,000	8,000	1,000	5,000	1,000
Total overhead	224,000	83,000	61,000	47,000	33,000
Apportioning of stores (Apportionment basis: ....)		31,000	16,000	(47,000)	
Apportioning of canteen (Apportionment basis: ....)		14,000	19,000		(33,000)
		128,000	96,000	–	–

📝 Test your understanding 1

A fair basis for apportioning the factory rental cost between the various cost centres in the business would be:

A   Building insurance

B   Machine value

C   Floor area

D   Number of staff

1.5   Absorption

Having collected all indirect costs in the production cost centres via overhead allocation and apportionment, the cost has to be spread over the output of the production cost centre.

The allotment of accumulated overhead costs to cost units is called overhead absorption. The absorption rate is normally calculated at the start of the period and therefore based on budgeted quantities. Various methods of absorption exist and the one most fitting should be chosen.

The following are the most common methods you will encounter.

(a)   **Rate per unit**

The simple unit rate is obtained by dividing total budgeted overheads by the number of units budgeted to be produced. However, where more than one product is produced, this is an unsatisfactory basis for absorbing overheads as it will not reflect the relative demands of each product on the production departments through which they pass.

(b)   **Alternative bases of absorption**

There are a number of bases commonly used as an alternative to the simple unit rate:

- rate per direct labour hour

- rate per machine hour

- percentage of material cost

- percentage of wage cost

- percentage of total direct cost (prime cost).

It is important to appreciate, however, that whichever method or combination of methods is used, the result will only be an approximate estimate of what that product actually costs.

In practice, many businesses use a 'direct labour hour rate' or 'machine hour rate' in preference to a rate based on a percentage of direct materials cost, direct wages or prime cost, as it may be possible to associate some overheads either with labour time or with machine time.

It may be possible to analyse the total overhead apportioned to each production department into fixed and variable elements. In this case a variable overhead rate per unit and a fixed overhead rate per unit can be calculated.

The absorption rates will normally be calculated at the beginning of a period and hence be based on budgeted costs and production levels. This can lead to problems when actual costs and volumes are not the same as budgeted leading to over- or under-absorption.

:Ò: Example

For the year ended 31 December 20X4 the budget for the Machining Cost Centre at Cuecraft Ltd was:

Overhead	£132,000
Volume of activity	15,000 machine hours

In January 20X4 the cost centre incurred £12,000 of overhead and 1,350 machine hours were worked.

Task

Calculate the pre-determined overhead absorption rate per machine hour and the overhead under or over-recovered in the month.

Solution

Absorption rate, based on the budget:

$$\frac{\text{Planned overhead}}{\text{Machine hours}} = \frac{£132,000}{15,000 \text{ machine hours}} = £8.80 \text{ per machine hour}$$

	£
Overhead absorbed	
1,350 machine hours at £8.80	11,880
Overhead incurred	12,000
	———
Under-absorption	(120)
	———

Here, the amount of overhead actually charged to production is £11,880, which is less than actual expenditure. We therefore have under-absorption of overhead.

Under-recovery of overheads is shown as a separate item in the costing income statement. Since production has been charged with fewer overheads than the amount of overheads incurred, an adjustment to profit for under-absorption is downwards. In other words, under-absorption is a 'loss' item.

 Example

The following example covers all stages of overhead allocation, apportionment and absorption summarised above. Work through it carefully to ensure you have fully understood this area.

SB Limited has two production departments (Assembly and Finishing) and two service departments (Maintenance and Canteen). The following costs are expected to be incurred during the next time period.

	£
Indirect materials	20,000
Rent	15,000
Electricity	10,000
Machine depreciation	5,000
Building depreciation	10,000
Direct labour	55,000

The following information is available.

	Assembly	Finishing	Maintenance	Canteen
Area (square metres)	1,000	2,000	0,500	0,500
Kw hours consumed	1,000	4,000	Nil	5,000
Machine value	£45,000	£35,000	£11,000	£9,000
Number of staff	20	30	10	4
Indirect materials consumed	7,000	8,000	3,000	2,000
Direct labour hours	10,000	2,000	0,500	0,200
Machine hours	1,000	5,000	–	–

The maintenance department spends 60% of its time servicing equipment for the assembly department and 40% of its time servicing equipment for the finishing department. The canteen equipment is serviced by outside specialist contractors.

(a) Calculate the total overheads in each cost centre.

(b) Reapportion the service centre costs to production cost centres.

(c) Calculate appropriate absorption rates for each production department.

(d) One of SB Ltd's products is the JK. Production details for each unit of JK are:

	Assembly	Finishing
Direct labour hours	4	1
Machine hours	0.5	2.5

How much overhead should be absorbed into each unit of JK?

Solution

(a)

Overhead	Total	Basis of apportionment (note)	Assembly	Finishing	Maintenance	Canteen
	£		£	£	£	£
Indirect materials	20,000	Allocate (i)	7,000	8,000	3,000	2,000
Rent	15,000	Area (ii)	3,750	7,500	1,875	1,875
Electricity	10,000	Kw hours (iii)	1,000	4,000	–	5,000
Machine depreciation	5,000	Machine value (iv)	2,250	1,750	550	450
Building depreciation	10,000	Area (v)	2,500	5,000	1,250	1,250
Direct labour	55,000	– (vi)	–	–	–	–
Total	60,000		16,500	26,250	6,675	10,575

Notes:

(i) We are given the amount of indirect materials used by each cost centre. This allows us to allocate the cost straight to each cost centre.

(ii) Rent is something that is shared by the whole factory and therefore the cost must be apportioned between the cost centres. The first thing to decide is what basis to use. Since rent is related to area, floor space would be a sensible basis to use (the bigger the area of a cost centre the more rent will be apportioned to it). The apportionment is carried out as follows.

- Calculate the total floor area for the factory.

- For each cost centre calculate what fraction of the total floor area this represents.

- Multiply this fraction by £15,000.

In the present case this would be as follows:

Total floor area =1,000 + 2,000 + 500 + 500 = 4,000 square metres.

Assembly is 1,000 square metres, i.e. 1,000/4,000 of the total area. Assembly is apportioned £15,000 × 1,000/4,000 = £3,750.

Similarly, finishing is apportioned £15,000 × 2,000/4,000 = £7,500 and Maintenance and Canteen are apportioned £15,000 × 500/4,000 = £1,875 each.

(iii) The most appropriate basis for apportioning the electricity between the cost centres will be the Kw hours consumed since these are a measure of the amount of electricity used.

The total Kw hours consumed = 1,000 + 4,000 + 0 + 5,000 = 10,000.

Assembly will be apportioned £10,000 × 1,000/10,000 = £1,000 etc.

(iv) Machine depreciation will be based on the value of the machinery and again needs to be apportioned between the cost centres.

The total machine value is £45,000 + £35,000 + £11,000 + £9,000 = £100,000.

This results in Assembly being apportioned £5,000 × 45/100 = £2,250 etc.

(v) Since the whole building is being depreciated, building depreciation should be related to the area of each cost centre. It does not matter that we have already used area once. There is no restriction against using it again if it is the most appropriate basis for apportioning this cost.

(vi) You may have thought that using number of employees was a good way to share out the direct wages bill, but remember that we are only interested here in overheads. Direct wages will already be included in the costs of the products that are made by the company. (Similarly direct materials are ignored for overheads.) If the question had included indirect labour then that would be included as an overhead and could be apportioned using the number of people working in each cost centre.

(b) A suitable basis for sharing out canteen costs is the number of employees. A suitable basis for sharing out the maintenance costs is the time spent servicing equipment.

First re-apportion canteen costs since the canteen provides services for maintenance but maintenance do not work for the canteen. Then re-apportion the maintenance work, which include a share of the canteen.

Overhead	Basis	Assembly £	Finishing £	Maintenance £	Canteen £
Total from above		16,500	26,250	6,675	10,575
Canteen	Personnel 20:30:10	3,525	5,288	1,762	(10,575)
Sub-total		20,025	31,538	8,437	
Maintenance	Time 60:40	5,062	3,375	(8,437)	
Total		25,087	34,913		

Total overhead = £60,000

(c) The assembly department seems to be labour based, therefore overhead is absorbed on the basis of labour hours:

Overhead absorption rate $\dfrac{£25,087}{10,000 \text{ hours}}$ = £2.51 per direct labour hour

The finishing department seems to be machine based, therefore overhead is absorbed on the basis of machine hours:

Overhead absorption rate $\dfrac{£34,913}{5,000 \text{ hours}}$ = £6.98 per machine hour

(d) Overhead absorbed per unit of JK:

(£2.51 × 4 hours) + (£6.98 × 2.5 hours) = £27.49

 Test your understanding 2

Which basis of absorbing factory overheads has traditionally been the most common?

A   Labour hours

B   Machine hours

C   Units of output

D   Units of inventory

Test your understanding 3

Lorus Limited

Lorus Limited makes cupboards. This involves three production departments (Sawing, Assembly and Finishing) together with two service departments (Maintenance and Materials handling).

Last year 4,000 cupboards were made.

Costs incurred:

	Sawing £	Assembly £	Finishing £
Materials	120,000	80,000	20,000
Wages	50,000	25,000	40,000
Overheads	75,000	50,000	20,000

Materials handling wages:	£9,000
Maintenance wages:	£20,000

The benefits derived from the service departments are estimated to be as follows:

	Sawing %	Assembly %	Finishing %	Materials handling %
Maintenance	30	40	20	10
Materials handling	50	20	30	

Required:

(a) Prepare a memorandum to the managing director, copied to each production head, showing the overheads allocated and apportioned to each production department.

(b) Calculate the unit cost of a cupboard.

Lorus Limited

(a) **MEMORANDUM**

To:

From:

Date:

Subject:

	Sawing	Assembly	Finishing	MH	Maintenance
	£	£	£	£	£
Overhead					
Apportion maintenance wages					
Apportion materials handling wages					
Total allotted				–	–

Note: Service department overhead has been apportioned to production departments on the basis of percentage estimates of relative benefit, as specified.

(b) 4,000 cupboards were produced with the following costs incurred:

	Sawing	Assembly	Finishing	Total	Unit cost
	£	£	£	£	£
Materials					
Wages					
Overheads					

The unit cost of a cupboard is £_____.

Test your understanding 4

Sandsend Engineers Ltd specialise in agricultural engineering. The business is divided into three cost centres: machining, fabrication and outside contract work.

The budgeted overhead for the quarter ended 31 March 20X3 shows:

Cost centre	Machining	Fabrication	Outside contracts	Total
	£	£	£	£
Allocated overhead	21,000	25,500	19,500	66,000
Apportioned overhead	15,000	16,100	9,100	40,200
	36,000	41,600	28,600	106,200
Budgeted machine hours	4,000	5,200		
Budgeted labour hours			1,950	

In early January, the company receives an order for a replacement door on a grain silo for a local farmer. The specification of costs includes:

Direct material	£3,100
Direct labour rate per hour	£7.50

Machine hours and labour hours per cost centre:

Machining	12 hours
Fabrication	8 hours
Outside contracts	6 hours

The business has a pricing policy based on full absorption costing principles. It adds 10% to production costs to cover for administration, selling and distribution. It then plans for profit based on 25% of the selling price or contract price.

Task

Determine, using absorption costing principles, the contract price of the replacement grain silo door. (Calculate to the nearest £.)

Overhead recovery rates for each cost centre:

Machining = £ _____ per machine hour

Fabrication = £ _____ per machine hour

Outside contract work = £ _____ per direct labour hour

Production cost of contract:

	£
Direct material	
Direct labour:	
Machining	
Fabrication	
Outside work	
Overheads:	
Machining	
Fabrication	
Outside work	
	———
Production cost	
Add 10% for admin, selling and distribution	
	———
Profit	
	———
Selling price/contract price	

Test your understanding 5

Refer again to the scenario in Test your understanding 4 – Sandsend Engineers Ltd.

The actual overhead incurred during the quarter ended 31 March 20X3 was:

	£
Machining	37,800
Fabrication	42,000
Outside work	29,100
	108,900

Overhead is recovered on machine hours in machining and fabrication, and labour hours on outside work.

The actual level of activity in the quarter was:

Machining	4,250 machine hours
Fabrication	5,300 machine hours
Outside work	1,975 labour hours

Task

Calculate the overhead recovered in each cost centre for the period.

Solution

Sandsend Engineers Ltd overhead recovered:

	£
Machining	
Fabrication	
Outside work	

Test your understanding 6

Luda Limited manufactures three products: P, Q and R. Each product is started in the machining area and completed in the finishing shop. The direct unit costs associated with each product, forecast for the next trading period, are as follows.

	P £	Q £	R £
Materials	18.50	15.00	22.50
Wages:			
Machining area @ £5 per hour	10.00	5.00	10.00
Finishing shop @ £4 per hour	6.00	4.00	8.00
	34.50	24.00	40.50

There are machines in both departments and the machine hours required to complete one of each product are:

	P	Q	R
Machining area	4.0	1.5	3.0
Finishing shop	0.5	0.5	1.0
Budgeted output in units	6,000	8,000	2,000

Fixed overheads:
Machining area £100,800
Finishing shop £94,500

Task

(a) Calculate the overhead absorption rate for fixed overheads using:

    (i) a labour hour rate for each department

    (ii) a machine hour rate for each department.

(b) Calculate the total cost of each product using:

    (i) the labour hour rate

    (ii) the machine hour rate

    as calculated in (a) above.

Solution

(a) **Fixed overhead absorption rates**

		Machine area £	Finishing shop £
Fixed overhead			
		Hours	Hours
(i) Labour hours	P		
	Q		
	R		
		————	————
		————	————
Overhead absorption rate per labour hour		————	————
(ii) Machine hours	P		
	Q		
	R		
		————	————
		————	————
Overhead absorption rate per machine hr		————	————

(b) **Product costs**

	P £	Q £	R £
Materials			
Wages			
Prime cost			

(i) *Labour hour rate absorption*

	P £	Q £	R £
Prime costs as above			
Fixed overheads:			
Machine area			
Finishing shop			

(ii) *Machine hour rate absorption*

	P £	Q £	R £
Prime costs as above			
Fixed overheads:			
Machine area			
Finishing shop			

1.6 Criticisms of absorption costs

Historically a direct labour rate for absorption of all fixed overheads was a very common method, as production tended to be highly labour-intensive. Such items as rent would be apportioned using the area involved, but the absorption rate would usually be labour hours. It was reasonable to assume that the more labour time spent on a product, the more production resources in general were being used. Thus a product with a higher labour content should be charged with a higher share of the overheads.

However, nowadays, production is far more mechanised. This has two impacts as follows:

(a) A higher proportion of the overhead is accounted for by machine-related costs (power, depreciation, maintenance, etc).

(b) The amount of labour time spent upon a unit is far less representative of its use of production resources.

To take a simple example, Product A may use 9 machine hours and 1 labour hour, whilst Product B requires 1 machine hour and 4 labour hours. The traditional approach would charge B with four times as much production overhead (including machine costs) as A, even though it takes half the time overall.

In this example, one solution would be to use machine hours as a basis. However, this still tries to relate all overhead costs, whatever their nature, to usage of one resource. This would not necessarily be appropriate for, say, costs of receiving and checking materials going into the production process. This will be more likely to depend upon the number of times an order of material is received into stores for a particular product.

2 Activity-based costing (ABC)

2.1 Activity-based costing (ABC) approach

Professors Robin Cooper and Robert Kaplan at the Harvard Business School developed a costing system called activity-based costing (ABC) which avoids the problems experienced by traditional costing methods. If management are keen to control costs, then it is vital that they should know the activities that cause costs to arise.

(a) **Cost drivers**

Those activities that are the significant determinants of cost are known as cost-drivers. For example, if production-scheduling cost is driven by the number of production set-ups, then that number is the cost-driver for the cost of production-scheduling. The cost-drivers represent the bases for charging costs in the ABC system, with a separate cost code established for each cost-driver.

(b) **Cost pools**

Where several costs are 'driven' by the same activity (e.g. engine oil, machine breakdown and repairs) then these costs are put into 'cost pools' and the total of the cost pool is absorbed by, say, machine hours.

2.2 Mechanics of ABC

The mechanics of operating an ABC system are similar to a traditional costing system. The significant cost drivers need to be ascertained and a cost centre is established for each cost driver. Costs are allocated to products by dividing the cost centre costs by the number of cost driving activities undertaken.

For example, in Plant Y a set up of a production run would be a cost driver. The cost of the engineers who do the set ups would be a cost centre. If the cost of the engineers is say £280,000 and the number of sets ups is 500, then the charging out rate is $\frac{280,000}{500}$ = £560. A product which has a number of small production runs will thus have a greater proportion of these costs relative to the quantity of the product produced, than a product with large production runs.

Other overheads will be allocated to products in a different way; which way depends upon the cost drivers which have been ascertained.

💡 Example

Plant Y produces about one hundred products. Its largest selling product is Product A; its smallest is Product B. Relevant data is given below.

	Product A	Product B	Total Plant Y
Units produced pa	50,000	1,000	500,000
Material cost per unit	£1.00	£1.00	
Direct labour per unit	15 minutes	15 minutes	
Machine time per unit	1 hour	1 hour	
Number of set ups p.a.	24	2	500
Number of purchase orders for materials	36	6	2,800
Number of times material handled	200	15	12,000
Direct labour cost per hour			£5

Overhead costs

	£
Set up	280,000
Purchasing	145,000
Materials handling	130,000
Machines	660,000
	1,215,000

Total machine hours are 600,000 hours.

Traditional costing (absorbing overheads on machine hours):

Unit cost	A £	B £
Material cost	1.00	1.00
Labour cost	1.25	1.25
Overhead per machine hour		
$\dfrac{1,215,000}{600,000} = 2.025$	2.025	2.025
	4.275	4.275

The above costings imply that we are indifferent between producing Product A and Product B.

Using an ABC approach would show:

Step 1 Calculate the direct material and labour costs as for the traditional approach.

Unit cost	A £	B £
Material cost	1.00	1.00
Labour cost	1.25	1.25
	2.25	2.25

Step 2 Calculate the overheads that will be charged to each product by:

(a) Calculating the overhead cost per cost driver for each type of over-head (e.g. cost per set-up).

(b) Charge cost to each unit by calculating the unit cost accordingly.

	A £	B £
Overheads:		
Set up		
$\dfrac{280,000}{500} = £560$ per set up		
$\dfrac{560 \times 24}{50,000}$	0.27	
$\dfrac{560 \times 2}{1,000}$		1.12

Purchasing:

$$\frac{145,000}{2,800} = £51.79 \text{ per purchase order}$$

$$\frac{36 \times 51.79}{50,000} \qquad\qquad 0.04$$

$$\frac{6 \times 51.79}{1,000} \qquad\qquad\qquad\qquad 0.31$$

Materials handling:

$$\frac{130,000}{12,000} = 10.83 \text{ per time}$$

$$\frac{200 \times 10.83}{50,000} \qquad\qquad 0.04$$

$$\frac{15 \times 10.83}{1,000} \qquad\qquad\qquad\qquad 0.16$$

Machines:

$\dfrac{660,000}{600,000} = £1.10$ per machine hour	1.10	1.10
	1.45	2.69
Add: Direct material and labour costs	2.25	2.25
	£3.70	£4.94

Common sense would lead us to conclude that ABC is a more accurate representation of the relative real costs of the two products.

What must be considered, however, is whether the benefits of this approach outweigh the costs of implementing and applying the system. The following example again contrasts a traditional product costing system with an ABC system and shows that an ABC system produces much more accurate product costs.

Example

Mayes plc has a single production centre and has provided the following budgeted information for the next period.

	Product A	Product B	Product C	Total
Production and sales (units)	40,000	25,000	10,000	75,000
Direct material cost per unit	£25	£20	£18	£1,680,000
Direct labour hours per unit	3	4	2	240,000
Machine hours per unit	2	4	3	210,000
Number of production runs	5	10	25	40
Number of component receipts	15	25	120	160
Number of production orders	15	10	25	50

Direct labour is paid £8 per hour.

Overhead costs in the period are expected to be as follows:

	£
Set-up	140,000
Machine	900,000
Goods inwards	280,000
Packing	200,000
Engineering	180,000
	1,700,000

What are the unit costs of each product using:

(a)   the traditional approach?

(b)   the ABC method?

Solution

(a) A traditional costing approach would cost each product as follows:

	Product A	Product B	Product C
	£	£	£
Direct materials	25.00	20.00	18.00
Direct labour (@ £8 per hour)	24.00	32.00	16.00
Overhead (@ £7.08 per hour) see below)	21.24	28.32	14.16
Total cost	70.24	80.32	48.16

Overhead recovery rate $= \dfrac{£1,700,000}{240,000} = £7.08$ per direct labour hour

(b) An ABC system needs to identify the cost drivers for the indirect overheads not driven by production volume. Assume that these are as follows.

Cost	Cost driver
Set-up	Number of production runs
Goods inwards	Number of receipts
Packing	Number of production orders
Engineering	Number of production orders

The machine overhead of £900,000 is likely to be related primarily to production volume, so it will be recovered on the basis of

machine hours used $= \dfrac{£900,000}{210,000} = £4.29$ per machine hour

(after rounding).

The cost per activity for each of the other cost centres is as follows.

Set-up cost $\dfrac{£140,000}{40} = £3,500$ per production run

Goods inwards $\dfrac{£280,000}{160} = £1,750$ per component receipt

Packing $\dfrac{£200,000}{50} = £4,000$ per production order

Engineering $\dfrac{£180,000}{50} = £3,600$ per production order

An ABC approach would allocate overheads to each of the product groups as follows:

	Product A £	Product B £	Product C £
Set-up costs			
5 × £3,500	17,500		
10 × £3,500		35,000	
25 × £3,500			87,500
Machine costs (rounded down)			
(2 × 40,000) × £4.29	343,200		
(4 × 25,000) × £4.29		429,000	
(3 × 10,000) × £4.29			128,700
Goods inwards costs			
15 × £1,750	26,250		
25 × £1,750		43,750	
120 × £1,750			210,000
Packing costs			
15 × £4,000	60,000		
10 × £4,000		40,000	
25 × £4,000			100,000
Engineering costs			
15 × £3,600	54,000		
10 × £3,600		36,000	
25 × £3,600			90,000
	———	———	———
Total overhead	500,950	583,750	616,200
	———	———	———
Average overhead per unit			
£500,950/40,000	£12.52		
£583,750/25,000		£23.35	
£616,200/10,000			£61.62
This compares to the traditional overhead absorption of:			
	£21.24	£28.32	£14.16

It can be seen that product C is significantly under-costed under the traditional system, while products A and B are over-costed. This situation arises because the large proportion of costs driven by product C is not picked up under the traditional costing system. Since it is the cost-drivers identified in the ABC system which generate the costs in the first place, the ABC system will produce a more accurate final analysis.

📝 Test your understanding 7

Which method of costing gives a more accurate product cost?

A   Activity based costing

B   Total absorption costing

C   Marginal costing

D   Standard costing

2.3   Advantages and disadvantages of activity based costing

ABC has a number of advantages:

- It provides a more accurate cost per unit. As a result, pricing, sales strategy, performance management and decision making should be improved.

- It provides much better insight into what causes (drives) overhead costs.

- ABC recognises that overhead costs are not all related to production and sales volume.

- In many businesses, overhead costs are a significant proportion of total costs, and management needs to understand the drivers of overhead costs in order to manage the business properly. Overhead costs can be controlled by managing cost drivers.

- It can be applied to calculate realistic costs in a complex business environment.

- ABC can be applied to all overhead costs, not just production overheads.

- ABC can be used just as easily in service costing as in product costing.

Disadvantages of ABC:

- ABC will be of limited benefit if the overhead costs are primarily volume related or if the overhead is a small proportion of the overall cost.

- It is impossible to allocate all overhead costs to specific activities.

- The choice of both activities and cost drivers might be inappropriate.

- ABC can be more complex to explain to the stakeholders of the costing exercise.

- The benefits obtained from ABC might not justify the costs.

2.4 The implications of switching to ABC

The use of ABC has potentially significant commercial implications:

- Pricing can be based on more realistic cost data.

  Pricing decisions will be improved because the price will be based on more accurate cost data.

- Sales strategy can be more soundly based.

  More realistic product costs as a result of the use of ABC may enable sales staff to:

  > target customers that appeared unprofitable using absorption costing but may be profitable under ABC

  > stop targeting customers or market segments that are now shown to offer low or negative sales margins.

- Decision making can be improved.

  Research, production and sales effort can be directed towards those products and services which ABC has identified as offering the highest sales margins.

- Performance management can be improved.

  Performance management should be enhanced due to the focus on selling the most profitable products and through the control of cost drivers.

  ABC can be used as the basis of budgeting and longer term forward planning of overhead costs. The more realistic budgeted overhead cost should improve the system of performance management.

📝 Test your understanding 8

P operates an activity based costing (ABC) system to attribute its overhead costs to cost objects.

In its budget for the year ending 31 August 20X6, the company expected to place a total of 2,895 purchase orders at a total cost of £110,010. This activity and its related costs were budgeted to occur at a constant rate throughout the budget year, which is divided into 13 four-week periods.

During the four-week period ended 30 June 20X6, a total of 210 purchase orders were placed at a cost of £7,650.

The over-recovery of these costs for the four-week period was:

A   £330

B   £350

C   £370

D   £390

📝 Test your understanding 9

Which of the following statements are correct (tick all that apply)?

		Correct?
(i)	A cost driver is any factor that causes a change in the cost of an activity.	☐
(ii)	For long-term variable overhead costs, the cost driver will be the volume of activity.	☐
(iii)	Traditional absorption costing tends to under-allocate overhead costs to low-volume products.	☐

Test your understanding 10

The accounting technician and the planning engineer have recently analysed the value adding processes and identified various activities, cost drivers within those activities and current volumes of production and decide to apply the ABC methodology.

Budget 20X3

	Activity	Cost pool £	Cost driver volume
(1)	Process set up	260,000	200 set ups
(2)	Material procurement	74,000	50 purchase orders
(3)	Maintenance	64,000	12 maintenance plans
(4)	Material handling	120,000	2,500 material movements
(5)	Quality costs	80,000	200 inspections
(6)	Order processing	30,000	1,000 customers
		628,000	

The company plans to produce 1,000 tonnes per month of a product which will require the following

   17 set ups

    4 purchase orders

    1 maintenance plan

210 material movements

   16 inspections

   80 customers

Task

(a) Calculate the cost driver rates.

(b) Determine the amount of overhead to be recovered per tonne of product.

Solution

(a) **Cost driver rates:**

Activity	Cost pool	Cost driver volume	Cost driver rate
	£		
Process set up			
Material procurement			
Maintenance			
Material handling			
Quality costs			
Order processing			

(b) Using the ABC method, the following overhead would be recovered for each 1,000 tonnes of output:

				£
	set ups	×		
	purchase orders	×		
	maintenance plan	×		
	material movements	×		
	inspections	×		
	customers	×		
				———
				———

Thus the overhead cost per tonne of product would be:

£ _____ per tonne.

3 Absorption costing and marginal costing

3.1 Introduction

We have discussed the idea of the collection of costs initially in cost centres and then attributing them to the cost units passing through those cost centres. But should all costs eventually be attributed to (absorbed by) cost units?

Two points should be noted regarding the absorption of costs into cost units:

*   **Production/selling costs** – in a manufacturing context, we have already seen that inventory of finished goods will never include an element of selling costs. The inventory will be valued at production costs only (including overheads). However, for pricing or profitability purposes, the cost of units sold may well include a selling cost element.

*   **Fixed/variable costs** – whether or not all production costs will be absorbed into cost units for inventory valuation will depend upon the particular system being used.

    (i) A total absorption costing (TAC) system absorbs all production costs (direct or indirect, fixed or variable) into cost units.

    (ii) A marginal costing (MC) system only absorbs variable production costs (direct and indirect) into cost units. Fixed costs are treated as period costs, and deducted as a 'lump sum' from the profits of the period concerned.

3.2 The main difference between absorption and marginal costing

The main difference between absorption and marginal costing is that under absorption costing the fixed production overheads are absorbed into the production cost of the units produced. They are thus treated as part of the cost per unit and are shown as part of the cost of sales.

Because the absorption rate for these costs is determined from the budgeted figures for output and the cost of the fixed overheads, there may be a difference between the amount absorbed into the units produced (which is based on the budgeted amounts) and the amount that should have been absorbed into the units produced if it had been based on the actual amounts. This may result in an over- or under-absorption of the production overheads which has to be corrected by an entry in the profit statement.

Example

A business has the following actual results (there are no opening or closing inventories).

Units produced and sold	5,000 (units)
Sales price per unit	£15
Direct materials (£4 per unit)	£20,000
Direct labour (£3 per unit)	£15,000
Variable production costs (£1 per unit)	£5,000
Fixed production costs incurred	£12,000
Admin and selling costs	£8,000

The budgeted production was 4,800 units.

Budgeted fixed overheads were £14,400.

Task

Prepare operating statements under absorption and marginal costing.

Solution

	Absorption £	Absorption £	Marginal £	Marginal £
Revenue (5,000 × £15)		75,000		75,000
Less cost of sales				
Materials	20,000		20,000	
Labour	15,000		15,000	
Variable overhead	5,000		5,000	
Fixed overhead absorbed (W2)	15,000			
		55,000		40,000
		20,000		35,000
Over-absorbed overhead (W3)		3,000		–
		23,000		
Fixed production costs		–		12,000
Admin and selling costs		8,000		8,000
		15,000		15,000

Workings:

1   Calculate the fixed production overhead absorption rate

= £14,400/4,800 = £3 per unit

2   Calculate the fixed production overhead absorbed into production under absorption costing

= actual units produced × absorption rate = 5,000 × £3 = £15,000

3   Calculate the over absorbed fixed overhead

Actual overhead	12,000
Absorbed overhead	15,000
Over absorbed	(3,000)

The overhead was over absorbed by £3,000 and this amount has to be added back to profit in the absorption statement to restore the figure to the actual amount.

3.3   The effect of changes in stock levels

The above example illustrated the difference between the two types of accounting but note that the profit figure at the end of the period was the same under both systems.

However, if inventory levels change in the period, the two systems will give a different figure for profit. This occurs because if inventory is carried forward under absorption costing, the inventory value will include some of the overheads incurred in the period. This effectively carries those overheads forward into the next period which reduces the overheads charged to profit in the first period thereby increasing the reported profit.

In the example above, if there had been no opening inventory but 500 units of inventory at the end of the period, the absorption statement would carry forward the production cost of this inventory to the next period including the fixed overhead element. The marginal statement would also carry forward the production cost of the inventory but there would be no fixed cost element.

Example

Consider the previous example with the business manufacturing 5,000 units, selling 4,500 units and carrying forward 500 units of inventory to the next period. All other facts are the same.

Task

Prepare operating statements under absorption and marginal costing.

Solution

	Absorption		Marginal	
	£	£	£	£
Revenue (4,500 × £15)		67,500		67,500
Less cost of sales				
Materials	20,000		20,000	
Labour	15,000		15,000	
Variable overhead	5,000		5,000	
Fixed overhead absorbed	15,000			
	―――		―――	
Less:	55,000		40,000	
closing inventory (W1)	(5,500)		(4,000)	
	―――	49,500	―――	36,000
		―――		―――
		18,000		31,500
Over-absorbed overhead		3,000		–
		―――		―――
		21,000		
Fixed production costs		–		12,000
Admin and selling costs		8,000		8,000
		―――		―――
		13,000		11,500
		―――		―――

Working:

Value of closing inventory

	Absorption	Marginal
	£	£
Cost per unit		
Materials	4	4
Labour	3	3
Variable overhead	1	1
Fixed overhead	3	Nil
	―	―
Unit cost	11	8
	―	―
Cost of 500 units	5,500 (500 × £11)	4,000 (500 × £8)

Test your understanding 11

Which gives the higher closing inventory valuation:

Marginal costing ☐

Absorption costing ☐

Test your understanding 12

X Ltd budgeted to spend £150,000 on fixed overheads in May, while producing 15,000 units.

During May, X Ltd actually produced 15,450 units and fixed overheads incurred were £152,500.

Required:

Fixed overheads were under/over absorbed (delete as appropriate) by
£ [_____]

Test your understanding 13

Y Ltd budgeted to spend £1,050,000 on fixed overheads in May, while producing 125,000 units.

During May, Y Ltd actually produced 112,000 units and fixed overheads incurred were £950,500.

Required:

Fixed overheads were under/over absorbed (delete as appropriate) by
£ [_____]

3.4 Marginal and absorption costing compared

Advantages of marginal costing

- Fixed overheads are the same regardless of output and are charged in full as a period cost. This avoids the need for apportionment and any under- or over-absorption.

- It focuses on variable costs and the concept of contribution, which can be much more useful for decision making.

Advantages of absorption costing

- Using absorption costing to value inventory is consistent with the valuation method used by financial accountants in International Accounting Standard (IAS) 2.

- In the long run a business needs to cover its fixed overheads to be profitable, so when setting a selling price, a management accountant needs to know the full product cost.

4 Contribution

 Definition

Contribution is defined as the **difference between selling price and the variable cost of producing and selling that item**. This is in contrast to profit per unit, which is the difference between selling price and the total absorption cost of producing and selling that item, which includes an element of fixed cost.

It is called contribution since it tells us how much each product contributes towards paying for the fixed costs of the business.

We need to decide between courses of action and **which course of action will be most beneficial**, looking at the revenues and costs under each alternative.

Fixed costs, by definition, are unavoidable and do not change with the level of production. Therefore, in any decision which is connected with varying the level of production, **fixed costs are not a relevant cost** as they do not change regardless of which course of action is taken.

Example

Katie is currently producing decorated mirrors. Each mirror sells at £10 each and has a variable cost of production of £8 per unit. Current production is 900 units per period. Fixed costs are expected to be £900 for the coming period, and therefore are charged at £1 per unit to production.

Katie has been approached to supply a new customer with 100 mirrors but at a discounted price of £8.25 per mirror.

Should she accept the order?

Solution

If we look at profit per unit, then the decision would be to **reject** the order, as we would not sell for £8.25 per unit something which has cost us (£8 + £1) = £9 to produce.

However, using contribution per unit might give us a different recommendation.

Contribution is calculated as selling price – variable cost. On a per unit basis for the contract, this is £8.25 – £8 = £0.25 contribution on each extra unit sold.

As we sell 100 units more, this generates a total increase in contribution (and profit) of £25 (100 × £0.25).We should **accept** the project.
The use of **contribution analysis** enables us to determine this quickly.

We could generate this answer by looking at total profits generated by the business before and after the acceptance of project:

	Reject £	Accept £
Revenue (900 @ £10)	9,000	9,000
(100 @ £8.25)		825
		9,825
Variable costs (900/1,000 @ £8)	(7,200)	(8,000)
Fixed costs	(900)	(900)
Profit	900	925

Therefore we can see that profits are improved by accepting the contract. Whilst revenue is increasing by £825, costs only increase by £800 as **fixed costs do not change**.

Test your understanding 14

Roger makes a single product, the Morton. During 20X9 he plans to make and sell 10,000 Mortons and accordingly has estimated the cost of each to be £50 (see below). Each Morton sells for £75.

	£
Materials	12
Labour	24
Variable overheads	10
Fixed overheads	4
Total absorption cost	50

Required:

(a) Calculate the contribution earned by each Morton.

(b) Calculate the total profit if Roger sells 2,000 Mortons.

Solution

(a) **Contribution per unit**

Selling price per unit – Variable cost per unit

= £_____

(b) **Profit**

Contribution – Fixed costs

= £_____

Test your understanding 15

Blidworth Loam Ltd manufacture a single product 'Cricketloam' and supply this product to cricket clubs.

Its cost specification includes the following budgeted details for the current year:

Direct labour hours	4.5
Labour rate per hour	£8.50
Direct material	1.1 tonnes per tonne of saleable output
Material cost	£25 per tonne
Variable production overheads (total)	£378,000
Fixed production overheads (total)	£250,000
Selling price per tonne	£132
Production volume	12,000 tonnes
Sales volume	11,500 tonnes

Task

Considering the above information, what is the budgeted marginal cost per tonne of product?

A   £65.75

B   £59.00

C   £97.25

D   £118.08

	£
Direct labour	
Direct material	
Variable overhead	
Marginal cost = Total variable costs per tonne	

Test your understanding 16

Task

Using the information in test your understanding 15, what is the contribution per tonne of product?

A   £66.25

B   £73.00

C   £13.92

D   £34.75

 Test your understanding 17

Task

Using the information in test your understanding 15 and 16:

(a)   Prepare a budgeted operating statement for the company in both marginal costing and full absorption costing format.

(b)   Reconcile the difference in reported profit shown in your two statements produced in part (a).

Solution

(a) **Blidworth Loam Ltd**

   Budgeted operating statement for the year

	Marginal costing format	Absorption costing format
Production (tonnes)		
	————	————
Sales (tonnes)		
	————	————
	£	£
Revenue		
	————	————
Variable costs		
Direct labour		
Direct material		
Variable overhead		
Closing inventory for marginal costing		
	————	
	————	
Contribution		
Fixed costs		
Closing inventory for absorption costing		
	————	————
Operating profit		
	————	————

(b) The difference in profit can be proved as:

5 Implications for pricing

5.1 Pricing considerations

The use of marginal cost is simpler as there is no need for the absorption of fixed overheads and could be argued to be more consistent with the use of contribution in decision making. The main difficulty lies in setting an appropriate margin or mark-up as this will need to ensure that fixed costs are covered. In practice the danger is often that prices are set too low. Marginal costing is particularly useful in short-term decisions concerning the use of excess capacity or one off contracts.

The use of full absorption cost ensures that all costs are incorporated into the pricing decision, so should ensure a profit is made, provided the target volume is achieved. However, to calculate the fixed cost per unit an assumption must be made concerning sales volumes, which in turn depend on the price, which depends on the cost per unit. A further criticism is that the method of absorbing overheads is somewhat arbitrary, so the prices obtained may not be very realistic when compared with what customers are willing to pay.

The use of ABC cost has the similar benefit to absorption costing in that all costs are incorporated into the pricing decision, so should ensure a profit is made. It is probably the most accurate cost and so therefore pricing, sales strategy, performance management and decision making should be improved. The issues are the same as listed earlier around complexity and ability to accurately allocate all overheads to specific activities.

6 Summary

This chapter has revised several fundamental cost accounting topics from your earlier studies, in particular the treatment of overheads including:

*   allocation/apportionment/absorption
*   service departments
*   over-/under-absorption
*   activity based costing
*   marginal costing and contribution.

Consideration of how the chosen method can impact selling price and therefore sales volume has also been reviewed.

Test your understanding answers

Test your understanding 1

C   Factory rental could be apportioned on the basis of the floor area occupied by the various cost centres.

Test your understanding 2

A   Traditionally, overheads have been absorbed as a rate per labour hour.

Test your understanding 3

Lorus Limited

(a)   **Memorandum re overheads**

MEMORANDUM

To: Managing Director

Copy: Production heads – sawing, assembly, finishing, materials handling (MH), maintenance

From: Management Accountant

Date: Today

Subject: Statement to show allotment of overhead

	Sawing £	Assembly £	Finishing £	MH £	Maintenance £
Overhead	75,000	50,000	20,000	9,000	20,000
Apportion maintenance department overhead	6,000	8,000	4,000	2,000	(20,000)
Apportion MH Overhead	5,500	2,200	3,300	(11,000)	–
Total allotted	86,500	60,200	27,300	–	–

Note: Service department overhead has been apportioned to production departments on the basis of percentage estimates of relative benefit, as specified.

KAPLAN PUBLISHING

(b) 4,000 cupboards were produced with the following costs incurred:

	Sawing £	Assembly £	Finishing £	Total £	Unit cost £
Materials	120,000	80,000	20,000	220,000	55.00
Wages	50,000	25,000	40,000	115,000	28.75
Overheads	86,500	60,200	27,300	174,000	43.50
	256,500	165,200	87,300	509,000	127.25

The unit cost of a cupboard is £127.25.

Test your understanding 4

Overhead recovery rates for each cost centre:

Machining $\dfrac{£36,000}{4,000 \text{ machine hours}}$ = £9.00 per machine hour

Fabrication $\dfrac{£41,600}{5,200 \text{ machine hours}}$ = £8.00 per machine hour

Outside contract work $\dfrac{£28,600}{1,950 \text{ labour hours}}$ = £14.67 per direct labour hr

Production cost of contract:

		£
Direct material		3,100
Direct labour:		
Machining	12 hours	
Fabrication	8 hours	
Outside work	6 hours	
	26 hours × £7.50	195
Overheads:		
Machining	12 hours × £9.00	108
Fabrication	8 hours × £8.00	64
Outside work	6 hours × £14.67	88
Production cost		3,555
Add 10% for admin, selling and distribution		356
Add 25% for profit (£3,911 × 25/75)		1,304
Selling price/contract price (£3,911/75) × 100 =		£5,215

Check:

	£
Contract price/selling price	5,215
Cost	3,911
Profit	£1,304

Profit = 25% of selling price as required.

Test your understanding 5

Sandsend Engineers Ltd overhead recovered:

		£
Machining	4,250 machine hours × £9.00	38,250
Fabrication	5,300 machine hours × £8.00	42,400
Outside work	1,975 labour hours × £14.67	28,973
		£109,623

Test your understanding 6

(a) Fixed overhead absorption rates

			Machining area £	Finishing shop £
Fixed overhead			100,800	94,500
			Hours	Hours
(i) Labour hours	P	6,000 units × 2, 1.5	12,000	9,000
	Q	8,000 units × 1, 1	8,000	8,000
	R	2,000 units × 2, 2	4,000	4,000
			24,000	21,000
Overhead absorption rate per labour hour			£4.20	£4.50

(ii) Machine hours

P	6,000 × 4, 0.5		24,000	3,000
Q	8,000 × 1.5, 0.5		12,000	4,000
R	2,000 × 3, 1		6,000	2,000
			42,000	9,000

Overhead absorption rate per machine hr £2.40 £10.50

(b) **Product costs**

	P £	Q £	R £
Materials	18.50	15.00	22.50
Wages	16.00	9.00	18.00
Prime cost	34.50	24.00	40.50

(i) *Labour hour rate absorption*

	P £	Q £	R £
Prime costs as above	34.50	24.00	40.50
Fixed overheads:			
Machine area £4.20 × 2, 1, 2	8.40	4.20	8.40
Finishing shop £4.50 × 1.5, 1, 2	6.75	4.50	9.00
	49.65	32.70	57.90

(ii) *Machine hour rate absorption*

	P £	Q £	R £
Prime costs as above	34.50	24.00	40.50
Fixed overheads:			
Machine area £2.40 × 4, 1.5, 3	9.60	3.60	7.20
Finishing shop £10.50 × 0.5,0.5,1	5.25	5.25	10.5
	49.35	32.85	58.20

Test your understanding 7

A   ABC gives the most accurate product costing.

 Test your understanding 8

A

Cost driver rate = 110,010 ÷ 2,895 = £38 for each order

	£
Cost recovered: 210 orders × £38	7,980
Actual costs incurred	7,650
Over-recovery of costs for four-week period	330

 Test your understanding 9

Which of the following statements are correct (tick all that apply)?

		Correct?
(i)	A cost driver is any factor that causes a change in the cost of an activity.	☑
(ii)	For long-term variable overhead costs, the cost driver will be the volume of activity.	☑
(iii)	Traditional absorption costing tends to under-allocate overhead costs to low-volume products.	☑

Statement (i) provides a definition of a cost driver. Cost drivers for long-term variable overhead costs will be the volume of a particular activity to which the cost driver relates, so Statement (ii) is correct. Statement (iii) is also correct. In traditional absorption costing, standard high-volume products receive a higher amount of overhead costs than with ABC. ABC allows for the unusually high costs of support activities for low volume products (such as relatively higher set-up costs, order processing costs and so on).

Test your understanding 10

(a) **Cost driver rates:**

Activity	Cost pool £	Cost driver volume	Cost driver rate
Process set up	260,000	200 set ups	£1,300/set up
Material procurement	74,000	50 purchase orders	£1,480 per purchase order
Maintenance	64,000	12 maintenance plans	£5,333 per plan
Material handling	120,000	2,500 material movements	£48 per movement
Quality costs	80,000	200 inspections	£400 per inspection
Order processing	30,000	1,000 customers	£30 per customer

(b) Using the ABC method, the following overhead would be recovered for each 1,000 tonnes of output:

			£
17 set ups	×	£1,300	22,100
4 purchase orders	×	£1,480	5,920
1 maintenance plan	×	£5,333	5,333
210 material movements	×	£48	10,080
16 inspections	×	£400	6,400
80 customers	×	£30	2,400
			———
			£52,233
			———

Thus the overhead cost per tonne of product would be:

£52,233/1,000 = £52.23 per tonne.

 Test your understanding 11

Absorption costing gives a higher inventory valuation than marginal costing since it includes fixed production costs which marginal costing does not.

Test your understanding 12

Budgeted absorption rate = £150,000/15,000 units = £10 per unit

		£
Actual expenditure		152,500
Overhead absorbed	15,450 units × £10	154,500
	Over absorbed	(2,000)

 Test your understanding 13

Budgeted absorption rate = £1,050,000/125,000 units = £8.40 per unit

		£
Actual expenditure		950,500
Overhead absorbed	112,000 units × £8.40	940,800
	Under absorbed	9,700

 Test your understanding 14

(a) **Contribution per unit**

Selling price per unit – Variable cost per unit

£75 – £46 = £29

(b) **Profit**

Contribution – Fixed costs

£29 × 2,000 – £40,000 = £18,000

Test your understanding 15

Answer is C.

		£
Direct labour	4.5 hours × £8.50	38.25
Direct material	1.1 tonnes × £25	27.50
Variable overhead	£378,000/12,000 tonnes	31.50
Marginal cost = Total variable costs per tonne		£97.25

Test your understanding 16

Answer is D.

Contribution per tonne	=	Selling price – Variable cost
	=	£132 – £97.25
	=	£34.75

Test your understanding 17

(a) **Budgeted operating statement for the year**

	Marginal costing format	Absorption costing format
Production (tonnes)	12,000	12,000
Sales (tonnes)	11,500	11,500
	£	£
Revenue (11,500 × 132)	1,518,000	1,518,000
Variable costs		
Direct labour (12,000 × 38.25)	459,000	459,000
Direct material (12,000 × 27.50)	330,000	330,000
Variable overhead (12,000 × 31.50)	378,000	378,000
Closing inventory for marginal costing (W1)	(48,625)	
	1,118,375	
Contribution	399,625	
Fixed costs	250,000	250,000
Closing inventory for absorption costing (W2)		(59,042)
Operating profit	149,625	160,042

(b) The difference in profit can be proved as 500 tonnes × £20.833 = £10,417.

Workings:

(W1) 500 tonnes × £97.25 = £48,625

(W2) Fixed production overheads are absorbed at £250,000 ÷ 12,000 = £20.833 per tonne

Inventory adjustment = 500 tonnes × (£97.25 + £20.833) = £59,042

Breakeven analysis

Introduction

How many units do we need to sell to make a profit? By how much will profit fall if price is lowered by £1? What will happen to our profits if we rent an extra factory but find that we can operate at only half capacity?

All of the above are **realistic business questions**. One solution would be to set up a model of the business on a PC and feed in the various pieces of information. Spreadsheet packages mean that this is an easy option.

But we have to appreciate that the PC is simply performing **cost-volume-profit (CVP) analysis** by another route. We can do this without a PC.

ASSESSMENT CRITERIA
Contribution per unit and per £ of turnover (1.3)
When to use contribution analysis as a decision making tool (1.3)
Break-even point and margin of safety (1.3 & 4.3)

CONTENTS
1   Cost-volume-profit (CVP) analysis
2   Breakeven analysis
3   Other considerations

1 Cost-volume-profit (CVP) analysis

1.1 Approach to CVP

*   Costs are assumed to be either **fixed** or **variable**, or at least **separable into these elements**.

*   Economies or diseconomies of scale are ignored; this ensures that **the variable cost per unit is constant**.

*   We look at the effect a change in volume has on **contribution** (not profit).

*   Contribution per unit = selling price per unit – total variable cost per unit.

2 Breakeven analysis

 Definition

Breakeven point

The breakeven point is the volume of sales at which neither a profit nor a loss is made.

Calculations are made easier, however, if we think in terms of contribution rather than profit. Breakeven is then the volume of sales at which total contribution (contribution per unit multiplied by number of units sold) is equal to fixed costs.

Note that fixed costs here are total fixed costs, i.e. fixed production and fixed selling costs.

The breakeven point can be found using the following formula.

$$\text{Breakeven point} = \frac{\text{Fixed cost}}{\text{Contribution/unit}}$$

Example

Breakeven point

Rachel's product, the 'Steadyarm', sells for £50. It has a variable cost of £30 per unit. Rachel's total fixed costs are £40,000 per annum.

What is her breakeven point?

Solution

To break even we want just enough contribution to cover the total fixed costs of £40,000.

We therefore want total contribution of £40,000.

Each unit of sales gives contribution of £50 – £30 = £20.

Therefore the breakeven point in units

$$= \frac{\text{Total fixed costs}}{\text{Contribution per unit}} = \frac{£40,000}{£20} = 2,000 \text{ units}$$

We can show that this calculation is correct as below.

	£
Total contribution (2,000 units × £20)	40,000
Total fixed costs	(40,000)
Profit/loss	NIL

2.1 Margin of safety

The margin of safety is the amount by which the anticipated (budgeted) sales can fall before the business makes a loss. It can be expressed in absolute units or relative percentage terms.

In units: Margin of safety = Budgeted sales units – Breakeven sales units

In %:   Margin of safety =

$$\frac{\text{Budgeted sales units} - \text{Breakeven sales units}}{\text{Budgeted sales units}} \times 100\%$$

For the 'Steadyarm' product above, if Rachel is expecting to achieve sales of 3,600 units:

Margin of safety (units) = 3,600 – 2,000 = 1,600 units

As a %: $\dfrac{1,600}{3,600} \times 100 = 44.4\%$

Actual sales can fall by 44.4% of the budgeted level before the Steadyarm will start to make a loss.

Margin of safety can also be expressed in sales revenue terms by taking the margin of safety in units and multiplying by the sales price (1,600 units × £50 = £80,000).

Test your understanding 1

Camilla makes a single product, the Wocket. During 20X5 she plans to make and sell 3,000 Wockets and has estimated the following:

	Cost per unit £
Material	3
Labour	5
Variable overhead	2
Total variable cost per unit	10

Total fixed costs are budgeted to be £12,000 and the estimated selling price £15.

Required:

(a) Calculate the contribution per unit earned by each Wocket.

(b) Calculate Camilla's budgeted profit.

(c) Calculate Camilla's breakeven point and margin of safety.

Solution

(a) **Contribution per unit**

= Selling price per unit – Variable cost per unit

= £_____

(b) **Budgeted profit**

= Total contribution – Fixed costs

= £_____

(c) **Breakeven point**

= Total fixed costs/Contribution per unit

= _____ units

Margin of safety

= (budgeted sales – breakeven point)/budgeted sales × 100%

= _____ %

2.2   Achieving a target profit

A similar approach can be used to find the sales volume at which a particular profit is made.

Sales volume to achieve a particular profit

$$= \frac{\text{Total fixed costs} + \text{required profit}}{\text{Contribution/unit}}$$

 Example

Achieving a target profit

Using the data from the previous example – Rachel, we now want to know how many units must be sold to make a profit of £100,000.

To achieve a profit of £100,000, we require sufficient contribution firstly to cover the fixed costs (£40,000) and secondly to give a profit of £100,000. Therefore our required contribution is £140,000.

Sales volume to achieve a profit of £100,000

$$= \frac{\text{Total fixed costs} + \text{required profit}}{\text{Contribution/unit}}$$

$$= \frac{£40,000 + £100,000}{£20}$$

= 7,000 units

We can show that this is the case with a summarised income statement.

	£
Revenue (7,000 × £50)	350,000
Variable cost (7,000 × £30)	(210,000)
Total fixed costs	(40,000)
Profit	100,000

2.3   C/S ratio

The C/S ratio is calculated by dividing contribution by sales value (either per unit in each part of the formula, or in total in both parts of the formula).

For example, if contribution per unit is £20 and the sales price per unit is £50 then the C/S ratio is 0.4 or 40%.

Test your understanding 2

A company budgets to sell 500 units but has calculated that it will breakeven at 400 units. The margin of safety is:

A   20%

B   25%

2.4   Breakeven point in terms of revenue

Another approach to the breakeven point is to calculate what sales revenue a company needs to achieve to break even.

$$\text{Breakeven point (rev)} = \frac{\text{Fixed cost}}{\text{C/S ratio}}$$

Alternatively it can also be found by using the breakeven point in units multiplied by the selling price.

 Example

Breakeven point

Rachel's product, the 'Steadyarm', sells for £50. It has a variable cost of £30 per unit. Rachel's total fixed costs are £40,000 per annum.

What is her breakeven point in revenue?

Solution

As before we want total contribution of £40,000.

The C/S ratio is £20/£50 = 0.4 or 40%

Therefore the breakeven point in revenue

$$= \frac{\text{Total fixed costs}}{\text{C/S ratio}} = \frac{£40,000}{0.4} = £100,000$$

Or Breakeven units × Selling price = 2,000 units × £50 = £100,000

Test your understanding 3

A company budgets to sell 16,000 units of a product at a selling price of £25. Variable costs are £15 per unit and fixed costs are £75,000 in total.

The contribution per unit is £ ☐

The breakeven point in units is ☐

The margin of safety in units is ☐

The margin of safety as a percentage (to 2 decimal places) is ☐

The contribution to sales (C/S) ratio (to 2 decimal places) is ☐

The break even sales are £ ☐

Test your understanding 4

A company budgets to sell 1,000 units of a product at a selling price of £2. Variable costs are £0.50 per unit and fixed costs are £900 in total.

The contribution per unit is £ [   ]

The breakeven point in units is [   ]

The margin of safety in units is [   ]

The margin of safety as a percentage (to 2 decimal places) is [   ]

The contribution to sales (C/S) ratio (to 2 decimal places) is [   ]

The break even sales are £ [   ]

3 Other considerations

3.1 Impact of costs structures on the breakeven point

Different organisations will have different cost structures. This will often be heavily influenced by the industry in which they operate. For example, a service company, such as a firm of accountants, will find that most of their costs are fixed costs such as salaries and rent. On the other hand, a retailer is likely to find that most of its costs are variable (such as the purchasing costs of the items it is selling). Other factors such as the level of computerisation and mechanisation will also impact on the cost structure.

The proportion of costs which are fixed is referred to as operating gearing. An organisation with a high operating gearing, such as a firm of accountants, will have a high proportion of costs which are fixed. An organisation with a low operating gearing will have a small proportion of fixed costs relative to variable costs.

Organisations with a high operating gearing will have a higher breakeven point than organisations with a low operating gearing. These organisations will also have a higher contribution margin meaning that small changes in revenue will have a large impact on profit. Therefore, as sales increase beyond the breakeven point profits and margins will increase greatly.

The opposite will be true for organisations with a low operating gearing. However, organisations with low operating gearing will perform better as sales fall (for example, in a recession) as they will be able to cut back on costs. For example, in a recession a supermarket can reduce its purchasing cost but an accountancy practice must still pay its salaries and rent.

3.2 Sensitivity analysis

Sensitivity (or 'What if?') analysis involves determining the effects of various types of changes in the CVP model. These effects can be determined by simply changing the constants in the CVP model, i.e., prices, variable cost per unit, sales mix ratios etc.

For example, it answers questions such as 'What will be the impact on our revenue if variable cost per unit increases by 30%?' The sensitivity of revenue to various possible outcomes broadens the perspective of management regarding what might actually occur before making cost commitments. This would be fairly easy with spreadsheets, or other software developed to handle these calculations.

 Example

Sensitivity

Rachel's product, the 'Steadyarm', sells for £50. It has a variable cost of £30 per unit. Rachel's total fixed costs are £40,000 per annum.

Her current breakeven point is 2,000 units.

What would be the impact on the breakeven point if the selling price was increase by 10%, the variable costs increase by 20% and fixed costs increased by 18.75%?

Solution

The selling price would now be: £50 × 1.1 = £55

The variable cost would now be £30 × 1.2 = £36

Giving a revised contribution of £55 – £36 = £19/unit

The fixed costs would now be £40,000 × 1.1875 = £47,500

$$= \frac{\text{Total fixed costs}}{\text{Contribution per unit}} = \frac{£47,500}{£19} = 2,500 \text{ units}$$

An increase of 500 or 25%.

 Example

Shifty is looking to increase its sales and profits. Current figures (per annum, unless stated otherwise) are as follows:.

Sales volume	2,000 units
Selling price	£15 per unit
Fixed overheads	£5,000
Labour	£2 per unit
Material	£1 per unit
Inventory levels	Nil

In order to increase sales to 2,500 units the selling price would need to fall to £14 per unit, the variable costs would fall by 10%, and fixed costs would fall by £500.

Extra investment in assets would be required of £10,000 which would be depreciated at 25% per annum.

KAPLAN PUBLISHING

The total annual change in profit would be:

(Negative figures should be entered using brackets.)

	Current	**Future**	**Change**
Revenue			
Material			
Labour			
Fixed overhead			
Depreciation			
Additional profit			

The return on the additional investment would be [   ] **%.**

Concerned that sales may not reach the 2,500 unit level, the Finance Director would like to know the break even volume.

Fixed costs	£
Contribution per unit	£
Break even volume (units)	

Solution

	Current	Future	Change
Revenue	2,000 × £15 = £30,000	2,500 × £14 = £35,000	£5,000
Material	2,000 × £1 = (£2,000)	2,500 × (£1 × 0.9) = (£2,250)	(£250)
Labour	2,000 × £2 = (4,000)	2,500 × (£2 × 0.9) = (£4,500)	(£500)
Fixed overhead	(5,000)	£5,000 – £500 = (£4,500)	£500
Depreciation		£10,000 × 25% = (£2,500)	(£2,500)
Additional profit			£2,250

The return on the additional investment would be 22.5% (2,250/10,000 × 100).

Fixed costs (4,500 + 2,500)	£7,000
Contribution per unit [(35,000 – 2,250 – 4,500)/2,500 units]	£11.30
Break even volume (units) = £7,000/£11.30 =	620

Test your understanding 5

Wat is looking to increase its sales and profits. Current figures (per annum, unless stated otherwise) are as follows:

Sales volume	10,000 units
Selling price	£20 per unit
Fixed overheads	£50,000
Labour	£2 per unit
Material	£10 per unit
Inventory levels	Nil

In order to increase sales to 10,500 units the selling price would need to fall to £19 per unit, the variable costs would fall by 10%, and fixed costs would fall by £1,000.

Extra investment in assets would be required of £20,000 which would be depreciated at 25% per annum.

The total annual change in profit would be:

(Negative figures should be entered using brackets.)

	Current	Future	Change
Revenue			
Material			
Labour			
Fixed overhead			
Depreciation			
Additional profit			

The return on the additional investment would be [   ] **%.**

Concerned that sales may not reach the 10,500 unit level, the Finance Director would like to know the break even volume.

Fixed costs	£
Contribution per unit	£
Break even volume (units)	

3.3 Advantages of CVP analysis

The major benefit of using breakeven analysis is that it indicates the lowest amount of activity necessary to prevent losses.

Breakeven analysis aids Decision Making as it explains the relationship between cost, production volume and returns.

It can be extended to show how changes in fixed costs, variable costs or in revenues will affect profit levels and breakeven points.

3.4 Disadvantages of CVP analysis

Any CVP analysis is based on assumptions about the behaviour of revenue, costs and volume. A change in expected behaviour will alter the breakeven point. In other words, profits are affected by changes in other factors besides volume. Other factors include unit prices of input, efficiency, changes in production technology, wars, strikes, legislation, and so forth. The following underlying assumptions will limit the precision and reliability of a given cost-volume-profit analysis.

(1) The behaviour of total cost and total revenue has been reliably determined and is linear over the relevant range.

(2) All costs can be divided into fixed and variable elements.

(3) Total fixed costs remain constant over the relevant volume range of the CVP analysis.

(4) Total variable costs are directly proportional to volume over the relevant range.

(5) Selling prices are to be unchanged.

(6) Prices of the factors of production are to be unchanged (for example, material, prices, wage rates).

(7) Efficiency and productivity are to be unchanged.

(8) The analysis either covers a single product or assumes that a given sales mix will be maintained as total volume changes.

(9) Revenue and costs are being compared on a single activity basis (for example, units produced and sold or sales value of production).

(10) Perhaps the most basic assumption of all is that volume is the only relevant factor affecting cost. Of course, other factors also affect costs and sales. Ordinary cost-volume-profit analysis is a crude oversimplification when these factors are unjustifiably ignored.

(11) The volume of production equals the volume of sales, or changes in beginning and ending inventory levels are insignificant in amount.

Test your understanding 6

Dandra S is a business that produces a single product; it has the following output levels and costs for the last 3 months.

Month	Activity (units)	Costs £
April	10,000	60,000
May	11,000	61,000
June	12,000	62,000

The fixed cost per month is £ [   ]

The CS ratio is budgeted to be 60%. Dandra S would like to maintain a minimum profit of £100,000 per month.

Complete the below sentences:

The contribution is £[   ] per unit.

Dandra S needs to sell [   ] units to achieve this minimum profit.

Budgeted sales for July are 75,000 units.

Complete the below sentences:

With sales of 75,000 units, the contribution needs to be £ [   ] per unit to achieve the minimum profit.

This means a selling price of £ [   ] per unit.

Test your understanding 7

B Company provides a single product to its customers. An analysis of its budget for the year ending 31 January 20X8 shows that, in Period 5, when the budgeted activity was 5,000 units with a sales value of £20 each, the margin of safety was 50%.

The budgeted contribution to sales ratio of the service is 25%.

Calculate the budgeted fixed costs in period 5. £ [   ]

Test your understanding 8

EJ Company makes and sells a single product to its customers, the AP. The budgeted sales are 50,000 units of AP per month. EJ has correctly calculated the following information.

The margin of safety for the coming period is 10,000 units and fixed costs are budgeted to be £80,000.

Calculate the contribution per unit. £ ☐ per unit.

Test your understanding 9

Mopit has a variety of costs making up the full cost of their single product.

	£
Selling price	25
Direct material cost per unit	6
Direct labour cost per unit	6

There are 2 different overhead costs, the first is entirely fixed, and the budgeted cost is £16,000 per month.

The second has the following costs from the last 2 months:

Activity level Units	Cost £
20,000	90,000
25,000	100,000

Complete the following table:

	£
Total variable cost per unit	
Contribution per unit	

The budgeted sales for the coming month are 20,000 units

Complete the following table:

	£
Breakeven point in units	
Margin of safety (%)	

4 Summary

This chapter has revised the fundamental cost accounting topic of breakeven analysis from your earlier studies.

Test your understanding answers

Test your understanding 1

(a) **Contribution per unit**

= Selling price per unit – Variable cost per unit

= £15 – £10 = £5

(b) **Budgeted profit**

= Total contribution – Fixed costs

= £5 × 3,000 – £12,000 = £3,000

(c) **Breakeven point**

= Total fixed costs/Contribution per unit

= £12,000/£5 = 2,400 units

Margin of safety

= (budgeted sales – breakeven point)/budgeted sales × 100%

= (3,000 – 2,400)/3,000 × 100% = 20%

Test your understanding 2

A   Budgeted sales – breakeven sales/Budgeted sales

= (500 – 400)/500

= 20%

Test your understanding 3

The contribution per unit is selling price – variable costs = £25 – £15 = £10

The breakeven point in units is fixed costs/contribution per unit = £75,000/£10 = 7,500

The margin of safety in units is budgeted sales – breakeven sales = 16,000 – 7,500 = 8,500

The margin of safety as a percentage (to 2 decimal places) is 8,500/16,000 × 100% = 53.13%

The contribution to sales (C/S) ratio is £10/£25 = 0.4

The breakeven sales is fixed costs/c/s ratio = £75,000/0.4 = £187,500

(Check this by taking breakeven units × selling price: 7,500 units × £25 = £187,500)

 Test your understanding 4

The contribution per unit is selling price – variable costs = £2 – £0.50 = £1.50

The breakeven point in units is fixed costs/contribution per unit = £900/£1.50 = 600

The margin of safety in units is budgeted sales – breakeven sales = 1,000 – 600 = 400 units

The margin of safety as a percentage (to 2 decimal places) is 400/1,000 × 100% = 40.00%

The contribution to sales (C/S) ratio is £1.50/£2.00 = 0.75

The breakeven sales volume is fixed costs/c/s ratio = £900/0.75 = £1,200

(Check this by taking breakeven units × selling price: 600 units × £2.00 = £1,200)

Test your understanding 5

	Current £	Future £	Change £
Revenue	10,000 × £20 = 200,000	10,500 × £19 = 199,500	(500)
Material	10,000 × £10 = (100,000)	10,500 × (£10 × 0.9) = (94,500)	5,500
Labour	10,000 × £2 = (20,000)	10,500 × (£2 × 0.9) = (18,900)	1,100
Fixed overhead	(50,000)	(49,000)	1,000
Depreciation	–	£20,000 × 25% = (5,000)	(5,000)
Additional profit			**2,100**

The return on the additional investment would be £2,100/£20,000 × 100 % = 10.5%.

		Workings
Fixed costs	**£54,000**	(£49,000 + £5,000)
Contribution per unit	**£8.20**	(£19 – £9.00 – £1.80)
Break even volume (units)	**6,586**	£54,000/£8.20

Test your understanding 6

Using the high-low method

Var cost = (62,000 – 60,000)/(12,000 – 10,000) = 2,000/2,000 = £1 per unit.

Fixed cost = 62,000– (12,000 × £1) = **£50,000**

As the variable cost is £1 per unit and the C/S ratio is 60%

	£	%
Selling price		100
Variable cost	1	40
Contribution		60

Selling price = 1/0.4 = £2.50 so the contribution = 2.50 – 1 = **£1.50 per unit.**

Units to achieve a target profit = (FC + Target profit)/contribution per unit

Units to achieve a target profit = (50,000 + 100,000)/1.50 = 150,000/1.50 = **100,000 units.**

Rearranging the target profit equation:

Contribution per unit = (FC + target profit)/number of units

= (50,000 + 100,000)/75,000

= **£2.00**

Contribution per unit = SP – var cost per unit

2.00 = SP – 1.00

SP = **£3.00 per unit**.

Test your understanding 7

Remember: **BEP (units) = Fixed costs/Contribution per unit**, so we need to use the information provided to find the BEP (units) and the contribution per unit.

If the MofS is 50% then BEP (units) = (100% – 50%) × 5,000 units = 2,500 units

Contribution per unit = 0.25 × 20 = £5

At the BEP, contribution is equal to the level of fixed costs.

Contribution at this volume is:

2,500 × £5 = £12,500

So the fixed costs are **£12,500**.

 Test your understanding 8

MofS (units) = BS – BEP

10,000 units = 50,000 units – BEP

BEP = 50,000 – 10,000 = 40,000 units

BEP = Fixed costs/contribution per unit

40,000 = 80,000/contribution per unit

Contribution per unit = £80,000/40,000 units = **£2.00**

Test your understanding 9

Using the high low method:

Variable cost per unit = (100,000 – 90,000)/(25,000 – 20,000) = 10,000/5,000 = £2

Total variable cost per unit = 6 + 6 + 2 = **£14**

Contribution per unit = 25 – 14 = **£11**

	£
Total variable cost per unit	**14**
Contribution per unit	**11**

Fixed costs:

Semi var = £100,000 – (25,000 × £2) = £50,000

Total Fixed cost = £16,000 + £50,000 = £66,000

BEP (units) = £66,000/£11 = **6,000 units**

MofS = (20,000 -6,000)/20,000 × 100 = **70%**

Breakeven point in units	**6,000**
Margin of safety (%)	**70**

Decision making techniques

Introduction

In the section on overheads we compared total absorption costing (TAC) with marginal costing (MC), where only directly attributable variable overheads are absorbed into cost units. The key reason for using MC is to assist in decision making. If a decision has to be made it is sensible only to take into account those costs which will actually be affected by the decision.

Within this chapter we will consider a number of different techniques that help a company make a decision.

ASSESSMENT CRITERIA
The optimal production mix when labour, materials or machine hours are restricted and opportunity costs of limited resources (1.3 & 4.3)
The outcomes of the various decision-making tools to aid the decision-making process (1.3)
The way to analyse decisions about: make or buy, closure of a business segment, automation (4.3)
The use of relevant and non-relevant costing information to aid decision making (4.3)
How analysis and calculations lead to recommendations (4.4)
Use the analysis to make reasoned recommendations and communicate them effectively (4.4)
Identify risks associated with a particular decision (4.4)

CONTENTS

1 Relevant costing

2 Limiting factor analysis

3 Make or buy decisions

4 Closure of a business segment

5 Further processing

1 Relevant costing

1.1 Introduction

When assisting management in making **short term** decisions only costs or revenues that are **relevant** to the decision should be considered. Any form of decision-making process involves making a choice between two or more alternatives.

For decision making, it is necessary to identify the costs and revenues that will be affected as a result of taking one course of action rather than another. The costs that would be affected by a decision are known as relevant costs.

Since relevant costs and revenues are those which are different, the term effectively means costs and revenues which change as a result of a decision.

Even though the costs and revenues are only being estimated it is important to ensure that the calculations are made knowing as much detail as possible or that any assumptions are stated. This will maintain the integrity of the information and should demonstrate professional competence.

1.2 Relevant costs and revenues

 Definition

Relevant costs and revenues are those costs and revenues that **change as a direct result of a decision that is taken**.

A relevant cost is a **future, incremental cash flow** arising as a direct result of a decision being taken:

- **Future costs and revenues** – costs and revenues that are going to be incurred sometime in the future due to the decision being taken.

- **Incremental costs and revenues** – any extra cost or revenue generated by the decision that would not arise otherwise e.g. an extra amount of fixed costs due only to the decision.

- **Cash flows rather than profits** – actual cash being spent or received should be used when making the decision. Profits can be manipulated by accounting concepts like depreciation. Cash flows are more reliable.

A relevant cost or revenue could also be referred to as an avoidable cost.

Definition

An **avoidable cost** is any cost that would only occur as a result of taking the decision. If the decision did not go ahead then the cost would not be incurred so it is avoidable.

1.3 Non-relevant costs and revenues

Costs or revenues that can be ruled out when making a decision come under the following categories:

- **Sunk costs** – past or historic costs that cannot be changed e.g. any cost incurred due to research and development that has already been carried out will not apply after the decision has been made.

- **Committed costs** – costs that are **unavoidable** and will be incurred whether or not the project is done.

- **Non-cash flow costs** – depreciation and carrying amounts are accounting concepts, not actual cash flows and are not relevant costs.

1.4 Fixed and variable costs

It is usually assumed that a **variable cost** will be **relevant** to a decision as when activity increases the total variable cost incurred increases. There is a direct relationship between production activity and variable costs. However there are some situations where this may not be true.

 Example

A company is considering a short-term pricing decision for a contract that would use 1,000 kg of material A. There are 800 kg of material A in inventory, which was bought some time ago for £3 per kg. The material in inventory could be sold for £3.50 per kg. The current purchase price of material A is £4.50.

What is the relevant cost of material A for this contract?

Solution

The cost per kg of material is considered to be a variable cost but you also need to consider whether the cost is a future cost for it to be relevant.

The company has already got 800 kg in inventory so this does not need to be purchased. The £3 per kg is an old purchase price i.e. a past or historic cost so it is not relevant. The material would therefore be valued at the current re-sale value of £3.50 per kg.

The company will need to buy a further 200 kg to complete the contract. This would be valued at the current purchase price of £4.50.

The total relevant cost of material A is:

800 kg × £3.50 = £2,800

200 kg × £4.50 = £900

Total = £3,700

Unless told otherwise variable costs and the variable element of the semi-variable costs are relevant to a decision.

Fixed costs tend to come under the umbrella of committed costs so are not relevant. Be careful though because if the fixed cost were to step up as a direct result of a decision taken then the extra cost would be relevant as it is an incremental cost.

 Example

MDCL Plc absorbs overheads on a machine hour rate, currently £20 per hour, of which £7 is for variable overheads and £13 is for fixed overheads. The company is deciding whether to undertake a contract in the coming year. If the contract is accepted it is estimated that the fixed costs will increase by £3,200 for the duration.

What are the relevant overhead costs for this decision?

Solution

The variable cost per hour is relevant as this cost would be avoided if the contract were not undertaken. The relevant cost is therefore £7 per machine hour.

The fixed cost per hour is an absorption rate. This is not an indication of how much actual overheads would increase by. The £3,200 extra fixed cost is relevant as it is an incremental or extra cost.

With regards to short-term decision making we assume that on the whole **fixed costs** are **non-relevant** costs so we can approach decisions using the **marginal costing technique**.

Test your understanding 1

As part of a new product development a company has employed a building consultant to perform an initial survey. This initial survey has cost £40,000. But there will be an ongoing need for her services if the company decides to proceed with the project. This work will be charged at a fixed rate of £20,000 per annum.

What relevant cost should be included for the building consultants services in the first year when considering whether the project should proceed?

A   £0

B   £20,000

C   £40,000

D   £60,000

 Test your understanding 2

A company which manufactures and sells one single product is currently producing 102,000 units per month and has capacity to produce up to 18,000 more. The current total monthly costs of production amount to £330,000, of which £75,000 are fixed and are expected to remain unchanged for all levels of activity up to full capacity.

A new potential customer has expressed interest in taking regular monthly delivery of 12,000 units at a price of £2.80 per unit.

All existing production is sold each month at a price of £3.25 per unit, the variable cost of production is £2.50 per unit. If the new business is accepted, existing sales are expected to fall by 2 units for every 15 units sold to the new customer.

What is the overall increase in monthly profit which would result from accepting the new business?

2 Limiting factor analysis

2.1 Single limiting factor

Since most overheads are fixed the decision to make one extra unit of production will not affect that cost, so it should be ignored. Only the marginal cost of making one extra unit should be considered in decision making and therefore should be added to the cost unit.

This approach to costing enables us to make decisions when there is a scarcity of resources, which is when the shortage of one resource means that that resource limits the entire capacity of the operation: this is the limiting factor.

A company may have two products, each requiring materials and labour. There may be a limit as to the amount of labour or materials that is available for the coming month. How can the company make the most profit when subject to such a constraint?

Since fixed costs are independent of production they are irrelevant (they will have to be paid however many units of each product are manufactured). The above problem therefore requires us to maximise contribution taking into account the limiting factor.

Example

Barbecue Limited manufactures two products for which the following details are available.

	Product X		Product Y
Selling price	£38		£38
Direct materials 8 units @ £1	£8	4 units @ £1	£4
Labour 4 hours @ £2	£8	6 hours @ £2	£12
Variable overhead 4 machine hours @ £3	£12	3 machine hours @ £3	£9
Fixed overheads	£5		£7

Maximum demand for X is 2,500 units.

Maximum demand for Y is 2,000 units.

Required:

Calculate the optimum production plan for Barbecue in each of the following two situations:

(a) Labour in the next period is limited to *16,000* hours, with no limit on machine hours.

(b) Machine hours in the next period are limited to *12,000* hours, with no limit on labour hours.

Solution

We would like to produce Xs and Ys up to the point where maximum demand is reached. (There is no point producing beyond this, because customers do not want any more.) So ideally we would like to produce 2,500 X and 2,000 Y.

To do this we would require the following resources.

	Labour hours	*Machine hours*
2,500 X	10,000	10,000
2,000 Y	12,000	6,000
	22,000	16,000

If labour is limited to 16,000 hours we will not have enough labour hours to achieve this. Similarly, if machine hours are limited to 12,000 our production will be restricted.

To tackle this problem we begin by calculating the contribution earned per unit of each product.

Contribution for each unit of X = £ (38 – 8 – 8 – 12) = £10 per unit

Contribution for each unit of Y = £ (38 – 4 – 12 – 9) = £13 per unit

(a) Labour is limited so we calculate the contribution earned per labour hour for each product.

X = £10/4 = £2.50 per labour hour

Y = £13/6 = £2.17 per labour hour

You get more contribution per labour hour for X than for Y so make as many Xs as possible.

Available hours = 16,000

2,500 Xs require 10,000 hrs

The remaining hours are all used to make as many Ys as possible.

Remaining Ys will take six hours each to make so produce 6,000/6 = 1,000 Ys.

Contribution = (2,500 × £10) + (1,000 × £13) = £38,000

(b) In this case, machine hours are the scarce resource so we calculate contribution per machine hour.

X = £10/4 = £2.50 per machine hour

Y = £13/3 = £4.33 per machine hour

Now it is better to make Ys. Making 2,000 Ys requires 2,000 × 3 = 6,000 machine hours. That leaves us a further 6,000 machine hours for making Xs.

6,000 remaining hours for X means making 6,000/4 = 1,500 Xs

Contribution = (1,500 × £10) + (2,000 × £13) = £41,000

Note that, in the assessment, if you are told the maximum demand for a product it is a big hint that this method should be used.

 Test your understanding 3

Roger makes three products – X Y and Z. He would like to make 500 of each product in the next year.

	X	Y	Z
Selling price	90	80	75
Materials (£3 per kg)	15	18	12
Labour	15	12	24
Variable overheads	8	6	10
Fixed overheads	4	4	4

Required:

(a) Calculate the contribution earned by each product.

(b) If material supplies are limited to 7,000 kg calculate the production plan which will optimise Roger's profit for the year.

Solution

(a) Contribution per unit = Selling price per unit – Variable cost per unit

	X	Y	Z
	£	£	£
Selling price			
Materials			
Labour			
Variable overhead			
Contribution			

(b)

Contribution			
Limiting factor			
Contribution per kg			
Rank			

Make _____ first using   kg

Make _____ next using   kg
                                        _____

                                        kg left

                                        _____

Available   7,000 kg
                            _____

The optimal production plan is _____

2.2 Opportunity costs of limited resources

It may be possible to buy extra materials or get extra time. An organisation would need to consider what was stopping them from producing more, for example if a company had more materials than they needed, there would be no value in buying anymore.

If materials was the limiting factor and there was the opportunity to buy more, perhaps from a different supplier, the key consideration would be how much the company would be willing to pay for it.

The calculation to work it out would be: (the contribution generated per kg plus the variable cost per kg) multiplied by the number of kg they were buying.

For labour, the calculation would be: (the contribution generated per hour plus the variable cost per hour) multiplied by the number of hours they required.

2.3 Absorption costing versus marginal costing in decision-making

We need to understand how absorption costing and marginal costing can be used in tasks which measure performance and which consider ways of enhancing value.

Absorption costing may be relevant for measuring the performance of a business and it may also be appropriate to use in enhancing value. For example, a product may be re-engineered in order to reduce production costs and it would be perfectly appropriate to consider the full absorption cost of the redesigned product.

Lifecycle costing (see later chapters) needs to consider both fixed and variable costs. However, it may be inappropriate to use absorption costing in certain circumstances. For example, if the business is considering contracting out the manufacture of a product, selling surplus capacity or some other limiting factor decision, then the marginal cost is the appropriate method as fixed costs will not change as a result of the decision.

However, it must be understood that certain fixed costs may change and the incremental cost in these circumstances may include both variable and fixed elements.

3 Make or buy decisions

3.1 Make or buy?

Sometimes a business will have to decide whether to make the product themselves or to buy it in from another company. This may be, for example, because they are already busy, because another company could produce it more cheaply or because the other company is a specialist.

Relevant costing should be used to resolve this decision. They include differences in variable costs and differences in directly attributable fixed costs.

3.2 Other considerations and risks associated with the decision

In addition to the relative cost of buying externally compared to making in-house, management must consider a number of other issues before a final decision is made.

- Reliability of external supplier: can the outside company be relied upon to meet the requirements in terms of:
  - quantity required
  - quality required
  - delivering on time
  - price stability.

- Specialist skills: the external supplier may possess some specialist skills that are not available in-house.

- Alternative use of resource: outsourcing will free up resources which may be used in another part of the business.

- Social: will outsourcing result in a reduction of the workforce? Redundancy costs should be considered.

- Legal: will outsourcing affect contractual obligations with suppliers or employees?

- Confidentiality: is there a risk of loss of confidentiality, especially if the external supplier performs similar work for rival companies.

- Customer reaction: do customers attach importance to the products being made in-house?

Example

Make or buy?

Dogbone makes two products X and Y. Next year the costs are expected to be:

	X	Y
Production (units)	1,000	2,000
	£	£
Direct materials	14	15
Direct labour	8	9
Variable production overhead	2	3
Directly attributable fixed costs	1,000	3,000

A subcontractor has offered to supply Dogbone with units of X and/or Y for £20 and £30 respectively. Should Dogbone make or buy the units?

	X	Y
	£	£
Variable cost of making	24	27
Variable cost of buying	20	30
Differential variable cost	4	(3)
Production (units)	1,000	2,000
Saving in variable cost by buying	4,000	(6,000)
Fixed cost saved by buying	1,000	3,000
Saving in total costs by buying	5,000	(3,000)

Dogbone should buy in units of X but should make units of Y.

Other considerations

• Is the supplier reliable with regards to delivery times and quality?

• Dogbone may have spare capacity now, which may lead to future job losses if other profitable activities cannot be found.

• Are the attributable fixed cost estimates reliable?

4 Closure of a business segment

4.1 Decisions about closure

The following difficult decisions might need to be made by a management accountant:

(a) Whether to close down a product line or department, perhaps because it appears to be making losses

(b) If the decision is to shut down, is it temporary or permanent?

A closure might result in

- savings in annual operating costs for a number of years

- unwanted non-current assets becoming available for sale

- employees being made redundant, relocated, re-trained or offered early retirement. There will be lump-sum cash outflows involved.

 Example

Shut down?

Dogbone makes two products X and Y. This year's annual profits are:

	X	Y	Total
	£	£	£
Sales	50,000	60,000	110,000
Variable costs	(30,000)	(40,000)	(70,000)
Contribution	20,000	20,000	40,000
Fixed costs	(15,000)	(25,000)	(40,000)
Profit / (loss)	5,000	(5,000)	Nil

Dogbone is concerned about Y's poor performance and is considering ceasing production of Y.

£15,000 of Y's fixed costs could be saved if production ceased i.e. there are some directly attributable fixed costs.

By stopping production of Y there would be a loss in profit of £5,000:

	£
Loss of contribution	(20,000)
Savings in fixed costs	15,000
Incremental loss	(5,000)

Another way of looking at this is that product X would now have to absorb some of Y's non-attributable fixed costs.

	£
Profit made by X	5,000
Companies fixed costs previously charged to Y (£25,000 – £15,000 attributable fixed costs)	(10,000)
Incremental loss (as above)	(5,000)

4.2 Other considerations and risks associated with the decision

Qualitative factors should be taken in to account alongside any numeric calculations, such as:

- Impact on employee morale
- Competitor reaction
- Customer reaction.

Non quantifiable costs and benefits of closure

- Some of the costs and benefits discussed above may be non-quantifiable at the point of making the shut-down decision:
  - penalties and other costs resulting from the closure (e.g. redundancy, compensation to customers) may not be known with certainty
  - reorganisation costs may not be known with certainty
  - additional contribution from the alternative use for resources released may not be known with certainty.
- Knock-on impact of the shut-down decision. For example, supermarkets often stock some goods which they sell at a loss. This is to get customers through the door, who they then hope will purchase other products which have higher profit margins for them. If the decision is taken to stop selling these products, then the customers may no longer come to the store.

4.3 Automation

Similar to closure of a business segment and with links to make or buy is automation.

Automation of a production process could involve closing down a production department to be replaced by a piece of machinery. The decision here could be whether to continue as we are now and incur the associated costs; or whether to automate the process and incur the associated costs.

As with earlier decisions in this chapter the business would need to consider other factors such as employee morale and customer reaction.

5 Further processing

Another type of decision to consider is whether a semi-finished product should be sold part way through production or whether it could be processed further and then sold at a higher price.

When deciding whether to process a particular product further or to sell at the end of the original processing **only future incremental cash flows** should be considered:

- Any difference in revenue and any extra costs associated with further processing.

- Any costs of making the original product are sunk at this stage and thus not relevant to the decision. (Note: if we are considering the viability of the whole process, then the costs to make the basic product would be relevant).

For example a piece of cheese can be sold as a block, or it could be cut into slices or grated for the customer.

Slicing or grating the cheese is processing the basic product further and will incur additional cost (potentially labour time or use of machinery), but the sliced or grated cheese will command a higher price for the convenience it provides to the customer.

Example

Further processing?

A firm makes three basic products, X, Y and Z, at a joint cost of £400,000. Joint costs are apportioned on the basis of weight. Products X and Z are currently processed further.

Product	Weight of basic product	Further processing costs (variable)	Sales revenue
	tonnes	£000	£000
X	600	800	980
Y	200	–	120
Z	200	400	600

An opportunity has arisen to sell all three products as the basic product for the following prices.

	£000
X	200
Y	120
Z	160

Which of the products, if any, should the firm process further?

Solution

The joint costs are not incremental and so can be ignored. The only incremental cash flows are as follows:

Product	X	Y	Z
	£000	£000	£000
Additional revenue from further processing	780	n/a	440
Less: additional cost from further processing	(800)	n/a	(400)
Benefit/(cost) of further processing	(20)		40

On financial grounds, only Z should be processed further.

Other considerations

• Are the products linked in anyway? By not processing X further the demand for Z could be reduced.

• Customer reaction, customers may be upset that the further processed version of X is no longer available.

• Use of spare capacity, the company could put the resources that previously processed X further to another use.

Test your understanding 4

The CS group is planning its annual marketing conference for its sales executives and has approached the VBJ Holiday Company (VBJ) to obtain a quotation. VBJ has been trying to win the business of the CS group for some time and is keen to provide a quotation which the CS group will find acceptable in the hope that this will lead to future contracts.

The manager of VBJ has produced the following cost estimate for the conference:

	£
Coach running costs	2,000
Driver costs	3,000
Hotel costs	5,000
General overheads	2,000
Subtotal	12,000
Profit (30%)	3,600
Total	15,600

You have considered this cost estimate but you believe that it would be more appropriate to base the quotation on relevant costs. You have therefore obtained the following further information:

Coach running costs represent the fuel costs of £1,500 plus an apportionment of the annual fixed costs of operating the coach. No specific fixed costs would be incurred if the coach is used on this contract. If the contract did not go ahead, the coach would not be in use for eight out of the ten days of the conference. For the other two days a contract has already been accepted which contains a significant financial penalty clause. A replacement coach could be hired for £180 per day.

Driver costs represent the salary and related employment costs of one driver for 10 days. If the driver is used on this contract the company will need to replace the driver so that VBJ can complete its existing work on the contract mentioned above. The replacement driver would be hired from a recruitment agency that charges £400 per day for a suitably qualified driver.

Hotel costs are the expected costs of hiring the hotel for the conference.

General overheads are based upon the overhead absorption rate of VBJ and are set annually when the company prepares its budgets.

The only general overhead cost that can be specifically identified with the conference is the time that has been spent in considering the costs of the conference and preparing the quotation. This amounted to £250.

Complete the statement showing the total relevant cost of the contract.

	£
Coach running costs	
Driver costs	
Hotel costs	
General overheads	
	———
Subtotal	
Profit	
	———
Total	
	———

Explain clearly the reasons for each of the values in your quotation and for excluding any of the costs (if appropriate).

6 Summary

This chapter has revised several fundamental cost accounting topics from your earlier studies including:

- relevant costing
- limiting factor analysis
- make or buy decisions
- closure of a business segment.

Answers to chapter test your understandings

Test your understanding 1

The correct answer is B.

The initial £40,000 fee will be deemed to be a sunk cost – it has already been committed and won't be affected by any decision to proceed from this point.

The £20,000 is a future cost. Despite the fact that it is called a fixed cost it will only be incurred if the project proceeds. It is therefore and extra or incremental cost of the project and should be included in any future decision making.

Test your understanding 2

As the spare capacity is 18,000 units, there is sufficient slack to meet the new order.

Variable cost per unit = £2.50

Contribution per unit from existing product = £3.25 – £2.50 = £0.75

Contribution per unit from new product = £2.80 – £2.50 = £0.30

	£
Increase in contribution from new product:	
£0.30 × 12,000 units	3,600
Fall in contribution from existing product:	
£0.75 × (12,000 × 2/15)	(1,200)
Net gain in contribution	2,400

Test your understanding 3

(a) **Contribution per unit**

Selling price per unit – Variable cost per unit

	X	Y	Z
	£	£	£
Selling price	90	80	75
Materials	(15)	(18)	(12)
Labour	(15)	(12)	(24)
Variable overhead	(8)	(6)	(10)
Contribution	52	44	29

(b)

Contribution	£52	£44	£29
Limiting factor	£15/£3 = 5 kg	£18/£3 = 6 kg	£12/£3 = 4 kg
Contribution per kg	£10.40	£7.33	£7.25
Rank	1	2	3

Make 500 X first using 500 × 5 kg =	2,500 kg
Make 500 Y next using 500 × 6 kg =	3,000 kg
	⎯⎯⎯
	5,500 kg
1,500 kg left	1,500 kg
	⎯⎯⎯
Available	7,000 kg
	⎯⎯⎯

Each Z requires 4 kg; therefore (1,500 kg/4 kg) = 375 Z can be produced.

Optimal production plan is 500 X, 500 Y and 375 Z.

Test your understanding 4

	£
Coach running costs: 1,500 + 360	1,860
Driver costs	800
Hotel costs	5,000
General overheads	–
Subtotal	7,660
Profit	–
Total	7,660

Coach running costs

The £1,500 fuel cost is directly traceable to the contract and is therefore relevant. The apportionment of annual fixed costs for operating the coach are not relevant. The total fixed cost would remain the same whether the contract were accepted or not.

The company should hire a replacement coach for two days @ £180 per day. This will ensure that any benefit on the other contract continues to be received. 2 × £180 = £360

Driver costs

The company's employed driver will be paid whether VBJ wins the contract or not. As a consequence of winning the contract, it would become necessary to hire a replacement driver for two days @ £400 per day to cover the existing work.

This incremental cost is relevant. 2 × £400 = £800

Hotel costs

The hotel cost is directly attributable to the contract and is therefore relevant.

General overheads

The general overhead that has been traced to the contract (£250) should be ignored as this cost is sunk.

Profit:

The profit is not a relevant cost.

Life cycle costing

Introduction

In this chapter we are going to revisit long-term investment decisions and focus on the use of life cycle costing. These techniques could be used on a decision to build a new factory or to whether or not to discontinue a product range.

There are different investment appraisal techniques that could be used but the discounted cashflow method is presented here. This was covered in Management Accounting: Costing and therefore should be revision.

ASSESSMENT CRITERIA
How costs change throughout the product life cycle (5.4)
Concepts of economies of scale, mechanisation and learning effect and how costs can switch between the variable and fixed through the stages of the product life cycle (5.4)
The stages of the product life cycle (5.4)
Identify the components of the life cycle cost of a product (5.1)
Calculate the discounted and non-discounted life cycle cost of a product (5.1)
Interpret the results of calculations of life cycle costs. (5.1)

CONTENTS

1. Predicting future cash flows
2. The time value of money and discounting
3. Long-term investments in more detail
4. Lifecycle costing
5. Product lifecycle

1 Predicting future cash flows

The first stage in evaluating a proposed investment is to estimate the future cash flows. This will involve estimating future sales, costs, capital expenditure and disposal proceeds.

As well as knowing what the future cash flows will be, we also need to know when they will occur. To simplify matters, we start the clock (time t = 0) when the initial investment happens.

To simplify things further, subsequent future cash flows are assumed to happen at year-ends, i.e. all of the sales and costs for the first year are assumed to occur at the end of the first year – call this t = 1.

If we do this for all the future cash flows of the project, then we will end up with the following:

	t = 0 £000	Year 1 (t = 1) £000	Year 2 (t = 2) £000	Year 3 (t = 3) £000	Year 4 (t = 4) £000	Year 5 (t = 5) £000
Investment	(100)					
Sales		40	50	60	50	40
Variable costs		(10)	(12)	(15)	(13)	(11)
Net cash flow	(100)	30	38	45	37	29

Note that when estimating future cash flows we want to identify what difference the project will make – only future, incremental cash flows are relevant, e.g. the factory rent may be unaffected by the proposed project and would not be included when assessing the investment.

2 The time value of money and discounting

2.1 The time value of money

A key concept in long-term decision-making is that of money having a time value.

Suppose you were offered £100 now or £100 in one year's time. Even though the sums are the same, most people would prefer the money now. The £100 in the future is effectively worth less to us than £100 now – the timing of the cash makes a difference.

The main reasons for this are as follows:

Investment opportunities: the £100 received now could be deposited into a bank account and earn interest. It would therefore grow to become more than £100 in one year.

Inflation: the £100 now will buy more goods than £100 in one year due to inflation.

Cost of capital: the £100 received now could be used to reduce a loan or overdraft and save interest.

Risk: the £100 now is more certain than the offer of money in the future.

What if the offer were changed to £100 now or £105 in one year? Many would still prefer the £100 now, even though it is the smaller amount!

To do calculations using the time value of money it needs to be expressed as an interest rate (often known as a cost of capital, a required return or a discount rate).

Suppose we felt that £100 now was worth the same to us as £110 offered in one year's time. We could say that our time value of money was 10% per annum.

While this would incorporate all four of the factors mentioned above (investment opportunities, inflation, costs of capital and risk), it is easiest to imagine that we have a bank account paying 10% interest per annum.

The £100 now could be invested for a year and would grow to £110.

Therefore £100 now is worth the same as £110 offered in one year. Alternatively we say that the £110 in one year has a 'present value' of £100. This process of taking future cash flows and converting them into their equivalent present value is called discounting.

To calculate the present value of any future cash flow we multiply the cash flow by a suitable discount factor (or present value factor):

Present value = future cash flow × discount factor

Discount factors are provided in assessments and simulations – you do not need to be able to calculate them.

For example, with a 10% discount rate, the discount factor for a cash flow at t = 1 is 0.909. Thus the offer of receiving £100 in one year's time is worth in today's terms:

Present value = 100 × 0.909 = £90.90

2.2 Net Present Value (NPV)

The main implication of the time value of money is that we cannot simply add up and net off cash flows at different times – they are not comparable.

To get round this we do the following:

Step 1 Identify future, incremental cash flows.

Step 2 Discount the cash flows so they are in today's terms (present values).

Step 3 Now the present values can be added up and netted off to give a net present value or NPV.

Step 4 If the NPV is positive, then it means that the cash inflows are worth more than the outflows and the project should be accepted.

Using the previous example with a discount rate of 10%, this could be set out as follows:

	$t = 0$ £000	Year 1 $(t = 1)$ £000	Year 2 $(t = 2)$ £000	Year 3 $(t = 3)$ £000	Year 4 $(t = 4)$ £000	Year 5 $(t = 5)$ £000
Net cash flow	(100)	30	38	45	37	29
Discount factor	1	0.909	0.826	0.751	0.683	0.621
Present value	(100)	27.3	31.4	33.8	25.3	18.0

Net Present Value = (100) + 27.3 + 31.4 + 33.8 + 25.3 + 18.0 = 35.8

This is positive, so the project should be undertaken.

An alternative layout could be as follows:

Time	Cash flow £000	Discount factor @ 10%	Present value £000
$t = 0$	(100)	1	(100)
$t = 1$	30	0.909	27.3
$t = 2$	38	0.826	31.4
$t = 3$	45	0.751	33.8
$t = 4$	37	0.638	25.3
$t = 5$	29	0.621	18.0
Net Present Value			35.8

Test your understanding 1

A machine costs £80,000 now. We expect cash receipts of £20,000 in one year's time, £50,000 in two years' time, £40,000 in three years' time and £10,000 in four years' time. The discount rate applicable is 15%. Should we accept or reject the investment?

The relevant discount factors are:

	Year 1	Year 2	Year 3	Year 4
15%	0.870	0.756	0.658	0.572

Year		Cashflow £	DF @ 15%	PV £
0	Cost			
1	Inflow			
2	Inflow			
3	Inflow			
4	Inflow			

NPV = _____

Since the net present value is _____ we should _____ the machine.

Test your understanding 2

Machine A costs £100,000, payable immediately. Machine B costs £120,000, half payable immediately and half payable in one year's time. (We can only acquire one machine.) The cash receipts expected are as follows.

	A £	B £
at the end of 1 year	20,000	–
at the end of 2 years	60,000	60,000
at the end of 3 years	40,000	60,000
at the end of 4 years	30,000	80,000
at the end of 5 years	20,000	–

With the discount rate at 5%, which machine should be selected?

The relevant discount factors are:

	Year 1	Year 2	Year 3	Year 4	Year 5
5%	0.952	0.907	0.864	0.823	0.784

Machine A   **Machine B**

Year	Cashflow £	DF @ 5%	PV £	Cashflow £	DF @ 5%	PV £
0						
1						
2						
3						
4						
5						

NPV = _____   NPV = _____

Since machine _____ has the higher NPV, our decision should be to select machine _____ .

Test your understanding 3

Highscore Ltd manufacture cricket bats. They are considering investing £30,000 in a new delivery vehicle which will generate savings compared with sub-contracting out the delivery service. The vehicle will have a life of six years, with zero scrap value.

The accounting technician and the transport manager have prepared the following estimates relating to the savings.

The cash flows from the project are:

		£
Year	1	9,000
	2	11,000
	3	10,000
	4	10,500
	5	10,200
	6	10,100

The business discount rate is 15%.

Required:

Prepare an appraisal of the project using the discounted cash flow (NPV method) technique.

The relevant discount factors are:

	Year 1	Year 2	Year 3	Year 4	Year 5	Year 6
15%	0.870	0.756	0.658	0.572	0.497	0.432

Highscore Ltd

Discounted cash flow – Net Present Value method – appraisal

Year	Cash flow	15% discount factor	PV
0			
1			
2			
3			
4			
5			
6			
		NPV	

 Test your understanding 4

Whitby Engineering Factors is considering an investment in a new machine tool with an estimated useful life of five years.

The investment will require capital expenditure of £50,000 and the accounting technician has prepared the following estimates of cash flow over the five-year period:

		£
Year	1	18,000
	2	20,000
	3	21,000
	4	22,000
	5	18,000

The firm's discount rate is considered to be 12% and it uses this rate to appraise any future projects.

Required:

Prepare an appraisal of the project using the discounted cash flow (NPV method) technique.

State with reasons whether you would accept or reject the project.

The relevant discount factors are:

	Year 1	Year 2	Year 3	Year 4	Year 5
12%	0.893	0.797	0.712	0.636	0.567

Discounted cash flow (NPV method)

Year	Cash flow	12% discount factor	PV
0			
1			
2			
3			
4			
5			
		NPV	‾‾‾‾

The business should therefore _____ the project.

🖉 Test your understanding 5

Four projects have been assessed using NPV. Assuming that we can invest in only one project which project should be chosen for investment?

A   £12,500

B   £33,450

C   (£44,777)

D   (£13,456)

2.3　Strengths and weaknesses of discounted cash flows

Strengths

(a)　Cash flows are less subjective than profits.

(b)　Profit measures rely on such things as depreciation and other policies which are to a certain extent subjective. Cash, being tangible, suffers from no 'definition' problems and hence leads perhaps to a more objective measure of performance.

Weaknesses

(a)　We are forced to make impractical assumptions or be faced with over-complicated calculations.

　　In the examples given so far we have assumed flows at yearly intervals, ignored taxation, ignored inflation – to mention just three simplifying assumptions.

(b)　Discounted cash flow as a concept is more difficult for a layman to grasp.

　　It would clearly be beneficial for the person on whose behalf we are performing the calculation to have a grasp of the basic concept underlying the technique.

2.4　Annuity factors

In the event of a cash flow occurring each year in a calculation it is time consuming to apply each individual years discount factor to each cash flow.

Annuity factors are cumulative discount factors. The net present value of a cash flow which occurs each year can be calculated in one, quick, step.

For example, using the individual discount factors:

Time	Cash flow £000	Discount factor @ 10%	Present value £000
t = 1	30	0.909	27.27
t = 2	30	0.826	24.78
t = 3	30	0.751	22.53
Net Present Value			74.58

However, given the annuity factor of 2.486 (0.909 + 0.826 + 0.751) this can be calculated much more quickly:

30 × 2.486 = 74.58 (as before)

If you were to need annuity factors in the assessment, the assessor would provide them.

2.5 Net present cost

Net present cost (NPC) is very similar to net present value, except that only costs are included in the calculation. Revenues or savings generated are not included, perhaps because they are too uncertain, or because they are the same under various options.

The calculation required will be performed in the same way as any other NPV calculation except that the answers would be negative. If you have to choose from a range of negative/cost alternatives, you should pick the smallest one.

This does not mean that the project should be rejected necessarily, since the savings or revenues were consciously left out of the decision for the earlier stated reasons.

This method could be used when a company is making a purchasing decision between two suppliers of a machine. They might both generate the same revenues or savings, but their investment and maintenance costs may be very different. Because the savings are the same they are omitted, and just the costs are discounted. Then the smallest negative NPC machine would be chosen.

2.6 Net terminal cost

Net terminal cost is very similar to net present cost except that instead of converting costs to their present value at time 0, they are compared at some time in the future.

In order to do this compounding must be used. This is the opposite of discounting. The formula for compounding is:

$(1 + r)^n$

The easiest way to calculate a terminal value is to work out the present value and then use the compounding formula.

For example, if a company has worked out that the proposed purchase of a machine and its maintenance costs has an NPV of £12,345 when discounted at 10%, then its net terminal cost after, say, 5 years would be:

£12,345 × $(1+ 0.1)^n$ where $n = 5$

= £19,882

Alternatively, using a different example, if the company had a potential cash outflow of, say, £10,000 in year 2 and they wanted to know what it was in year 4, with a discount factor of 10%, then

£10,000 × 1.10 × 1.10

= £12,100

Test your understanding 6

A company is considering whether to buy a machine for £20,000 today with maintenance costs of £1,000 per year for 3 years. It will be sold at the end of the third year for £3,000. The company uses a discount rate of 10%.

(a)   What is the net present cost?

(b)   What is the net terminal cost?

Discount factors are:

Year	1	2	3
	0.909	0.826	0.751

 Test your understanding 7

The net terminal cost for two projects has been calculated. For Project A it was (£12,000) and for Project B it was (£15,000). Which project should be accepted?

3 Long-term investments in more detail

 Definition

Capital investment project

The key characteristic of a capital investment project is the commitment of capital for a number of years, in order to earn profits or returns over the period. Terminating the project earlier than originally intended will normally cause the return on investment to be considerably lower and may even cause a loss.

This differentiates business investments from those more commonly undertaken by individuals, such as the purchasing of shares or depositing money at a building society, where the capital can often be recovered with a reasonable return at any time.

3.1 What will the capital be invested in?

The most common investment you will encounter will be in **tangible fixed assets**, such as a new machine, factory or premises from which to operate a new service business.

Other less tangible forms of investment include **research and development**, **patent rights or goodwill** obtained on the purchase of an existing business.

3.2 What form will the returns take?

The purchase of a new fixed asset will often be with the intention of starting a new line of business – say the manufacturing of a new product, or the provision of a new or extended service. The returns will be the **net income** generated by the new business.

Alternatively, the investment may be to benefit the existing operations, such that **revenues are increased** (where existing products/services are improved technologically or in quality) or **costs are reduced** (where production processes are updated or personnel reorganised). The returns will be measured as the **increase in net income or net reduction in costs** resulting from the investment.

3.3 Authorisation for a capital project

For projects involving a significant amount of capital investment, **authorisation** for its go-ahead will usually be given by the main board, or a sub-committee formed from the board for this purpose. Smaller projects (such as the replacement of an existing machine) may be within the authorisation limits of the manager of the area of business involved.

The decision will be based upon a **project proposal** using methods such as discounted cash flow.

3.4 Importance of non-financial factors

Although appraisal methods will usually give a basis for a **recommendation as to whether or not the project should be accepted,** they will only be able to take account of monetary costs and benefits. **Qualitative factors** will also need to be considered when reaching a final decision – such as possible effects on staff morale (for example, if the project involves increased automation or considerable overtime), the environment, customer satisfaction and the business's status/reputation.

4 Lifecycle costing

4.1 Discounted approach

Lifecycle costing is the forecasting of costs for assets over their entire life, so that decisions concerning the acquisition, use or disposal of the assets can be made in a way that achieves the optimum asset usage at the lowest possible cost to the entity. (It is simply a net present cost (NPC).)

For example, when buying a machine, a business might be offered either a poor quality machine for £20,000 or a high quality machine for £50,000. If the poor quality machine is expected to continually break down and need to be repaired all the time, while the high quality machine is expected never to break down, then life cycle costing might argue that the high quality machine should be bought, despite it being more expensive, since its total cost of ownership over its entire life will be less than the poor quality alternative.

 Test your understanding 8

A company is going to renew a machine and is undecided between two options.

Machine A costs £50,000 immediately while machine B costs £80,000. Both machines will last 4 years. They will generate net savings after maintenance costs of:

	Machine A	Machine B
Year 1	£20,000	£30,000
Year 2	£20,000	£20,000
Year 3	£20,000	£20,000
Year 4	£10,000	£20,000

At the end of their lives they will be disposed of, generating an inflow of £10,000 for machine A and £30,000 for machine B.

Task

Calculate the Life Cycle Cost (LCC) of the two proposals when the interest rate is 10%.

The relevant present value factors are:

	Year 1	Year 2	Year 3	Year 4
10%	0.909	0.826	0.751	0.683

	Cashflow	DF	PV	Cashflow	DF	PV
Y0						
Y1						
Y2						
Y3						
Y4						
		LCC	£		LCC	£

Therefore machine _____ is the better option.

4.2 Non-discounted approach

The discounted approach based around annual periods may give a misleading impression of the costs and profitability of a product. This is because systems are based on the financial accounting year, and dissect the product's lifecycle into a series of annual sections. Not all costs will happen at the beginning or the end of a year.

The non-discounted approach however, tracks and accumulates costs and revenues attributable to each product **over its entire product lifecycle**.

Lifecycle cost of a product per unit

$$= \frac{\text{Total costs of the product over its entire life}}{\text{Total number of units of the product}}$$

Example

The following details relate to a new product that has finished development and is about to be launched

	Costs to date	Year 1	Year 2	Year 3	Year 4
R&D costs (£ million)	20				
Marketing costs (£ million)		5	4	3	0.9
Production cost per unit (£)		1.00	0.90	0.80	0.90
Production volume (millions)		1	5	10	4
Clean up costs (£ million)					1

The launch price in the first year is proving a contentious issue between managers.

The marketing manager is keen to start with a low price of around £8 to gain new buyers and achieve target market share.

The accountant is concerned that this does not cover costs during the launch phase and has produced the following schedule to support this:

Year 1		£ million
Amortised R&D costs	(£20,000,000/4 years)	5.0
Marketing costs		5.0
Production costs	1,000,000 × £1.00 per unit	1.0
		‾‾‾
Total		11.0
		‾‾‾

Total production units   1 million
Cost per unit =   11,000,000/1,000,000 = **£11.00**

Prepare a revised cost per unit schedule looking at the whole lifecycle and comment on the implications of this cost with regards to the pricing of the product during the launch phase.

Solution

Lifecycle costs		£ million
Total R&D costs		20.0
Total marketing costs	5 + 4 + 3 + 0.9	12.9
Total production costs	(1 × 1) + (5 × 0.9) + (10 × 0.8) + (4 × 0.9)	17.1
Clean up costs		1.0
		————
Total life cycle costs		51.0
		————

Total production units =   1 + 5 +10 + 4 = 20 million

Cost per unit =   51,000,000/20,000,000 = **£2.55**

Comment

The cost was calculated at £11 per unit during the launch phase. Based on this cost, the accountant was right to be concerned about the launch price being set at £8 per unit.

However, looking at the whole lifecycle the marketing manager's proposal seems more reasonable.

The average cost per unit over the entire life of the product is only £2.50 per unit. Therefore, a starting price of £8 per unit would seem reasonable and would result in a profit of £5.50 per unit.

4.3   Implications of Lifecycle costing

Design costs out of the product

Around 90% of a product's costs are often incurred at the design and development stages of its life. Decisions made then commit the organisation to incurring the costs at a later date, because the design of the product determines the number of components, the production method, etc. It is absolutely vital therefore that design teams do not work in isolation but as part of a cross functional team in order to minimise costs over the whole life cycle.

Minimise the time to market

In a world where competitors watch each other keenly to see what new products will be launched, it is vital to get any new product into the marketplace as quickly as possible. The competitors will monitor each other closely so that they can launch rival products as soon as possible in order to maintain profitability. It is vital, therefore, for the first organisation to launch its product as quickly as possible after the concept has been developed, so that it has as long as possible to establish the product in the market and to make a profit before competition increases. Often it is not so much costs that reduce profits as time wasted.

Maximise the length of the life cycle itself:

Generally, the longer the life cycle, the greater the profit that will be generated. This assumes that production ceases once the product goes into decline and becomes unprofitable. One way to maximise the life cycle is to get the product to market as quickly as possible because this should maximise the time in which the product generates a profit.

Another way of extending a product's life is to find other uses, or markets, for the product. Other product uses may not be obvious when the product is still in its planning stage and need to be planned and managed later on. On the other hand, it may be possible to plan for a staggered entry into different markets at the planning stage.

Many organisations stagger the launch of their products in different world markets in order to reduce costs, increase revenue and prolong the overall life of the product. A current example is the way in which new films are released in the USA months before the UK launch. This is done to build up the enthusiasm for the film and to increase revenues overall. Other companies may not have the funds to launch worldwide at the same moment and may be forced to stagger it. Skimming the market is another way to prolong life and to maximise the revenue over the product's life.

5 Product lifecycle

5.1 Revenue forecasts

When forecasting revenue figures, consideration should be given to the position of the product within its lifecycle. Some products have a limited life and there are generally thought to be five stages of the product lifecycle – development, launch (or introduction), growth, maturity and decline, each of which will have different characteristics.

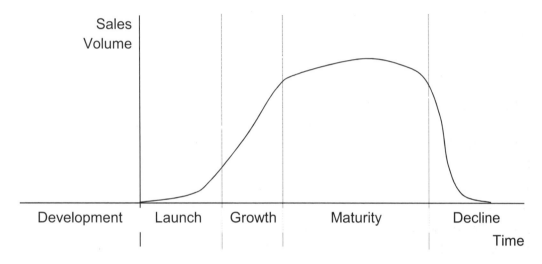

5.2 Development stage

During this time of the product's life there is likely to be a large amount of cost incurred on research and development but no revenue will be generated yet.

5.3 Launch stage

In the early stages of the product's life, immediately after its launch, sales levels are likely to be quite low. However, some eagerly awaited products, for example the PlayStation 3 games console, have had incredibly high sales levels in the launch stage.

Advertising costs will be very high, as will production costs building up inventory ready for the launch.

5.4 Growth stage

If the product is successfully launched then the product is likely to show fairly large increases in revenue indicated by a steep upward trend. However, such large revenue increases are unlikely to continue indefinitely.

As revenues increase, production will increase in order to match demand. Mechanisation may be preferred over labour intensive processes in order to speed up production. Economies of scale may be achieved through discounts received on bulk purchases of materials.

For labour intensive processes the learning effect is likely to reduce costs. Workers will become more familiar with their roles they are likely to work faster and make fewer mistakes.

5.5 Maturity stage

During this stage the demand for the product is likely to start to slow or at least become more constant. The trend line in this stage will not show such a steep curve. It is probable that Heinz Baked Beans are at this stage.

Advertising costs are low and economies of scale have been achieved, any further cost reduction from the learning effect will likely cease at this stage. There will probably be a switch from traditionally variable costs to fixed costs, for materials and labour, as production levels are now stable. Profits are probably maximised in this stage.

5.6 Decline stage

Most products will eventually reach the end of their life and revenues will begin to decline, with the trend line now also declining.

Costs will also fall as production stops and the remaining inventory is sold off. Profits will reduce considerably possibly to a loss.

5.7   Time series analysis and product lifecycle

Due to the changes in sales demand throughout the lifecycle of a product, care should be taken when using time series analysis to estimate the trend of future revenues. If the time series figures are based upon the growth stage then the trend line in this stage is unlikely to continue but will be likely to become less steep.

 Test your understanding 9

Enrono is an accounting software package which has a six year product lifecycle. The following are the yearly costs, estimated for the entire length of the packages life:

Costs in £000	Year 1	Year 2	Year 3	Year 4	Year 5	Year 6
R&D costs	275					
Design costs		120				
Production cost			120	200	200	
Marketing cost			125	170	130	60
Distribution cost			20	20	15	10
Customer service cost			5	15	30	45

The company that make Enrono expect to sell 150,000 units across its entire life.

(a)   Calculate the life cycle cost per unit.

Life cycle costs	£000
R&D costs	
Design costs	
Production cost	
Marketing cost	
Distribution cost	
Customer service cost	
Total life cycle cost	

(b)　Comment on the uses of this information for the company.

(c)　Comment on the implications for planning at the different stages of the products life.

Introduction	Growth	Maturity	Decline

Test your understanding 10

The stage in the product lifecycle with the highest unit sales is:

Introduction   ☐

Growth   ☐

Maturity   ☐

Decline   ☐

Test your understanding 11

A transport company is considering purchasing an automatic vehicle-cleansing machine. At present, all vehicles are cleaned by hand.

The machine will cost £80,000 to purchase and install in year 0 and it will have a useful life of four years with no residual value.

The company uses a discount rate of 10% to appraise all capital projects.

The cash savings from the machine will be:

Year	£
0	–
1	29,600
2	29,200
3	28,780
4	28,339

Task

As assistant management accountant, you are asked to carry out an appraisal of the proposal to purchase the machine and prepare a report to the general manager of the company. Your report should contain the following information:

(1) the net present value of the cash flows from the project

(2) a recommendation whether or not the proposal should be accepted.

In your calculations, you should assume that all cash flows occur at the end of the year.

Note: The present value of £1 at a discount rate of 10% is as follows:

Number of years from the present	£
1	0.909
2	0.826
3	0.751
4	0.683

Transport company

REPORT

To: General Manager
From: Assistant management accountant
Date: 13 June 20X4
Subject: Report on proposal to purchase vehicle cleansing machine

Appendix: Appraisal calculations

Year	Total cash flow £	Discount factor	Present value £
0			
1			
2			
3			
4			
Net present value			

Test your understanding 12

RBG plc is a large quoted company using a 25% rate of interest for appraising capital projects. One of its divisional directors has put forward plans to make a new product, the Al. This will involve buying a machine specifically for that task. The machine will cost £600,000 and have a life of 5 years. However, because of the nature of the product, the machine will have no residual value at any time.

The annual cash flow will be as follows:

	£
Turnover per annum	380,000
Material	(90,000)
Labour	(30,000)
Overheads	(20,000)
Annual cash inflow	£240,000

Task

You are asked to write a report to the divisional accountant appraising the divisional director's proposal using the net present value method of evaluating discounted cash flows and interpreting the result.

For the calculation of the net present value, it can be assumed that cash flows occur at the end of each year. The present value of £1 at a discount rate of 25% is as follows:

End of year	£	End of year	£
1	0.800	4	0.410
2	0.640	5	0.328
3	0.512	6	0.262

REPORT

To:

From:

Date:

Subject:

Appendix 1 Investment appraisal (£)

End of year	Cash flow £	Discount factor	Discounted cash flow
0			
1			
2			
3			
4			
5			
		NPV =	

6 Summary

In this chapter we have considered the mechanics, the advantages and the disadvantages of the Discounted Cash Flow (DCF) or Net Present Value (NPV) technique.

The Net Present Value is an appraisal technique that takes the time value of money into account. As a general rule, if a project has a positive NPV, then it should be accepted, whereas a project with a negative NPV should be rejected.

Lifecycle costing and how it can be used to aid cost management has been considered.

This chapter has also considered the product lifecycle and how costs will change throughout the life of a product.

Test your understanding answers

Test your understanding 1

Year		Cash flows	DF @ 15%	Present value
		£		£
0	Cost	(80,000)	1	(80,000)
1	Inflows	20,000	0.870	17,400
2		50,000	0.756	37,800
3		40,000	0.658	26,320
4		10,000	0.572	5,720
			NPV =	7,240

Since the net present value is positive we should accept the machine.

Test your understanding 2

Machine A

Year	Cash flows	DF @ 5%	Present value
	£		£
0	(100,000)	1	(100,000)
1	20,000	0.952	19,040
2	60,000	0.907	54,420
3	40,000	0.864	34,560
4	30,000	0.823	24,690
5	20,000	0.784	15,680
		NPV =	48,390

Machine B

Year	Cash flows	DF @ 5%	Present value
	£		£
0	(60,000)	1	(60,000)
1	(60,000)	0.952	(57,120)
2	60,000	0.907	54,420
3	60,000	0.864	51,840
4	80,000	0.823	65,840
		NPV =	54,980

Since machine B has the higher NPV, our decision should be to select machine B.

Test your understanding 3

Discounted cash flow – Net Present Value method – appraisal

Year	Cash flow	15% discount factor	PV
0	(30,000)	1.000	(30,000)
1	9,000	0.870	7,830
2	11,000	0.756	8,316
3	10,000	0.658	6,580
4	10,500	0.572	6,006
5	10,200	0.497	5,069
6	10,100	0.432	4,363
		NPV =	£8,164

Test your understanding 4

Discounted cash flow (NPV method)

Year	Cash flow	12% discount factor	PV
0	(50,000)	1.00	(50,000)
1	18,000	0.893	16,074
2	20,000	0.797	15,940
3	21,000	0.712	14,952
4	22,000	0.636	13,992
5	18,000	0.567	10,206
		NPV	£21,164

As the NPV is positive, the project is achieving a rate of return in excess of 12% – the business' cost of capital.

The business should therefore accept the project.

 Test your understanding 5

Project B has the highest NPV and should be selected.

 Test your understanding 6

(a)   The net present cost is: £20,233.

Year	Cost	DF @ 10%	PC
0	(20,000)	1.000	(20,000)
1	(1,000)	0.909	(909)
2	(1,000)	0.826	(826)
3	2,000	0.751	1,502
		NPC =	(20,233)

(b)   The net terminal cost is:

$(20{,}233) \times 1.1^{n}$ where n is 3

= (£26,930)

Test your understanding 7

Project A is the least cost and should be selected.

Test your understanding 8

	Cashflow	DF	PV	Cashflow	DF	PV
0	(£50,000)	1.000	(50,000)	(£80,000)	1.000	(80,000)
1	£20,000	0.909	18,180	£30,000	0.909	27,270
2	£20,000	0.826	16,520	£20,000	0.826	16,520
3	£20,000	0.751	15,020	£20,000	0.751	15,020
4	£20,000	0.683	13,660	£50,000	0.683	34,150
		LCC	£13,380		LCC	£12,960

Therefore machine A is the better option.

Test your understanding 9

(a)

Life cycle costs	£000
R&D costs	275
Design costs	120
Production cost	520
Marketing cost	485
Distribution cost	65
Customer service cost	95
Total life cycle cost	1,560

Lifecycle cost per unit = 1,560,000/150,000 = £10.40

(b) Lifecycle costing clearly takes into consideration the costs of the package incurred during the entire lifecycle – over £1.5 m. accordingly, from lifecycle costing, the management can know whether the revenue earned by the product is sufficient to cover the whole costs incurred during its life cycle.

When viewed as a whole, there are opportunities for cost reduction and minimisation (and thereby scope for profit maximisation) in several categories of cost:

For example, initiatives could be taken to reduce testing costs and therefore the 'Research and Development' category.

Likewise, proper planning and a tight control on transportation and handling costs could minimise distribution costs.

(c) These opportunities for cost reduction are unlikely to be found when management focuses on maximising profit in a period by period basis. Only on knowing the lifecycle costs of a product can a business decide appropriately on its price. This, coupled with planning of the different phases of the product's life, could give rise to the following tactics:

Introduction	Growth	Maturity	Decline
High prices to recoup high development costs; High returns before competitors enter the market.	Competition increases; reduce price to remain competitive.	Sales slowdown and level off; the market price is maintained. Upgrades and/or new markets should be considered.	Superior products appear – our prices must be cut to maintain sales.

 Test your understanding 10

The maturity stage has the highest unit sales.

Test your understanding 11

M E M O R A N D U M

To: General Manager

From: Assistant management accountant

Date: 13 June 20X4

Subject: Report on proposal to purchase vehicle cleansing machine

(1)   The results of the investment appraisal

I have carried out an appraisal of this proposal using the net present value method. The results of my calculations are shown in the Appendix.

The project generates a positive net present value of £11,995. This means that the wealth of the company would be increased by this amount if the project is undertaken.

(2)   A recommendation concerning the proposal

Since the proposal is forecast to result in a positive net present value, I recommend that it should be accepted.

If I can be of any further assistance in this matter, please do not hesitate to contact me.

Appendix: Appraisal calculations

The net present value of the cash flows from the project

Year	Total cash flow £	Discount factor	Present value £
0	(80,000)	1.000	(80,000)
1	29,600	0.909	26,906
2	29,200	0.826	24,119
3	28,780	0.751	21,614
4	28,339	0.683	19,356
Net present value			11,995

Test your understanding 12

MEMORANDUM

To: The divisional accountant

From: Assistant management accountant

Date: Today

Subject: Capital appraisal of new machine

As a result of using discounted cash flow, the net present value of the project is £45,600 and so the proposal appears to be worthwhile. This amount represents the gain to the company in the equivalent of pounds today from carrying out the proposal.

Taking risk into account brings in greater complexities. Although not always so, risk often increases with time. The further into the future are the cash flows, the more uncertain they tend to become.

Recommendation

Given that the proposal has a positive Net Present Value at 25 per cent, it meets the company's requirements for investment proposals and should go ahead.

Appendix 1 Investment appraisal (£)

End of year	Cash flow £	Discount factor	Discounted cash flow
0	(600,000)	1.000	(600,000)
1	240,000	0.800	192,000
2	240,000	0.640	153,600
3	240,000	0.512	122,880
4	240,000	0.410	98,400
5	240,000	0.328	78,720
Net Present Value			45,600

Target costing

Introduction

Target costing involves setting a target cost by subtracting a desired profit from a competitive market price. It has been described as a cost management tool for reducing the overall cost of a product over its entire life-cycle with the help of production, engineering, research and design. Real world users include Sony, Toyota and the Swiss watchmakers, Swatch. In effect it is the opposite of conventional 'cost plus pricing'.

ASSESSMENT CRITERIA	CONTENTS
The concepts behind target costing, including value analysis and value engineering (5.2)	1 Cost reduction and value enhancement
Analyse and evaluate target costs (5.2)	
Identify components of a target cost (5.2)	

1 Cost reduction and value enhancement

1.1 Introduction

There are few organisations which would not benefit from real efforts to keep costs to a minimum. Businesses will make more money that way, assuming quality is not compromised.

Not-for-profit organisations will make their funds go further in providing necessary services, and will be better able to meet the requirements for 'good stewardship' normally imposed on them.

 Definitions

Cost reduction is a process which leads to the achievement of real and permanent reductions in the unit costs of goods manufactured or services rendered without impairing their suitability for the use intended.

Cost control, on the other hand, aims simply to achieve the target costs originally accepted.

Note that cost reduction is aiming to reduce unit costs, i.e. the cost per item of output. (It would be possible for a cost reduction programme to increase the total costs incurred if the output volume rose even higher, so that the unit cost was reduced.)

1.2 Implementing a cost reduction programme

Once an organisation has adopted an objective of reducing costs, the following conditions need to apply if it is to be successful.

- A clear purpose – say, to reduce labour costs by 20%, or materials by 15%.

- A good reason – economic survival, say, or the ability in the future to compete with competitors with a lower cost base.

- Commitment and involvement by senior managers.

- Excellent and positive communication with workforce and, if possible, consultation.

- Gradual introduction.

1.3 Application of cost reduction techniques

All areas of businesses and not-for-profit organisations are open to the use of cost reduction techniques.

Three important cost reduction techniques are target costing, value analysis and value engineering.

(a) **Target costing**

Target costing starts by subtracting a desired profit margin from the market price at which an item can be sold; this gives the target cost. It is then up to the designers to plan how the product can be manufactured for that cost. If the product is currently planned to cost more than the target cost, then the plan must be modified (which may mean that it is abandoned).

For example, if customers have indicated that they would pay £100 a new product, and the company that developed it aims to make a 20% profit margin on each product they sell, then the product would have to be manufactured for £80. If this was impossible, then the product would not make it as far as the production stage.

(b) **Value engineering**

Value engineering is a philosophy of designing products which meet customer needs at the lowest cost while assuring the required standard of quality and reliability. The idea is to understand what it is that customers want from your products, and save costs by eliminating items that add no value in customers' eyes. For example, a manufacturer of computer components may decide that its customers place no value on a paper instruction manual or on fancy packaging, and will decide to sell its products with no manual and in a plain cardboard box.

(c) **Value analysis**

Value analysis is similar to value engineering, but relates to existing products, while value engineering relates to products that have not yet been produced. A company may sell a product with a feature that they discover adds no value to the customer, but incurs cost to include in the product. Using value analysis they would remove this feature, thus saving money, without harming the value of the product to the customer.

1.4 Value enhancement

The 'flip side' of cost reduction is value enhancement namely, getting the best value from the resources that are used in the organisation. Value added can be defined as revenue less the cost of bought in materials. Use of performance indicators that we will see in Chapter 16 (for example productivity and efficiency) provides useful comparative measures to assess value enhancement before and after an active 'value-for-money' programme. It should be emphasised that cost reduction and value enhancement are not just the responsibility of the accounts department of a business. All the functional specialists (designers, marketing, engineering, quality control, etc) must pool their knowledge and work side-by-side to achieve the required objectives.

1.5 Benchmarking

One way of closely monitoring one's own business is to compare the results in your business by department or division (internal benchmarking) or against a competitor (competitive benchmarking).

Benchmarking is the establishment of targets and comparators, through whose use relative levels of performance (particularly areas of under-performance) can be identified. By the adoption of identified best practices it is hoped that performance can be improved.

One common example is internal benchmarking, where a company is split up into business divisions, all operating in more or less the same industry, and performance indicators are calculated and compared for each division. Perhaps it is then found that one division has receivables of four months revenue, while all the other divisions have receivables of less than two months revenue. The division with abnormally high receivables should be able to improve its liquidity by tightening up its credit control procedures.

🗒 Test your understanding 1

Revenue less the cost of bought-in materials and services is called:

Value added	☐
Cost reduction	☐
Value enhancement	☐

Test your understanding 2

A cost reduction method whereby the starting point is the selling price followed by the deduction of a margin is called?

Target costing	
Loss leading	
Competitor pricing	

Test your understanding 3

A new product has been developed. After extensive research it has been estimated that the future selling price will be £200 with a demand of 1,000 units. Other useful information is below:

Material	4 litres at £10 per litre
Labour	5 hours
Fixed costs	£10 per unit
Profit margin required	25%

Calculate the target labour cost per hour.

	£
Selling price	
Profit margin at 25%	
Total costs	
Material cost	
Fixed costs	
Maximum labour cost	
Target labour cost per hour	

2 Summary

Target costing reverses the traditional approach to setting a selling price, by identifying a competitive selling price and the desired profit first then working backwards to get the target cost.

One of the key components is the process involved in making sure the company achieve that target cost, by using cost reduction, value engineering and value analysis.

Answers to chapter test your understandings

Test your understanding 1

Value added equals revenue less the cost of bought-in materials and services.

Test your understanding 2

Target costing is the idea of identifying the cost at which a product must be made, and then choosing a design and production method that will meet that cost. This differs from the traditional idea of producing an item, seeing how much it has cost, and then adding a profit margin to set the selling price.

Test your understanding 3

	£
Selling price	200
Profit margin at 25%	(50)
Total costs	150
Material cost	(40)
Fixed costs	(10)
Maximum labour cost	100
Target labour cost per hour	20

Trend analysis

Introduction

We use the time series techniques to forecast future trends.

You may be asked to use the results of the linear regression (covered later) technique to produce a trend for a series of data.

You should be able not only to use the time series techniques to forecast future trends and seasonal variations but also understand the weaknesses of time series analysis and the problems of using historical data to predict the future.

<table>
<tr><td>

ASSESSMENT CRITERIA

Calculate time series analysis – moving averages, seasonal variations and trend information (3.1)

Calculate the outputs from various statistical calculations (3.1)

Know the key statistical indicators to forecast income and costs and recommend actions (3.2)

Know the reason for their recommendations (3.2)

Know the key variations (seasonal, cyclical and random) (3.2)

</td><td>

CONTENTS

1 Time series analysis

2 Isolating the trend

3 Moving averages

4 Finding the seasonal variations

5 Forecasting with time series analysis

6 Collecting information

</td></tr>
</table>

1 Time series analysis

1.1 Introduction

The process of forecasting will inevitably involve some analysis of historic data (revenues, costs, share prices, etc) in order that future values may be predicted.

The data may concern the economy as a whole, the particular industry with which the organisation is involved (or wants to be) or the organisation itself.

Definitions

A **time series** is a set of values for some variable (e.g. monthly production) which varies with time. The set of observations will be taken at specific times, usually at regular intervals. Examples of figures which can be plotted as a time series are:

- monthly rainfall in London
- daily closing price of a share on the Stock Exchange
- monthly revenues in a department store.

Time series analysis takes historic data and breaks it down into component parts that are easier to extrapolate (predict future values of). In particular, it will isolate the underlying trend.

1.2 Plotting the graph of a time series

The pattern of a time series can be identified by plotting points of the values on a graph, such as below.

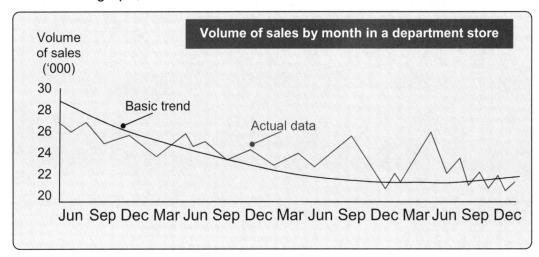

KAPLAN PUBLISHING

In such a graph time is always plotted on the horizontal x axis. Each point is joined by a straight line hence the typically 'jagged' appearance. Don't try to draw a smooth curve which will pass through all the points on a time series graph. You will find it practically impossible and, in any case, it is incorrect to do so. The only reason for joining the points at all is to give a clearer picture of the pattern, which would be more difficult to interpret from a series of dots.

On the graph above you will see that, having completed the time series graph, we have sketched in a 'basic trend' line. But what does it tell us? We need to look in more detail at what factors are at play in a time series.

1.3 Characteristic time series components

Analysis of time series has revealed certain characteristic movements or variations, the components of the time series. Analysis of these components is essential for forecasting purposes.

The four main types of component are as follows:

- basic trend (long-term)
- cyclical variations (not so long-term)
- seasonal variations (short-term)
- random variations (short-term).

1.4 Basic trend

The basic trend refers to the general direction in which the graph of a time series goes over a long interval of time once the short-term variations have been smoothed out. This movement can be represented on the graph by a basic trend curve or line.

1.5 Cyclical variations

Cyclical variations refer to long term swings around the basic trend. These cycles may or may not be periodic; they do not necessarily follow exactly similar patterns after equal intervals of time. In business and economic situations movements are said to be cyclical if they recur at time intervals of more than one year. A good example is the trade cycle, representing intervals of boom, decline, recession, and recovery which has, historically, followed an approximate seven year cycle.

1.6 Seasonal variations

Seasonal variations are the identical, or almost identical, patterns which a time series follows during corresponding intervals of successive periods. Such movements are due to recurring events such as the sudden increase in department store sales before Christmas. Although, in general, seasonal movements refer to a period of three months, this is not always the case and periods of hours, days, weeks and months, may also be considered depending on the type of data available.

1.7 Random variations

Random variations are the sporadic motions of time series due to chance events such as floods, strikes or elections.

By their very nature they are unpredictable and therefore cannot play a large part in any forecasting, but it is possible to isolate the random variations by calculating all other types of variation and removing them from the time series data. It is important to extract any significant random variations from the data before using them for forecasting.

Random and cyclical variations will not feature in your assessment.

2 Isolating the trend

There are three main ways of isolating the trend:

- using a line of best fit
- using moving averages
- using linear regression.

2.1 Line of best fit – sketching a basic trend line

A basic trend line was drawn in on the time series graph shown earlier in this chapter. Indeed one way of isolating the trend is simply to draw it in freehand on the graph. This is called a 'line of best fit'.

This is actually a very helpful method. Once a time series has been prepared as a graph, it is usually a fairly simple matter to sketch in a basic trend line which manages to echo the overall long-term trend of the time series. There are some advantages to doing it this way:

- It is quick and easy.
- It allows one to interpolate a value easily. If you have monthly data for, say, Months 1, 3, 5, 7, 9 and 11 only, plotting those values and sketching a trend line will allow you to see what the likely value for months 2, 4, 6, 8 and 10 might have been. On the graph below you will see that we have interpolated the values of £125,000 for Month 6 of 20X4, and 175,000 for Month 12 of 20X4.

- It is possible to extrapolate a figure past the end of the data available (see the dotted line on the graph below). It is always worth bearing in mind, however, that data cannot be extrapolated very far ahead. Common sense suggests, for instance, that the trend line in the graph below is unlikely to continue in a horizontal line for very long – it is bound either to rise or fall. So the extrapolation of 175,000 for Month 7 in 20X5 is not unreasonable, but it would not be helpful to extrapolate the line and make the same prediction for, say, Month 1 of 20X6.

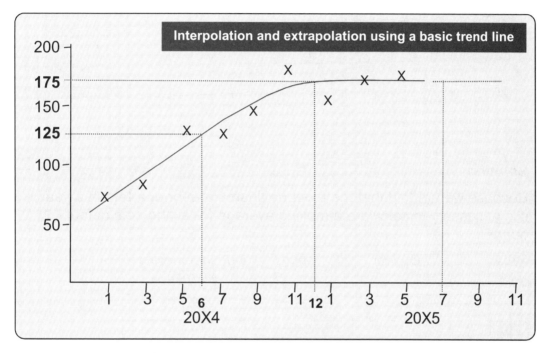

Interpolation and extrapolation using a basic trend line

---

3 Moving averages

3.1 Introduction

By using moving averages, the effect of any seasonal variation in a time series can be eliminated to show the basic trend. This elimination process will only work if the moving average is calculated over the correct number of values (being the number of values in one complete cycle). For instance, if a seasonal variation present in a time series is repeated every fourth period, then moving averages with a cycle of four should be used.

This will become clearer as you follow through this simple example.

Example

The following time series shows a set of revenue figures for eight quarters which are clearly increasing. At first sight, however, this increase appears to be quite erratic. We can however produce this trend by the use of moving averages.

Year	Quarter	Revenues £000
20X4	1	3
	2	5
	3	5
	4	5
20X5	1	7
	2	9
	3	9
	4	9

Solution

Because we are told that the revenue figures are for quarters of a year, it is necessary to calculate a moving average for all the sets of four quarters.

Year	Quarter	Revenues £000	4-quarter moving average £000
20X4	1	3	
	2	5	
			4½ (W1)
	3	5	
			5½
	4	5	
			6½
20X5	1	7	
			7½
	2	9	
			8½
	3	9	
	4	9	

Workings:

The moving average for the first four quarters is calculated as

$$\frac{3+5+5+5}{4} = 4½$$

Each moving average value is calculated and then placed in the centre of the numbers that were used in the calculation. For example, the first 4-value moving average is calculated as the average of the first four numbers, and then placed mid-way between the 2nd and 3rd quarter values of 20X4.

The moving average of four values captures the steadily increasing basic trend.

It will usually be fairly obvious which is the appropriate order in an examination question due to the way in which the data are presented, e.g. in 'quarters' (order 4) or days of the working week (order 5).

Be sure that you have understood the positioning of the moving averages in the above table. Each average has been written exactly opposite the middle of the figures from which it has been calculated. This results in the moving averages for even numbers of values (four in this case) being suspended halfway between two of the original figures.

Where you have a moving average for an even number of values, it is necessary to realign the moving averages so that they fall opposite the original values by calculating a centred moving average for every two moving average values.

Year	Quarter	Original time series	Moving average (4 values)	Centred moving average order 4
20X4	1	3		
	2	5		
			4½	
	3	5		5 (W)
			5½	
	4	5		6
			6½	
20X5	1	7		7
			7½	
	2	9		8
			8½	
	3	9		
	4	9		

As you can see by the centring process, the centred moving average is the basic trend.

(W) $(4½ + 5½) \div 2 = 5$

3.2 Disadvantages of moving averages

- Values at the beginning and end of the series are lost – therefore the moving averages do not cover the complete period.

- The moving averages may generate cycles or other variations that were not present in the original data.

📝 Test your understanding 1

Using the table below, calculate the moving average of the following sales figures to:

(a)   order 3

(b)   order 4.

Month	Value £
1	10
2	12
3	14
4	17
5	21
6	19
7	17
8	17

Solution

Month	Value £000	Moving average order 3	Moving average order 4
1	10		
2	12		
3	14		
4	17		
5	21		
6	19		
7	17		
8	17		

Test your understanding 2

Ski Fun Ltd owns a number of chalets in Switzerland that it lets out for holidays. Given below is data showing the number of people who stayed in the chalets each quarter.

	Quarter 1	Quarter 2	Quarter 3	Quarter 4
20X1			92	195
20X2	433	324	95	202
20X3	486	347	98	218
20X4	499	360	104	236

Calculate the trend of the number of visitors. Use a four-period moving average and round to the nearest whole number where necessary.

Ski Fun Ltd

Quarter	Numbers	Four-period moving total Step 1	Four-period moving average Step 2	Trend Step 3
20X1 – 3	92			
4	195			
		☐	☐	
20X2 – 1	433			☐
		☐	☐	
2	324			☐
		☐	☐	
3	95			☐
		☐	☐	
4	202			☐
		☐	☐	
20X3 – 1	486			☐
		☐	☐	
2	347			☐
		☐	☐	
3	98			☐
		☐	☐	
4	218			
		☐	☐	

20X4 –	1	499		
	2	360		
	3	104		
	4	236		

4 Finding the seasonal variations

4.1 Introduction

Having isolated the trend we need to consider how to deal with the seasonal variations. We will look at two models – the additive model and the multiplicative model.

The additive model is the simplest model and is satisfactory when the variations around the trend are within a constant band width.

4.2 The additive model – finding the seasonal variations

The additive model we will use expresses variations in absolute terms, with above and below average figures being shown as positives or negatives.

The four components of a time series (T = trend; S = seasonal variation; C = cyclical variation; R = random variation) are expressed as absolute values which are simply added together to produce the actual figures:

Actual data (time series) = T + S + C + R

For unsophisticated analyses over a relatively short period of time cyclical variations (C) and random variations (R) are ignored. Random variations are ignored because they are unpredictable and would not normally exhibit any repetitive pattern, whereas cyclical variations (long-term oscillations) are ignored because their effect is negligible over short periods of time. The model therefore simplifies to:

Actual data = T + S

The seasonal variation is therefore the difference between the computed trend figure and the original time series figure. Thus:

S = Actual – T

Example

The seasonal variations can be extracted by subtracting each trend value from its corresponding time series value.

Solution

Quarter	Original time series	Underlying trend	Seasonal variation (S)
	(a)	(b)	(a) – (b)
3	94	100	(6)
4	127	102	25
1	84	106	(22)
2	106	111	(5)

5 Forecasting with time series analysis

5.1 Introduction

Earlier we noted that the analysis of a time series into its component parts would make extrapolation easier for forecasting future values for planning purposes.

In general, for short-term forecasts, only the trend and seasonal variations will be used; the cyclical variations will only have a significant effect over quite a long period of time and the random variations are, by their very nature, unpredictable.

Thus the approach to forecasting will be to:

* extrapolate the trend to the appropriate future time; and

* adjust the extrapolated trend value by the appropriate seasonal variation.

5.2 Extrapolating the trend

There is no unique method for extrapolation of the basic trend, as it will very much depend upon its particular shape (if, indeed, it has a discernible shape).

In practice, computers will be of great help in producing various possible equations for the trend, which can be rapidly tested against the data available to determine which fits best.

If the moving averages method has been used, a certain amount of judgement will be necessary. Possible approaches include the following:

- Plot the trend values on a graph and extrapolate by eye. (In fact, an initial sketch graph can be useful anyway to get a visual impression of the trend, before using one of the following methods to predict it.)

- Look at the increments between each trend value for any approximate pattern (e.g. roughly equal, which makes the trend approximately linear or steadily increasing) and continue this pattern to the future time required.

5.3 Seasonal variations and the multiplicative model

In the assessment you may be given the trend figures and seasonal variations but, instead of the seasonal variations being given in absolute figures as in the additive model that we have used so far, the seasonal variations may be given as percentage figures. This is the case if the multiplicative model is used for the time series analysis.

In order to find the forecast figures in this case, simply multiply the trend figure by the seasonal variation percentage and either add it to the trend or deduct it from the trend.

 Example

Given below are the estimated trend figures for a company's revenue for the next four quarters:

20X3	Trend £
Quarter 1	560,000
Quarter 2	580,000
Quarter 3	605,000
Quarter 4	632,000

The seasonal variations have been calculated as:

Quarter 1	+ 15%
Quarter 2	+ 10%
Quarter 3	– 5%
Quarter 4	– 20%

Calculate the forecast revenue figures for each of the next four quarters.

Solution

Quarter 1	£560,000 + (560,000 × 0.15) =	£644,000
Quarter 2	£580,000 + (580,000 × 0.10) =	£638,000
Quarter 3	£605,000 – (605,000 × 0.05) =	£574,750
Quarter 4	£632,000 – (632,000 × 0.20) =	£505,600

5.4 Problems with forecasting

There are a number of problems with using time series analysis in order to estimate or forecast future results.

- The main problem is the inherent weakness of extrapolation. In order to estimate the trend for the future the trend line is extended on the graph and the figures read off. However, although the time series has moved in that particular manner in the past, it does not necessarily mean that it will continue to do so in the future.

- The seasonal adjustments used to find the forecast for the future are again based upon historic figures that may well be out of date. There is no guarantee that the seasonal variations will remain the same in the future. If the time series has a large cyclical or random variation element, then this will make any forecasts even less reliable.

Test your understanding 3

Eastoft Feeds and Fertilisers Ltd uses a number of standard raw materials for its product range. Product F4's main raw material is 'EF1'. The average price per tonne for this material, which is subject to seasonal change, for each quarter during 20X1, was as below. The material is in short supply.

20X1	Q1	Q2	Q3	Q4
Average price per tonne	£40	£44	£64	£76
Seasonal variation	–£4	–£8	+£4	+£8

Task

(a) Determine the seasonally adjusted price per tonne for raw material 'EF1' for each of the four quarters of 20X1.

(b) If a similar pattern of price movements were to continue, determine the likely purchase price per tonne for each of the four quarters of 20X2.

Solution

(a) **20X1**

	Q1	Q2	Q3	Q4
Actual price per tonne				
Seasonal variation				
Trend				

(b) **20X2**

Trend				
Seasonal variation				
Forecast price per tonne				

6 Collecting information

6.1   Introduction

As we have seen, the purpose of the management information system and the management accountant is to provide useful information to the management of the business. In order to do this the management accountant will have to collect the information in the first place. However, before collecting information, it will be necessary to determine what the population is that we are interested in.

 Definition

The population is simply all of the items of information that the collector is interested in. For example, if the management accountant wanted to know the proportion of defective units produced by a machine in a day then the population would be all of the units of product produced by the machine in the day.

6.2   Census or sampling approach

If information is required about a particular topic then there are two main approaches to obtaining the information, the census approach or the sampling approach.

The question here is whether we examine every item in the population; the census approach, or take a sample of the population. In business contexts it is rare to use the census approach so some form of sampling technique will be used. When sampling is used only a small number of items in the population are examined or tested.

Care must be taken when selecting a sample as the reliability of the results will be dependent upon how unbiased the sample is.

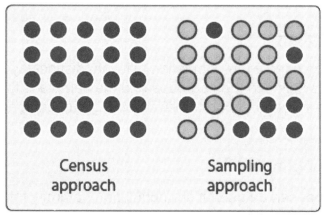

The census approach examines every item in the population

6.3 Random sampling

Random sampling is the best method of producing a totally unbiased sample; each item in the population has an equal chance of being included in the sample. In order for random sampling to be used each item in the population must be known and must have a consecutive number assigned to it. The sample is then chosen by random numbers taken from random number tables or a random number generator (your scientific calculator).

It is rare in practice for all items of the population to be known and for pure random sampling to be used. Therefore there are a number of other quasi-random methods of sampling that could be used:

- systematic sampling
- stratified sampling
- multi-stage sampling.

6.4 Systematic sampling

Systematic sampling is a simpler method of random sampling where again all of the items in the population must be known and each item must have a consecutive number assigned to it. Under systematic sampling the first item in the sample is chosen using a random number. Thereafter, every nth item in the population is taken to make up the sample. For example, the 14th item followed by every 50th item would produce a sample of 20 items from a population of 1,000 items.

6.5 Stratified sampling

Stratified sampling can be used if the population falls into distinct layers or groups. The population is split into these groups and the sample is then chosen from each group in proportion to the size of the group compared to the total population.

6.6 Multi-stage sampling

Again this is a method that can be used if the population naturally fall into fairly large groups or areas. Initially a number of groups or areas are selected randomly. The next stage is to take each group that has been selected and to split them into smaller groups from which again a sample is chosen randomly. This can be done any number of times until the final sample has been chosen.

6.7 Non-random sampling methods

In some instances it may not be cost effective to carry out random sampling techniques and therefore some form of non-random sampling is used. These methods will not produce such accurate results as the random sampling methods but the information collected can still be useful. Typical non-random sampling methods that can be used are:

- quota sampling

- cluster sampling.

6.8 Quota sampling

This is particularly useful when market research is being carried out. Quota sampling can be used when there are a number of different groups in the population, for example men under 30, women over 30, etc. The number of sample members required from each group is determined and these samples are taken on a non-random basis from the group until the required number has been reached.

6.9 Cluster sampling

Cluster sampling is where one or more areas of the population are determined to be representative of the population as a whole and therefore the sample is taken from that group alone. For example, if a business was carrying out market research into the buying habits of supermarket shoppers countrywide then it may be decided that customers shopping at three different supermarkets in Birmingham are representative of nationwide supermarket shoppers and the sample can then be taken from shoppers at these three supermarkets only.

 Test your understanding 4

The method of sampling that assumes that specific groups of the population will be representative of the population as a whole and selected items are taken from specified groups rather than the entire population is:

A   Random sampling

B   Quota sampling

C   Cluster sampling

D   Stratified sampling

 Test your understanding 5

A method of sampling whereby each item in the population has an equal chance of being included in the sample is called:

A   Random sampling

B   Systematic sampling

C   Stratified sampling

D   Quota sampling

7 Summary

Forecasts of future events are normally based on historical information. Information may be available from a wide variety of sources both internal and external to the business.

Time series analysis helps with the isolation of trends, although these still may not be easy to extrapolate into the future. Remember that you are using historic data which will not reflect future economic and environmental changes.

Also, you must be able to calculate the seasonal variations and be able to de-seasonalise data if required.

In this chapter we also looked briefly at sampling techniques and you should be aware of the definitions of the main sampling methods.

Test your understanding answers

Test your understanding 1

Month	Value £000	Moving average order 3	Moving average order 4
1	10		
2	12	12.0	
			13.25
3	14	14.3	
			16.00
4	17	17.3	
			17.75
5	21	19.0	
			18.50
6	19	19.0	
			18.50
7	17	17.6	
8	17		

Test your understanding 2

Ski Fun Ltd

Quarter		Numbers	Four-period moving total Step 1	Four-period moving average Step 2	Trend Step 3
20X1 –	3	92			
	4	195			
			1,044	261	
20X2 –	1	433			262
			1,047	262	
	2	324			263
			1,054	264	
	3	95			271
			1,107	277	
	4	202			280
			1,130	283	

20X3 –	1	486				283
			1,133	283		
	2	347				285
			1,149	287		
	3	98				289
			1,162	291		
	4	218				293
			1,175	294		
20X4 –	1	499				295
			1,181	295		
	2	360				298
			1,199	300		
	3	104				
	4	236				

Test your understanding 3

(a) 20X1

	Q1	Q2	Q3	Q4
Actual price per tonne	£40	£44	£64	£76
Seasonal variation	– £4	– £8	+ £4	+ £8
Trend	£44	£52	£60	£68

(b) 20X2

	Q1	Q2	Q3	Q4
Trend (+ £8 per quarter)	£76	£84	£92	£100
Seasonal variation	– £4	– £8	+ £4	+ £8
Forecast price per tonne	£72	£76	£96	£108

Test your understanding 4

C Cluster sampling makes the assumption that specific groups of the population will be representative of the population as a whole and selects items from specified groups rather than the entire population.

 Test your understanding 5

A Random sampling is a method of sampling whereby each item in the population has an equal chance of being included in the sample.

Linear regression

Introduction

Another way of isolating a trend is to use a mathematical technique called 'linear regression'. Only a broad understanding of linear regression is required in the context of producing a trend for a time series.

Regression analysis is a technique for estimating the line of best fit, given a series of data. It is essentially a statistical technique, and the description that follows is only a working guide for applying the technique in the assessment.

KNOWLEDGE
Use the regression equation (3.1)
Calculate the outputs from this statistical calculation (3.1)
Know the key statistical indicators to forecast income and costs and recommend actions (3.2)
Know the reason for their recommendations (3.2)

CONTENTS
1   Linear regression

1 Linear regression

1.1 Equation of the regression line

The general equation for the regression line is given as:

$$y = a + bx$$

Where:

x is the independent variable

y is the dependent variable

a is the fixed element

b is the variable element

You do not have to understand how this equation is calculated, but you do need to be able to use it.

In particular, you must understand that the independent variable (x) in some way causes the dependent variable (y) to have the value given by the equation.

Thus, if we were calculating the value of umbrellas sold for given amounts of monthly rainfall, the rainfall would be the independent variable (x) and the sales value would be the dependent variable (y) (rainfall causes umbrella sales and not vice versa).

KAPLAN PUBLISHING

Example

X Ltd is forecasting its sales for the four quarters of 20X5. It has carried out a linear regression exercise on its past revenue data and established the following:

a = 20

b = 0.7

The equation of the regression line is therefore:

y = 20 + 0.7x

Where x is number of the quarter and y is revenue in £000s.

Calculate the revenue for each of the quarters in 20X5.

Solution

		£000
Quarter 1	y = 20 + (0.7 × 1) =	20.7
Quarter 2	y = 20 + (0.7 × 2) =	21.4
Quarter 3	y = 20 + (0.7 × 3) =	22.1
Quarter 4	y = 20 + (0.7 × 4) =	22.8

Test your understanding 1

Regression line

A regression line has been calculated as y = 192 + 2.40x, where x is the output and y is the total cost. You are required to:

(a)   Fill in the blanks:

In the formula y = a + bx, y represents total cost (the _____ variable), x represents the units of activity (the _____ variable), 192 represents the _____ cost element (£), 2.40 represents the _____ cost per unit (£).

(Choose from: Variable, Fixed, Dependent, Independent)

The formula is estimating a linear relationship between activity level and total cost.

(b)   Use it to predict the total cost for (i) 500 units and (ii) 1,500 units.

(i)   x   =   500

        y   =

              = £ _____

(ii)   x   =   1,500

        y   =

              = £ _____

1.2   The assumptions of regression analysis

Regression analysis is based on sample data and if we selected a different sample it is probable that a different regression line would be constructed. For this reason, regression analysis is most suited to conditions where there is a relatively stable relationship between variables

Assumptions we are making:

•   The relationship is a linear one

•   The data used is representative of future trends.

2 Summary

Forecasts of future events are normally based on historical information. Information may be available from a wide variety of sources both internal and external to the business.

Linear regression is a way of using historic information to help understand what may happen in the future and therefore help an organisation make decisions like how many units should be made. While it is a very useful tool, it is not without its limitations.

Test your understanding answers

Test your understanding 1

Regression line

(a) In the formula y represents total cost (the dependent variable), x represents the units of activity (the independent variable), 192 represents the fixed cost element (£), 2.40 represents the variable cost per unit (£).

   The formula is estimating a linear relationship between activity level and total cost.

(b) (i)   x   =   500

            y   =   192 + 2.40 (500)

                 =   £1,392

     (ii)   x   =   1,500

            y   =   192 + 2.40 (1,500)

                 =   £3,792

Index numbers

Introduction

We have seen that the trend of revenue or costs can be estimated using time series analysis. However, this method is quite complex and time-consuming. There are other methods of indicating the trend of figures for income or costs and one of these is to use index numbers.

KNOWLEDGE
Calculate index numbers (3.1)
Calculate the outputs from various statistical calculations (3.1)
Know the key statistical indicators to forecast income and costs and recommend actions (3.2)
Know the reason for their recommendations (3.2)

CONTENTS
1   Index numbers
2   Statistical technique questions

1 Index numbers

1.1 Use of index numbers

A time series of figures for costs or income can be easily converted into an index. This is done firstly by choosing a base period and allocating to this period's figure an index of 100. Each subsequent period's figure is then converted into an index number using the formula:

$$\text{Index} = \frac{\text{Current period figure}}{\text{Base period figure}} \times 100$$

 Example

The materials costs for a business for the last six months were:

	£
March	427,000
April	442,000
May	460,000
June	433,000
July	447,000
August	470,000

If the index for March is 100, what are the index numbers of the costs for each of the subsequent months and what do these index numbers tell us?

Solution

Month		Index
March	Base year	100.0
April	$\dfrac{442,000}{427,000} \times 100$	103.5
May	$\dfrac{460,000}{427,000} \times 100$	107.7
June	$\dfrac{433,000}{427,000} \times 100$	101.4
July	$\dfrac{447,000}{427,000} \times 100$	104.7
August	$\dfrac{470,000}{427,000} \times 100$	110.1

The index shows that the materials costs are generally rising although there is a fall back in June which has been made up for by the highest level yet in August.

1.2 Indices to measure inflation

Published indices that can be useful to the management accountant are the Consumer Price Index (CPI) and the Retail Price Index (RPI). These indices published on a monthly basis by the Government and are used as measures of general price changes and inflation.

If we have a series of cost or revenue figures measured over a fairly long time period then they could have been distorted by price changes over the period and may not necessarily show the correct position.

We can use the RPI to adjust all of the figures in the time series into current day prices by using the formula:

$$\text{Current price adjusted figure} = \text{Actual revenue} \times \frac{\text{RPI in current year}}{\text{RPI in year of sales}}$$

Example

Suppose that a company has recorded annual revenue over the last six years as follows:

	£
20X0	735,000
20X1	764,000
20X2	791,000
20X3	811,000
20X4	833,000
20X5	856,000

The average RPI for each of those years was as follows:

	RPI
20X0	144.3
20X1	149.8
20X2	153.0
20X3	157.2
20X4	161.9
20X5	170.0

Show the revenue for the last six years in terms of current year (20X5) prices and explain what this shows.

Solution

	Actual revenue £	RPI adjustment	Price adjusted revenue £
20X0	735,000	× 170.0/144.3	865,900
20X1	764,000	× 170.0/149.8	867,000
20X2	791,000	× 170.0/153.0	878,900
20X3	811,000	× 170.0/157.2	877,000
20X4	833,000	× 170.0/161.9	874,700
20X5	856,000		856,000

The original, unadjusted figures indicated a fairly substantial increase in revenue over the period, but once the revenues are adjusted to current prices, a different picture appears. In fact the revenue increased very gradually until 20X2 and has been in decline for the last three years.

When comparing costs or revenue over time the accountant should consider the effects of either general inflation by using the RPI or more specific price changes that affect the cost or revenue by using a price index specifically related to that cost or revenue.

Test your understanding 1

Price indices

A product which cost £12.50 in 20X0, cost £13.65 in 20X1. Calculate the simple price index for 20X1 based on 20X0.

Simple price index $= \dfrac{P_1}{P_0} \times 100$

$= \underline{\hspace{3cm}}$

This means that the price has increased by $\underline{\hspace{3cm}}$% of its base year price of £12.50.

 Test your understanding 2

If a machine costs £2,000 on 1 January 20X2 and the relevant cost index has risen from 125.0 to 133.4 from January to April 20X2, how much would the machine be expected to cost in April 20X2?

 Test your understanding 3

Restating revenue figures

Given below are the revenue figures of an organisation and the Retail Price Index for a number of years.

	Revenues £000	Retail Price Index
20X1	500	131
20X2	510	139
20X3	540	149
20X4	580	154
20X5	650	164

Restate the revenue figures for each year on the following bases:

(a) deflating each year's revenue in order to take out the effect of inflation

(b) restating each year's figures in terms of *20X5* prices.

Comment on your findings.

Restating revenue figures

(a) **Deflation of figures**

20X1 £500,000 × $\dfrac{131}{131}$ = £500,000

20X2 £510,000 × _____ =

20X3 £540,000 × _____ =

20X4 £580,000 × _____ =

20X5 £650,000 × _____ =

(b) **Inflation to current year prices**

20X1 £500,000 ×   =

20X2 £510,000 ×   =

20X3 £540,000 ×   =

20X4 £580,000 ×   =

20X5 £650,000 ×   =

Comment

Test your understanding 4

Index numbers

Complete the table below by converting the cost per kilogram for each of the months to index numbers using January X2 as the base month. The price per kilogram at January X2 was £96.00. Round your answers to two decimal places.

	June X2 £	July X2 £	August X2 £
Cost per kg	99.00	99.40	99.80
Index			

1.3 Contracts

Indices can be used as a method of securing contracts to reduce the risk of rising prices. Particularly in the building industry, some building contracts may span several years. For example the building of the Olympic village for the 2012 Olympic Games in London has taken several years. The price of the contract will probably have been agreed up front. If there is inflation then the final receipt will be worth less than when the contract price was agreed years earlier. It is for this reason that often inflation is built into the contract, whereby the final price paid will be increased according to an agreed change in an index.

Test your understanding 5

Eastoft Feeds and Fertilisers uses a system of standard costing as a basis for its monthly management reporting.

Costs are revised on a quarterly basis to account for changes in price based on an index for specific categories of cost. The following information relates to current costs.

Category of cost	Standard
Direct labour rate per hour	£7.00
Raw material cost per tonne	£55.00
Fixed overhead recovery rate per hour	£12.50

The price index for these categories and the index for each quarter were:

	Current	Q1	Q2	Q3	Q4
Direct labour	105.00	108.15	108.15	108.15	108.15
Raw material	110.00	112.75	113.87	114.45	114.45
Fixed overhead	108.00	109.08	109.62	110.17	110.50

Task

Revise the standards for each quarter on the basis of the changes in the index for each category of cost shown above.

Revision of standards based on changes in the index

Category of cost	Current standard	Revised standards			
		Q1	Q2	Q3	Q4
Direct labour hour rate					
Raw material cost/tonne					
Fixed overhead recovery rate per hour					

2 Statistical technique questions

2.1 Exam style questions

This chapter is the final chapter covering the statistical techniques relevant to the MDCL syllabus. The tasks in the exam usually incorporate aspects of each of the three chapters on statistical techniques.

Test your understanding 6

Bex-Index-Perplex Co have been purchasing a valuable material for use in the manufacture of their products for many years, in 20X2 they started to look at the price index for the product. The price in 20X2 (the base year) was £320 per kg. It is now 20X8, following a computer error they have incomplete records regarding the prices paid and the price index for the material over the years.

(a) Complete the table below:

Give index numbers and prices to the nearest whole number.

Year	Index	Price per kg £
20X4	108	
20X5		350
20X6		380
20X7	116	

T-Rex-Pex Ltd have a table showing the index of prices for a certain commodity over the last five years (base 20X1):

Year	20X3	20X4	20X5	20X6	20X7
Index	102	120	110	125	115

The price was £52 per kg in 20X5.

(b) Complete the following sentences (to 2 decimal places):

The percentage increase in price from 20X3 to 20X5 is   %.

The price in 20X7 is £   per kg.

Reggie Quackton Co has found that production costs vary linearly according to the regression equation $y = a + bx$, where x = production volume. Total production costs of 500 units and 4,000 units are £17,500 and £35,000 respectively.

(c)   Calculate the values of a and b.

Value of a	
Value of b	

(d)   Complete the below sentences:

A down-turn in the size of the population is an example of   .

long term trend / cyclical variation / seasonal variation / random variation.

If the regression equation linking sales (Y) to advertising expenditure (X) is given by $Y = 4,000 + 12X$, the sales when £150 is spent on advertising, to the nearest £ is £   .

(e)   Insert the appropriate three month moving averages into the table below:

Month	Sales (units)	Three month moving average (units)
February	12,003	
March	12,204	
April	12,306	
May	12,603	
June	13,209	

3   Summary

Index numbers measure how a group of related commercial quantities vary, usually over time.

As with trend analysis they can be very useful to help use historic information to extrapolate future economic and environmental changes.

Test your understanding answers

 ### Test your understanding 1

Price indices

$$\text{Simple price index} = \frac{P_1}{P_0} \times 100$$

$$= \frac{13.65}{12.50} \times 100$$

$$= 1.092 \times 100$$

$$= 109.2$$

This means that the price has increased by 9.2% of its base year price of £12.50.

 ### Test your understanding 2

$$£2,000 \times \frac{133.4}{125.0} = £2,134.40$$

Test your understanding 3

Restating revenue figures

(a) **Deflation of figures**

$$20X1 \quad £500,000 \times \frac{131}{131} = £500,000$$

$$20X2 \quad £510,000 \times \frac{131}{139} = £480,647$$

$$20X3 \quad £540,000 \times \frac{131}{149} = £474,765$$

20X4 £580,000 × $\dfrac{131}{154}$ = £493,377

20X1 £500,000 × $\dfrac{131}{131}$ = £500,000

20X5 £650,000 × $\dfrac{131}{164}$ = £519,207

(b) **Inflation to current year prices**

20X1 £500,000 × $\dfrac{164}{131}$ = £625,954

20X2 £510,000 × $\dfrac{164}{139}$ = £601,727

20X3 £540,000 × $\dfrac{164}{149}$ = £594,362

20X4 £580,000 × $\dfrac{164}{154}$ = £617,662

20X5 £650,000 × $\dfrac{164}{164}$ = £650,000

Comment

The revenue figures alone show increases year after year. However, once inflation is taken into account the result is different.

Both sets of figures, once deflated by one method or the other, show that in real terms revenues decreased in *20X2* and *20X3* and increased again in *20X4* and *20X5*. By *20X5,* even in real terms, revenues were higher than in *20X1.*

Test your understanding 4

Index numbers

	June X2 £	July X2 £	August X2 £
Cost per kg	99.00	99.40	99.80
Index	103.13	103.54	103.96

Test your understanding 5

Revision of standards based on changes in the index.

Category of cost	Current standard	Revised standards			
		Q1	Q2	Q3	Q4
Direct labour hour rate	£7.00	£7.21 (W1)	£7.21	£7.21	£7.21
Raw material cost/tonne	£55.00	£56.38	£56.94	£57.23	£57.23
Fixed overhead recovery rate per hour	£12.50	£12.63	£12.69	£12.75	£12.79

Working:

(W1) $£7 \times \dfrac{108.15}{105.00} = £7.21$

The other numbers are obtained in a similar manner.

 Test your understanding 6

(a)

Year	Index	Price per kg £
20X4	108	**346**
20X5	**109**	350
20X6	**119**	380
20X7	116	**371**

108/100 × 320 = 345.6

350/320 × 100 = 109.375

380/320 × 100 = 118.75

116/100 × 320 = 371.2

(b) The percentage increase in price from 20X3 to 20X5 is **7.84%**.

110/102 = 1.0784

The price in 20X7 is £**54.36** per kg.

52/110 × 115 = 54.3636

(c)

Value of a	**15,000**
Value of b	**5**

Var cost (b) = (35,000 – 17,500)/(4,000 – 500) = 17,500/3,500 = 5

Fixed cost = 35,000 – (5 × 4,000) = 15,000

(d) A down-turn in the size of the population is an example of **long term trend**

If the regression equation linking sales (Y) to advertising expenditure (X) is given by Y = 4,000 + 12X, the sales when £150 is spent on advertising, to the nearest £ is £**5,800**.

Y = £4,000 + 12 × £150 = £4,000 + £1,800 = £5,800

(e)

Month	Sales (units)	Three month moving average (units)
February	12,003	
March	12,204	**12,171**
April	12,306	**12,371**
May	12,603	**12,706**
June	13,209	

March = (12,003 + 12,204 + 12,306)/3 = 12,171

April = (12,204 + 12,306 + 12,603)/3 = 12,371

May = (12,306 + 12,603 + 13,209)/3 = 12,706

Cost variance analysis

Introduction

Earlier we looked at standard costing, in this chapter, we examine how and why the actual results may vary from the standard.

Assessments for Decision and Control will tend to concentrate on the calculation of variances for materials, labour, variable and fixed overheads and the intelligent interpretation of these variances. Note that variances for revenue are not examined in Decision and Control.

ASSESSMENT CRITERIA	CONTENTS
Calculate raw material variances (total raw material, price and usage) (2.3)	1 Cost variances
Calculate labour variances (total, rate, idle time and efficiency) (2.3)	2 Variance analysis – absorption costing
Calculate variable overhead variances (total, rate, and efficiency) (2.3)	3 Raw material variances
Know how variances may interrelate (2.5)	4 Material variances with inventory
Identify what causes standard costing variances such as wastage, economies of scale, learning effect inflation and skills mix (2.5)	5 Labour variances
	6 Variable overhead variances

1 Cost variances

1.1 Introduction

 Definition

A cost variance is the difference between the standard cost of a product and its actual cost.

Cost variances are usually calculated for each element of cost separately, e.g. material, labour, variable overheads and fixed overheads.

We have seen how management will develop standard costs in advance of the period under review. During the course of that period actual costs will then be compared with standard costs, and any differences isolated for investigation as to their causes. This will then enable any corrective action to be taken as soon as possible.

If we consider top level management within the firm, perhaps the board of directors, then they will want to see a clear and succinct summary of the results for a given period. In particular they will wish to see a reconciliation between budgeted profit and actual profit that highlights the factors causing the difference.

1.2 Diagrammatic view of cost variances

Consider the cost of materials for producing 1,000 units of product X.

The standard cost of one unit is calculated as 2 kg of material at £2 per kg = £4 per unit.

To produce 1,000 units in period 1, the process actually uses 2,200 kg which cost £2.30 per kg.

The actual and standard costs for materials can be calculated as follows:

Standard cost of 1,000 units = 2,000 kg × £2 = £4,000

Actual cost of 1,000 units = 2,200 kg × £2.30 = £5,060

Total cost variance £1,060 (adverse)

This can be shown in a diagram as follows:

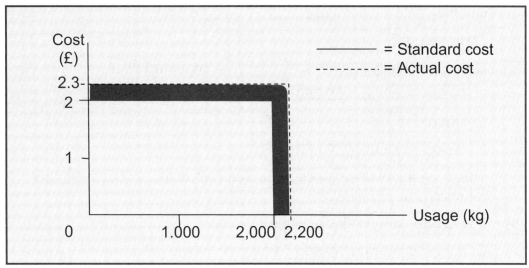

The shaded area shows the excess of the total actual cost over the total standard cost.

We need to analyse this into two parts:

(a)   the price variance, i.e. the amount of the excess cost caused by actually paying £2.30 rather than standard £2.00 per unit

(b)   the usage variance, i.e. the amount of the excess cost caused by actually using 2,200 kg rather than the standard 2,000 kg.

This is shown in the diagram by dividing the shaded area of total excess cost into two parts as shown below:

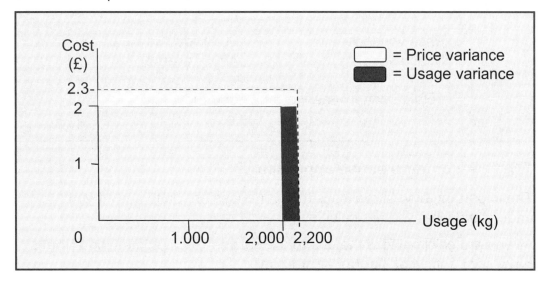

(a) The price variance is calculated as:

Quantity actually purchased × Actual price

Compared to:

Quantity actually purchased × Standard price

2,200 kg × £2.30 = £5,060

Compared to:

2,200 kg × £2.00 = £4,400

This is an adverse variance of £660 as we actually paid more than we should have paid.

(b) The usage variance is calculated as:

Quantity actually purchased × Standard price

Compared to:

Quantity that should have been used × Standard price

2,200 kg × £2.00 = £4,400

Compared to:

1,000 units × 2 kg × £2.00 = £4,000

This is an adverse variance of £400 as we actually used more than we should have used.

The two variances give the total variance as follows:

	£
Price variance	660 (adverse)
Usage variance	400 (adverse)
Total material variance	£1,060 (adverse)

1.3 A common sense approach

The important thing to realise is that variances are quite easy if you understand what you are calculating.

All you are calculating is the difference between what something **should have cost** and what it **actually did cost**.

We shall see this time and time again as we work through the variances.

2 Variance analysis – absorption costing

2.1 Illustration

The following illustration will be used to show the computation of all cost variances.

Katzman Ltd produces soap in bulk.

The standard cost per drum of soap is made up as follows:

Raw materials   100 kg costing £2 per kg

Labour   12 hours costing £3 per hour

Variable overheads   12 hours costing £2 per hour

Fixed production costs per month are budgeted at £90,000. For April 20X8, budgeted production was 7,500 drums.

The actual costs incurred in the month were:

Raw materials (900,000 kg purchased)	£1,755,000
Labour (110,000 hours worked and paid)	£341,000
Variable production overheads	176,500
	£2,272,500
Fixed production costs	£86,000
	£2,358,500

During April 7,800 drums of soap were actually produced. There were no raw materials in stock at the start or end of the period.

2.2 Standard cost card

When standards have been set for individual operations or items of material, they can be combined to give the standard costs for products, components or other units of output.

The standard cost card for a drum of soap would appear as below:

	£
Raw materials (100 kg × £2)	200
Labour (12 hours × £3)	36
Variable production overheads (12 hours × £2)	24
Fixed production overheads (12 hours × £1) (see working below)	12
Standard cost per drum	272

Working:

The only figure requiring explanation here is the hourly fixed production overhead rate.

Based on our budgeted output, we planned to produce 7,500 drums, each taking 12 hours. Thus, budgeted hours are (7,500 × 12) = 90,000.

This gives us a standard fixed overhead absorption rate per hour of

$$\frac{£90,000}{90,000} = £1/\text{hour}$$

Notice here that we have assumed two things:

- we are operating a total absorption costing system, so that all production costs are absorbed into units produced; and

- the basis for absorbing fixed overheads is labour hours.

2.3 A simplistic comparison

Let us now compare the standard total costs with the actual total costs.

	Standard	Actual	Variance	
Output (drums)	7,500	7,800	300	F
	£	£	£	
Direct materials	1,500,000 (W1)	1,755,000	255,000	A
Labour	270,000 (W2)	341,000	71,000	A
Variable production overheads	180,000 (W3)	176,500	3,500	F
Fixed production overheads	90,000	86,000	4,000	F
	2,040,000	2,358,500	318,500	A

(A = Adverse, F = Favourable)

Workings:

(W1) Total direct materials at standard = 7,500 drums × (100 kg × £2) = £1,500,000

(W2) Total labour cost at standard = 7,500 drums × (12 hours × £3) = £270,000

(W3) Total variable cost at standard = 7,500 drums × (12 hours × £2) = £180,000

The standard and actual costs are not directly comparable. The budgeted activity level was 7,500 drums, but 7,800 were actually produced. It is not surprising therefore that total actual costs exceed the budget.

It would be much more useful to management to compare the actual costs of producing 7,800 drums with the standard costs of producing that same quantity.

2.4 A better comparison

A better comparison as suggested above is to compare the standard and actual costs of the actual quantity produced. This is done by what is known as 'flexing the budget'.

	Standard cost of budgeted output	Standard cost of actual output	Actual cost of actual output	Variance	
Output (drums)	7,500	7,800	7,800	–	
	£	£	£	£	
Direct materials	1,500,000	1,560,000 (W1)	1,755,000	195,000	A
Labour	270,000	280,800 (W2)	341,000	60,200	A
Variable production overhead	180,000	187,200 (W3)	176,500	10,700	F
Fixed production overheads	90,000	93,600 (W4)	86,000	7,600	F
	2,040,000	2,121,600	2,358,500	236,900	A

Workings:

(W1) 7,800 drums × 100 kg × £2 = 1,560,000

(W2) 7,800 drums × 12 hours × £3 = 280,800

(W3) 7,800 drums × 12 hours × £2 = £187,200

(W4) 7,800 drums × 12 hours × £1 = £93,600.

The above table shows the revised variances caused by comparing the standard and actual costs for the actual output of 7,800 drums.

Note: The preparation of variances may be beginning to seem a little arbitrary; we appear to be able to compare different things and produce a different version of what the variances are – surely there must be a right way of doing it? The important point to remember is that you are trying to produce the most useful information for management. There is no right way of doing this. The most useful way to produce the variances is to 'flex the budget' and that is how variances are normally produced.

3 Raw material variances

3.1 Introduction

Let us now begin our detailed analysis of the difference between standard and actual cost, by looking at raw materials.

3.2 Total material cost variance

To produce 7,800 drums we should have used (7,800 × 100 kg)

= 780,000 kg. The material should have cost £2 per kg.

	£
Therefore, 7,800 drums should have cost 780,000 kg × £2 =	1,560,000
To produce 7,800 drums we actually used 900,000 kg. This actually cost	1,755,000
Total cost variance (adverse)	195,000

The budgeted level of 7,500 drums is irrelevant here, since we must compute the standard cost for **actual** production.

We shall now analyse this total variance into a price and usage variance.

3.3　Materials price variance

We actually purchased 900,000 kg.

The price variance is simply the difference between what 900,000 kg should have cost and what they did actually cost.

	£
At actual price per kg, they did cost	1,755,000
Actual quantity × Standard price	1,800,000
900,000 kg × £2	
Price variance (favourable)	45,000

Therefore, there is a favourable price variance of £45,000.

This means that the actual price per kg purchased must have been less than standard. We can compute the actual price as follows:

$$\frac{\text{Actual cost}}{\text{Quantity purchased}} = \frac{£1,755,000}{900,000} = £1.95\,/\,kg$$

Thus, for every kg we purchased, we actually paid £0.05 less than the standard price. This is a cost saving and gives rise to a favourable variance.

3.4　Materials usage variance

We actually produced 7,800 drums.

	£
Actual quantity × Standard price	
900,000 kg × £2	= 1,800,000
Standard quantity × Standard price	= 1,560,000
7,800 units × 100 kg × £2	
Usage variance (adverse)	240,000

This over-usage is valued at the standard price per kg.

Clearly, the variance is adverse, since the additional usage above standard incurs extra cost.

Reconciliation

We can summarise the above computations as follows:

		Calculations		£	
Step 1	Actual quantity purchased at actual cost	900,000 kg		1,755,000	Price variance £45,000 F
Step 2	Actual quantity purchased at standard cost	900,000 kg × £2		1,800,000	Usage variance £240,000 A
Step 3	Standard quantity that should have been used at standard cost	780,000 kg × £2		1,560,000	Total variance £195,000 A

This tabulation is the method that we will use to compute the variances.

Thus, what we have really done is the following:

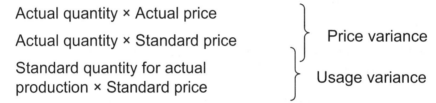

Actual quantity × Actual price

Actual quantity × Standard price — Price variance

Standard quantity for actual production × Standard price — Usage variance

---

🖉 Test your understanding 1

The standard direct material usage per unit of product K is 0.4 tonnes. The standard price of the material is £30/tonne.

During April, 500 units of K were produced using 223 tonnes of material costing £6,913. Calculate the direct material usage variance.

Standard usage of 500 units of K:

    Actual usage

           —————

    Excess usage   tonnes

           —————

    Valued at standard price of £30/tonne:

    Direct material usage variance is:

    £_____

3.5 Assessment style question – materials

A typical example is shown below for materials.

Example

Materials Ltd makes boxes and the budget and actual results for June 20X8 were as follows.

	Budget		Actual	
Production (units)	1,000		1,200	
Direct materials	500 kgs	£5,000	530 kgs	£5,700

Calculate the following variances:

Variance	£	A/F
Direct material price	400	A
Direct material usage	700	F

Workings:

Standard price of materials per kilogram £5,000/500 kg = £10/kg

Standard usage for one unit = 500 kg/1,000 = 0.5 kg

Standard usage for actual production = 0.5 × 1,200 = 600 kg

(a) **Direct materials price variance**

530 kg did cost	£5,700
530 kg should have cost 530 × £10	£5,300
	___
Price variance	400 (A)
	___

(b) **Direct materials usage variance**

1,200 units did use 530 kg	
which should have cost at standard price 530 × £10	£5,300
1,200 units should have used 600 kg	
which should have cost at standard price 600 × £10	£6,000
	___
Usage variance	£700 (F)
	___

Tutorial note:

You are not asked to reconcile the total materials variance, but you could do this as follows.

Total material budget cost of 1,200 units from data in question =

(£5,000/1,000 units) × 1,200 units =	£6,000
Total actual cost from data in question	£5,700
Total variance	£300 (F)
Variances per answer	
Price	£400 (A)
Usage	£700 (F)
	£300 (F)

3.6 Interpretation of the variances

The variances computed in 3.4 above act as error signals to management. They in no way explain why we have used more material than the standard allowed, or why we have succeeded in purchasing material more cheaply than the standard price.

If management decided that these exceptional performances (compared to budget) demanded explanation, then investigation would have to be carried out as to their causes. This would enable responsibility for the variance to be identified, and management could then take any preventative action considered necessary.

Some possible causes of the variances in 3.4 above are listed below.

Price variance

• Purchase of a cheaper substitute than the material per the standard cost and specification. Such an action may be a deliberate policy of the buying department (and therefore controllable), or may result from uncontrollable external factors such as market shortages.

• Bulk buying leading to discounts that the standard had not envisaged. This is sometimes referred to as economies of scale.

• Market factors leading to a lower price than anticipated (this would apply for example where raw materials depend upon random factors such as the weather affecting harvests).

- Using different suppliers from normal.

- The standard may have been set at a 'mid-year' price, anticipating future price rises. Thus we would expect favourable variances initially.

Usage variance

- Sub-standard raw materials. Notice the possibility here of interdependence between the variances. If the favourable price variance is due to buying a cheaper substitute, this may well cause operating inefficiencies leading to an adverse usage variance. Thus, in allocating responsibility for the variances, after investigation we may hold the purchasing manager responsible for the usage variance!

- Mechanical breakdown leading to spoilage of raw materials.

- The standard itself could be too tight (is it an ideal standard that is unattainable in practice?).

- Measurement errors. For example, if there are raw materials closing stocks that have not been recorded, this would overstate actual usage for the current period, but underestimate usage in the next period. Widely fluctuating variances from period to period may be indicative of such errors.

- Operating inefficiencies could lead to increased wastage of materials.

- The learning effect, as workers become more familiar with a material or a process they may make fewer mistakes leading to reduced wastage of material.

 Test your understanding 2

Total material variance

The standard direct material cost of product A is £5. During August 600 units of product A were made (standard usage of material is 1 kg per unit) and the actual direct material cost was £3,200. Calculate the direct material total cost variance for the period.

Variance	£	F/A
Direct material total cost		

Test your understanding 3

Materials price and usage variance

A raw material, used in the manufacture of product F, has a standard price of £1.30 per litre. During May, 2,300 litres were bought and used at a cost of £3,128. The 600 units made should have used 4 litres per unit. Calculate the direct material price and usage variances for May.

Variance	£	*F/A*
Direct material price		
Direct material usage		

Test your understanding 4

A company bought 112,000 kilograms of material paying £4 per kilogram. It managed to make 2,100 units whilst the budget had been for 1,900 units. The standard quantity of material allowed for in the budget was 56 kilograms per unit, and the budgeted price per kilogram was £4.50.

Complete the following table.

			£
Budgeted/Standard cost of materials for actual production			
Variances	F	A	
Direct materials price			
Direct materials usage			
Total variance			
Actual cost of materials for actual production			

Test your understanding 5

A company bought 2,000 kilograms of material paying £5 per kilogram. It managed to make 400 units whilst the budget had been for 420 units. The standard quantity of material allowed for in the budget was 6 kilograms per unit, and the budgeted price per kilogram was £5.50.

Complete the following table.

			£
Budgeted/Standard cost of materials for actual production			
Variances	F	A	
Direct materials price			
Direct materials usage			
Total variance			
Actual cost of materials for actual production			

 Materials variances with inventory

4.1 Introduction

So far we have only considered an example where all the materials purchased were used so that there is no inventory at the end of the period.

We need to consider cases where all the materials purchased are not used and inventory therefore remains at the end of the period.

4.2 Materials price variance calculated on purchases

The most important thing to understand is that the materials price variance is calculated on the total of all the materials purchased in the period, whether they are used or not.

This means that any inventory carried to the next period is carried at its standard cost.

Note that the materials usage variance is based on the quantity of materials used as before.

Example

X Ltd purchases 4,000 kg of material at a cost of £8,400. It uses 3,300 kg to produce 600 of product A. Product A's standard cost card for material is as follows:

	Standard cost per unit £
Material – 5 kg at £2 per kg	10.00

Calculate:

(a)   the price variance

(b)   the usage variance

(c)   the value of closing inventory in the cost records.

Solution

(a)   **Price variance**

This is calculated on all the materials purchased whether they are used in production or not.

				£	
Actual cost of 4,000 kg			=	8,400	
Actual quantity purchased × Standard price		= 4,000 × £2	=	8,000	
				———	
Price variance (adverse)				400	(A)
				———	

(b) **Usage variance**

			£	
Actual quantity used × Standard price	= 3,300 kg × £2	=	6,600	
Standard cost of producing 600 units	= 600 × 5 kg × £2	=	6,000	
			——	
Usage variance (adverse)			600	(A)
			——	

(c) **Closing inventory**

Closing inventory will be valued at standard cost

Purchased   4,000 kg
Used   3,300 kg
Closing inventory   700 kg

Value per cost accounts = 700 × £2 = £1,400.

 Test your understanding 6

Y Ltd

Y Ltd produces a product B which has the following standard cost for materials.

Standard cost per unit
£

Material – 5 kg at £3 per kg   15.00

Y Ltd produces 100 units of B in a period. It purchased 750 kg of material at a cost of £2,500 and used 600 kg for production.

Calculate:

(a) the price variance

(b) the value of closing inventory of material in the cost records

(c) the usage variance.

Solution

(a)

	£
Actual cost of materials purchased	
Standard cost of materials purchased	
Price variance	

(b)   Closing inventory (kg)   =   Purchase quantity – quantity used

=   _____

Valued at standard cost, this gives a closing inventory valuation of

£ _____.

(c)

	£
Actual materials used at standard price	
Standard cost of producing 100 B	
Usage variance	

5   Labour variances

5.1   Total labour cost variance

Referring back to the original example, you will see that the standard for labour per drum of soap is 12 hours at £3 per hour.

The actual results were:

Hours paid	110,000	costing £341,000
Actual production	7,800 drums	

Total labour cost variance

To produce 7,800 drums we should have taken (7,800 × 12 hours) = 93,600 hours.

	£
This did cost	341,000
This should have cost, at the standard rate, (93,600 × £3)	280,800
Total cost variance (adverse)	60,200

Note that, just as for materials variances:

- the variance is adverse because the actual labour cost exceeds the standard cost for actual production

- the budgeted production level of 7,500 drums is again irrelevant

- again, we would obtain more useful management information if we could analyse the total cost variance further into the rate of pay and efficiency variances.

5.2   Labour rate variance

We actually paid for 110,000 hours.

	£
This did cost	341,000
At standard rate per hour, this should have cost (110,000 × £3)	330,000
Rate variance (adverse)	11,000

This means that the actual rate of pay per hour must have been more than the standard.

The actual rate is $\dfrac{\text{Actual cost}}{\text{Hours paid}} = \dfrac{£341,000}{110,000} = £3.10/\text{hour}$

Thus, for every hour paid for, we have actually paid £0.10 more than the standard price, and so the labour rate of pay variance is adverse.

5.3 Labour efficiency variance

We actually produced 7,800 drums.

		£
This did take 110,000 hrs which should have cost £3/hr	=	330,000
At standard efficiency, this should have taken (7,800 × 12) 93,600 hrs which should have cost £3/hr	=	280,800
Efficiency variance (adverse)		49,200

This variance is adverse, because we have taken more hours, and therefore incurred more cost, to produce 7,800 drums than the standard allowed.

Reconciliation

We can summarise the above computations as follows:

			£	£
Step 1	Actual hours paid at actual rate (actual cost)	110,000 hrs	341,000	11,000 A Rate of pay variance
Step 2	Actual hours paid at standard rate	110,000 hrs × £3	330,000	
Step 3	Standard hours that should have been paid at standard rate (standard cost)	93,600 hrs × £3	280,800	49,200 A Efficiency variance
				Total variance 60,200 A

Again, we can show the above in 'shorthand' as:

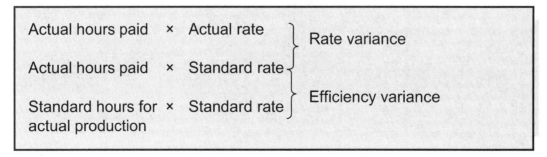

     KAPLAN PUBLISHING

Test your understanding 7

The standard direct labour cost of product H is £7. During January 450 units of product H were made and the actual direct labour cost was £3,450. Calculate the direct labour total cost variance of the period.

	£
Standard direct labour cost of 450 units:	
Actual direct labour cost	
Direct labour total cost variance	

5.4 Assessment style question – labour

Example

Labour Ltd makes boxes and the budget and actual results for June 20X8 were as follows.

	Budget		Actual	
Production (units)		1,000		1,200
Direct labour	300 hrs	£4,500	340 hrs	£5,440

Calculate the following

(a) Direct labour rate variance

(b) Direct labour efficiency variance.

Solution

Variance	£	A/F
Direct labour rate	340	A
Direct labour efficiency	300	F

Standard labour rate per hour

£4,500/300 hr = £15 per hr

Standard labour hours for one unit = 300/1,000 = 0.3 hrs

Standard labour hours for actual production = 0.3 × 1,200 = 360 hrs

(a) **Direct labour rate variance**

340 hrs did cost	£5,440
340 hrs should have cost 340 × £15 =	£5,100
Labour rate variance	£340 (A)

(b) **Direct labour efficiency variance**

1,200 units did use 340 hrs	
which should have cost at standard price 340 × £15	£5,100
1,200 units should have used 360 hrs	
which should have cost at standard rate 360 × £15	£5,400
Labour efficiency variance	£300 (F)

Tutorial note:

Reconciliation:

Total labour budget cost of 1,200 units from data in question

= (£4,500/1,000 units) × 1,200 units =	£5,400
Total actual cost from data in question	£5,440
Total variance	£40 (A)

Variances per answer:

£340A + £300F = £40A

5.5 Idle time

The labour force can be paid for a greater number of hours than they actually work. This may be due to a late delivery of raw materials preventing production and causing the workers to stand idle. If this is the case, then this idle time affects the labour efficiency variance and needs to be separated from it.

> Actual hours paid × actual labour rate
>   Rate variance
> Actual hours paid × standard labour rate
>   Idle time variance
> Actual hours worked × standard labour rate
>   Efficiency variance
> Standard labour hours × standard labour rate

For example, if the labour force were paid a standard rate of £10 per hour and in January they were paid for 6500 hours, but only worked 6000 hours. During the month 620 units were made that take 10 hours each.

Calculate the idle time and efficiency variances.

6,500 × £10 = £65,000
            Idle time = £5,000 A
6,000 × £10 = £60,000
            Efficiency = £2,000 F
620 × 10 × £10 = £62,000

In the assessment all idle time variances will be adverse.

5.6   Interpretation of labour variances

Some possible causes of labour variances may be:

Rate of pay variances

(i)   Failure to include overtime premiums in the standard, or failure to allow for pay increases (e.g. inflation) during the period.

(ii)   Rush orders necessitating costly overtime working.

(iii) Using different grades of labour (skills mix) compared to that budgeted for, which could of course lead to an adverse or favourable variance.

Idle time variances

(i)   Shortage of work

(ii)   Machine breakdown

(iii) Shortage of material.

Efficiency variances

(i)   Good quality raw materials could lead to favourable labour efficiency, or of course sub-standard materials could cause inefficiencies. Time could be lost in setting up machines after breakdowns, or rectifying poor quality output.

(ii)   The learning effect, as the workers become more familiar with a process this could lead to reductions in the time taken to do the work.

(iii) Random fluctuations such as high morale due to the local football team's winning streak.

Although this last example is somewhat flippant, it does illustrate an important point. We are dealing here with labour – a human asset. As such its efficiency will depend greatly upon behavioural factors.

The plan itself could be wrong! Remember that to compute the variance we compare standard labour time with actual labour time. If the standard represents an ideal time, then adverse variances are inevitable. Alternatively, if the standard is outdated due to technical innovations or revised working practices, then again we would expect to see variances.

✏️ Test your understanding 8

The following data relates to product C:

Actual production of C (units)	700
Standard wage rate/hour	£4
Standard time allowance per unit of C (hours)	1.50
Actual hours worked	1,000
Actual hours paid	1,050
Actual wage cost	£4,200

Calculate (a) the direct labour rate variance, (b) the idle time variance and (c) the efficiency variance from the above data.

(a) Actual hours paid did cost

     Actual hours paid should cost

                             _____

     Rate variance

                             _____

(b) Idle time:

     Hours paid

     Hours worked

                             _____

     Idle time variance

                             _____

(c) Efficiency:

     Standard hours produced

     Actual hours worked

                             _____

     Efficiency variance

                             _____

Test your understanding 9

Compute labour variances for the following examples:

(a)
Standard	2 hours per unit at £3 per hour
Labour hours	5,000 hours, cost £14,000
Units produced	2,800 units

Variances	£	A/F
Direct labour rate		
Direct labour efficiency		

(b)
Standard	3 hours per unit, £12 per unit
Original budget	20,000 units
Production	18,000 units
Hours worked	48,000 hours
Hours paid	50,000 hours, cost £210,000

Variances	£	A/F
Direct labour rate		
Idle time		
Direct labour efficiency		

Test your understanding 10

A company used 2,000 hours of labour paying £10 per hour. During this time the company made 2,050 units whilst the budget had been for 2,500 units. The standard number of hours allowed was one hour per unit, and the budgeted rate per hour was £9.80.

Complete the following table.

			£
Budgeted/Standard cost of labour for actual production			
Variances	F	A	
Direct labour rate			
Direct labour efficiency			
Total variance			
Actual cost of labour for actual production			

Test your understanding 11

A company used 24,000 hours of labour paying £8 per hour. During this time it managed to make 400 units whilst the budget had been for only 190 units. The standard number of hours allowed was 50 per unit, and the budgeted rate per hour was £8.50.

Complete the following table.

			£
Budgeted/Standard cost of labour for actual production			
Variances	**F**	**A**	
Direct labour rate			
Direct labour efficiency			
Total variance			
Actual cost of labour for actual production			

5.7 Labour variances – ratios

Three control ratios can be used to measure productivity, as follows:

Labour Activity ratio: $\dfrac{\text{Standard hours for actual production}}{\text{Budgeted hours}} \times 100$

Labour Efficiency ratio: $\dfrac{\text{Standard hours for actual production}}{\text{Actual hours worked}} \times 100$

Idle time ratio: $\dfrac{\text{Idle hours}}{\text{Total hours}} \times 100$

Example

	Budget	Actual
Output (units)	10,000	9,000
Hours worked	200	190
Hours paid	200	195

Calculate:

(a) the labour activity ratio

(b) the labour efficiency ratio

(c) the idle time ratio

Solution

(a) Standard time for one unit: $\dfrac{200}{10,000} = 0.02$ hours per unit

Actual output in standard hours: $9,000 \times 0.02 = 180$ hours

Labour activity ratio: $\dfrac{180}{200} = 90\%$

In other words, the production level was only 90% of the budgeted level.

(b) Labour efficiency ratio: $\dfrac{180}{190} = 94.74\%$

According to the budget, 50 units should have been produced in an hour and therefore in the 190 hours that were actually worked, 9,500 units should have been produced. Only 94.74% of that quantity (9,000) were actually produced.

(c) Idle time ratio: $\dfrac{195-190}{195} = 2.56\%$

Only 2.56% of hours paid were idle.

6 Variable overhead variances

6.1 Total variable overhead variance

Referring back to the original example, you will see that the standard for variable overheads per drum of soap is 12 hours at £2 per hour.

Total variable overhead variance

To produce 7,800 drums we should have taken (7,800 × 12 hours) = 93,600 hours.

	£
This did cost	176,500
This should have cost, at the standard rate, (93,600 × £2)	187,200
Total variable cost variance (favourable)	10,700

Note that, just as for materials or labour variances:

- the variance is favourable because the actual variable overhead cost is less than the standard cost for actual production

- the budgeted production level of 7,500 drums is again irrelevant

- again, we would obtain more useful management information if we could analyse the total cost variance further into expenditure and efficiency variances.

Variable overhead variances are usually calculated on the **labour hours worked**.

6.2 Variable overhead expenditure variance

	£
This did cost	176,500
At standard rate per hour, this should have cost (110,000 hrs × £2)	220,000
Expenditure variance (favourable)	43,500

This variance is favourable because we incurred less cost, to produce 7,800 drums, than the standard allowed.

6.3 Variable overhead efficiency variance

We actually produced 7,800 drums.

		£
This did take 110,000 hrs which should have cost £2/hr	=	220,000
At standard efficiency, this should have taken (7,800 × 12) 93,600 hrs which should have cost £2/hr	=	187,200
Efficiency variance (adverse)		32,800

This variance is adverse because we have taken more hours (as per the labour efficiency variance) and therefore incurred more cost to produce 7,800 drums, than the standard allowed.

Reconciliation

We can summarise the above computations as follows:

			£	£
Step 1	Actual hours paid at actual rate (actual cost)	110,000 hrs	176,500	43,500 F Expenditure variance
Step 2	Actual hours paid at standard rate	110,000 hrs × £2	220,000	
Step 3	Standard hours that should have been paid at standard rate (standard cost)	93,600 hrs × £2	187,200	32,800 A Efficiency variance

Again, we can show the above in 'shorthand' as:

Actual hours worked	×	Actual rate	Expenditure variance
Actual hours worked	×	Standard rate	Efficiency variance
Standard hours for actual production	×	Standard rate	

6.4 Assessment style question – variable overheads

Example

Skill Ltd makes bags and the budget and actual results for June 20X2 were as follows.

		Budget		Actual
Production (units)		1,000		1,200
Variable overheads	3,000 hrs	£4,500	3,400 hrs	£5,440

Calculate the following:

(a) Variable overhead expenditure variance

(b) Variable overhead efficiency variance

Solution

Variance	£	A/F
Variable overhead expenditure	340	A
Variable overhead efficiency	300	F

Standard labour rate per hour

£4,500/3,000 hr = £1.50 per hr

Standard labour hours for one unit = 3,000/1,000 = 3 hrs

Standard labour hours for actual production = 3 × 1,200 = 3,600 hrs

(a) **Variable overhead expenditure variance**

3,400 hrs did cost	£5,440
3,400 hrs should have cost 3,400 × £1.50 =	£5,100
	————
Variable overhead expenditure variance	£340 (A)
	————

(b) **Variable overhead efficiency variance**

1,200 units did use 3,400 hrs	
which should have cost at standard rate 3,400 × £1.50	£5,100
1,200 units should have used 3,600 hrs	
which should have cost at standard rate 3,600 × £1.50	£5,400
	————
Variable overhead efficiency variance	£300 (F)
	————

6.5 Interpretation of variable overhead variances

Some possible causes of variable overhead variances may be:

Expenditure variances

(i) Failure to allow for rate increases during the period.

Efficiency variances

(i) Good quality raw materials could lead to favourable labour and variable overhead efficiency, or of course sub-standard materials could cause inefficiencies. Time could be lost in setting up machines after breakdowns, or rectifying poor quality output, all affecting labour hours and therefore the labour and variable overhead efficiency variances.

(ii)   The plan itself could be wrong! Remember that to compute the variance we compare standard labour hours with actual labour hours. If the standard represents an ideal time, then adverse variances are inevitable. Alternatively, if the standard is outdated due to technical innovations or revised working practices, then again we would expect to see variances.

You should see from the above that many of the factors affecting the labour efficiency variances are the same for the variable overhead efficiency variance.

✎ Test your understanding 12

Compute the variable overhead variances for the following examples:

(a)   Standard   2 hours per unit at £4 per hour
       Hours worked   3,000 hours, cost £12,000
       Units produced   1,400 units

Variances	£	A/F
Variable overhead expenditure		
Variable overhead efficiency		

(b)   Standard   5 hours per unit, £10 per unit
       Original budget   10,000 units
       Production   9,500 units
       Hours worked   48,000 hours, cost £90,000

Variances	£	A/F
Variable overhead expenditure		
Variable overhead efficiency		

---

7   Summary

We have examined the causes of variances and outlined techniques which may be used to decide whether to investigate them.

We have revised the computation and interpretations of material, labour and variable overhead variances.

Test your understanding answers

Test your understanding 1

Standard usage of 500 units of K:

500 × 0.4 tonnes	200 tonnes
Actual usage	223 tonnes
Excess usage	23 tonnes

Valued at standard price of £30/tonne:

Direct material usage variance is:

23 tonnes × £30/tonne = £690 Adverse

i.e.: (Standard usage − actual usage) × standard price = (200 − 223) × £30 = £690 Adverse.

Test your understanding 2

Total material variance

	£
Actual direct material cost	3,200
Standard direct material cost of 600 units i.e. standard cost of actual production £5 × 600	3,000
Direct material total cost variance – Adverse	200

Test your understanding 3

Material price variance

	£
Actual cost of 2,300 litres	3,128
Standard cost of 2,300 litres:	
2,300 litres × £1.30/litre	2,990
Direct material price variance – Adverse	138

Material usage variance

	£
Actual usage 2,300 × £1.30	2,990
Standard usage 600 × 4 × £1.30	3,120
Materials usage variance – Favourable	130

Test your understanding 4

AQ × AP

112,000 × £4 = £448,000

AQ × SP

112,000 × £4.50 = £504,000   Price variance = £56,000 F

SQ × SP

2,100 × 56 × £4.50 = £529,200   Usage variance = £25,200 F

			£
Budgeted/Standard cost of materials for actual production			529,200
Variances	F	A	
Direct materials price	56,000		
Direct materials usage	25,200		
Total variance	81,200		81,200
Actual cost of materials for actual production			448,000

Test your understanding 5

AQ × AP

2,000 × £5 = £10,000

AQ × SP

2,000 × £5.50 = £11,000   Price variance = £1,000 F

SQ × SP

400 × 6 × £5.50 = £13,200   Usage variance = £2,200 F

	F	A	£
Budgeted/Standard cost of materials for actual production			13,200
Variances	**F**	**A**	
Direct materials price	1,000		
Direct materials usage	2,200		
Total variance	3,200		3,200
Actual cost of materials for actual production			10,000

Test your understanding 6

Y Ltd

(a)

	£
Actual cost of materials purchased =	2,500
Standard cost of materials purchased = 750 × £3 =	2,250
	————
Price variance	250 (A)
	————

(b) Closing inventory (kg) = Purchase – quantity used

        = 750 – 600

        = 150 kg

Valued at standard cost, this gives a closing inventory valuation of 150 × 3 = £450

(c)

	£
Actual materials used at standard price 600 kg × £3	1,800
Standard cost of producing 100 B	1,500
100 × 5 kg × £3	————
Usage variance	300 (A)
	————

Test your understanding 7

	£
Actual direct labour cost	3,450
Standard direct labour cost of 450 units:	
£7 × 450	3,150
	————
Direct labour total cost variance – Adverse	300
	————

Test your understanding 8

(a)   Actual hours paid did cost   £4,200
      Actual hours paid should cost
            1,050 × £4 =   £4,200
                                                                          ———
      Rate variance   NIL
                                                                          ———

(b)   Idle time:
      Hours paid = 1,050 × £4 = £4,200
      Hours worked 1,000 × £4 = £4,000

                                                                          £200 A

(c)   Standard hours produced:
      700 units × 1.50 standard hours = 1,050 standard hours
      Actual hours worked = 1,000, thus efficiency variance
      1,000 × £4 = £4,000
      1,050 × £4 = £4,200
      = £200 favourable – the hours worked were less than those
      allowed.

Test your understanding 9

(a)

	Hours	£
Actual hours paid at actual rate per hour	5,000	14,000
Actual hours paid at standard rate per hour 5,000 × £3	5,000	15,000
Direct labour rate variance	–	1,000 F
Actual hours worked at standard rate per hour	5,000	15,000
Standard hours for production achieved at standard rate per hour 2,800 × 2 hrs × £3	5,600	16,800
Direct labour efficiency variance	600	1,800 F

(b)

	Hours	£
Actual hours paid at actual rate per hour	50,000	210,000
Actual hours paid at standard rate per hour	50,000	200,000
50,000 × £4 per hour		
Direct labour rate variance	–	10,000 A

		£
Actual hours paid at standard rate per hour		200,000
Actual hours worked at standard rate per hour		192,000
48,000 × £4		
Idle time variance		8,000 A

	Hours	£
Actual hours worked at standard rate per hour	48,000	192,000
Standard hours for production achieved at standard rate per hour	54,000	216,000
18,000 × 3 hrs × £4		
Direct labour efficiency variance	6,000	24,000 F

Test your understanding 10

AH × AR
2,000 × £10 = £20,000
AH × SR
2,000 × £9.80 = £19,600   Rate variance = £400 A
SH × SR
2,050 × 1 × £9.80 = £20,090   Efficiency variance = £490 F

			£
Budgeted/Standard cost of labour for actual production			20,090
Variances	F	A	
Direct labour rate		400	
Direct labour efficiency	490		
Total variance	490	400	90
Actual cost of labour for actual production			20,000

Test your understanding 11

AH × AR

24,000 × £8 = £192,000

AH × SR

24,000 × £8.50 = £204,000   Rate variance = £12,000 F

SH × SR

400 × 50 × £8.50 = £170,000   Efficiency variance £34,000A

			£
Standard cost of labour			170,000
Variances	**F**	**A**	
Direct labour rate	12,000		
Direct labour efficiency		34,000	
Total variance	12,000	34,000	22,000
Actual cost of labour for actual production			192,000

Test your understanding 12

(a)

	Hours	£
Actual hours at actual rate per hour	3,000	12,000
Actual hours at standard rate per hour 3,000 × £4	3,000	12,000
Variable overhead expenditure variance	–	Nil
Actual hours at standard rate per hour	3,000	12,000
Standard hours for production achieved at standard rate per hour 1,400 × 2 hrs × £4	2,800	11,200
Variable overhead efficiency variance	200	800 A

(b)

	Hours	£
Actual hours at actual rate per hour	48,000	90,000
Actual hours at standard rate per hour	48,000	96,000
48,000 × £2 per hour	———	———
Variable overhead expenditure variance	–	6,000 F
	———	———
Actual hours at standard rate per hour	48,000	96,000
Standard hours for production achieved at standard rate per hour	47,500	95,000
9,500 × 5 hrs × £2	———	———
Variable overhead efficiency variance	500	1,000 A
	———	———

Fixed overhead variances

Introduction

In this chapter, we look at fixed overhead variances, there are lots of different types of fixed overhead variances, depending on how the overhead is absorbed into production.

Again assessments for Decision and Control will tend to concentrate on the calculation of these variances and then the intelligent interpretation of them.

ASSESSMENT CRITERIA
Calculate fixed production variances (total, expenditure and volume) (2.3)
Know how variances may interrelate (2.5)
Identify what causes standard costing variances such as wastage, economies of scale, learning effect, inflation and skills mix (2.5)

CONTENTS
1   Fixed overheads

1 Fixed overheads

1.1 Introduction

Remember that, in order to set a fixed overhead absorption rate per hour, we had to make an estimate of the activity level in hours, as well as of the fixed cost itself.

The relevant information from the example is:

Budgeted fixed production costs	=	£90,000
Standard hours per drum	=	12 hours
Budgeted production	=	7,500 drums
The actual results were:		
Labour	=	110,000 hours paid
Fixed production costs	=	£86,000
Production	=	7,800 drums

From these estimates we obtained the standard fixed overhead absorption rate per hour:

$$\frac{\text{Budgeted cost}}{\text{Budgeted hours}} = \frac{£90,000}{(7,500 \times 12)} = £1/\text{hour}$$

This means that, as units are produced, we will absorb £12 (12 hours at the standard of £1) per unit. Thus, there may be a variance due to the over or under absorption of fixed overheads.

For example, if actual fixed costs were exactly as per budget of £90,000, but we actually produced 8,000 units, then we would absorb 8,000 × 12 hours × £1 = £96,000.

Thus we would have over-absorbed £6,000, due to the increased production compared to budget. Finished goods will therefore be valued at £6,000 more than the actual cost, and so a favourable variance would be needed to reduce this standard cost back to the actual cost. This variance is called the volume variance, and only arises because we have chosen to absorb fixed overheads into production.

1.2 Fixed overheads – total cost variance

	£
The actual cost was	86,000
In producing 7,800 drums we have absorbed (7,800 × £12)	93,600
	———
Total cost variance (favourable)	7,600
	———

1.3 Fixed overhead expenditure variance

Since fixed costs do not vary with the level of production, the expenditure variance is simply a comparison of budgeted and actual fixed costs.

	£
Actual total cost	86,000
Budgeted cost	90,000
	———
Expenditure variance (favourable)	4,000
	———

Thus we have actually incurred, regardless of activity level, £4,000 less fixed costs than budgeted. The variance is therefore favourable.

1.4 Fixed overhead volume variance

We actually produced 7,800 drums.

	£
Budgeted absorption (7,500 × £12)	90,000
Actual absorption (7,800 × £12)	93,600
	———
Volume variance (favourable)	3,600
	———

Remember that the variance is favourable because we have over absorbed fixed overheads. We thus require a favourable variance to compensate for this over-absorption.

We have produced 300 units more than budget, thus over-absorbing fixed overheads by 300 × the standard rate of £12 per unit i.e. £3,600 favourable volume variance.

Further reading: Sub-division of the volume variance

This is no longer required for MDCL, but is included for reference

The volume variance as computed above can be subdivided further to explain why the level of activity was different from budget. In other words, how did we manage to produce 300 units more than the budget of 7,500?

- **Capacity variance**

This compares actual hours worked with the budgeted hours, and is favourable where actual hours exceed budgeted hours since squeezing more hours out of our factory enables us to make extra units.

- **Efficiency variance**

This compares standard hours that should have been worked with actual hours worked, and so is the usual measure of efficiency seen already for both labour and variable overheads.

These sub-variances can be calculated as shown below:

Capacity variance

	Hours	*£*
Budgeted hours at the standard rate	90,000	90,000
Actual hours worked at the standard rate	110,000	110,000
Capacity variance (favourable)	20,000	20,000

Efficiency variance

	Hours	*£*
Actual hours worked at the standard rate	110,000	110,000
Standard hours that should have been worked at the standard rate	93,600	93,600
Efficiency variance (adverse)	16,400	16,400

Thus, if we absorb fixed overheads on the basis of labour hours it enables us to split the volume variance further into capacity and efficiency elements. The total cost variance must remain the same. The 'variance tree' below may help as a convenient way of remembering this.

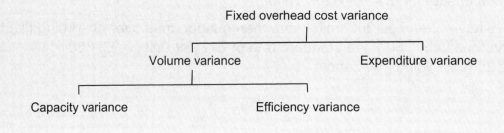

1.5 Assessment style question – fixed overheads

Example

Fixed Ltd makes boxes and the budget and actual results for June 20X8 were as follows

		Budget		Actual
Production (units)		1,000		1,200
Fixed overheads		£2,000		£2,500

Calculate the following

(a) Budgeted overhead absorption rate per unit

(b) Fixed overheads absorbed into actual production

(c) Fixed overhead expenditure variance

(d) Fixed overhead volume variance.

Solution

(a) Budgeted overhead absorption rate per unit

£2,000/1,000 = £2 per unit

(b) Fixed overheads absorbed into actual production

Units actually produced = 1,200 units

Overheads absorbed into actual production = 1,200 × £2 = £2,400

(c) Fixed overhead expenditure variance

£2,000 – £2,500 = £500 (A)

(d) Fixed overhead volume variance

Actual overhead absorbed =	£2,400
Budgeted overhead =	£2,000
Variance	£400 (F)

Tutorial note:

You are not asked to reconcile the fixed overhead variance, but you could do this as follows.

Overhead absorbed	2,400
Actual overhead	2,500
Total variance	£100 (A)
Variances per answer	
Expenditure variance	£500 (A)
Volume variance	£400 (F)
	£100 (A)

1.6 Usefulness of fixed overhead variances

We must be clear throughout the above analysis that we are dealing with a fixed cost. Refer back to the earlier sections on materials and labour and you will see that there are no volume variances for these items. The volume variance arises for fixed overheads purely because of our desire to absorb fixed costs into production, and the consequent setting up of an arbitrary absorption basis such as labour hours.

Conflict

Thus we are really seeing a conflict between the use of standard costing for control purposes, and the use of standards for product costing. We may for example base our selling price on cost plus a fixed mark-up, in which case a production cost inclusive of fixed costs may be desired. However, for control purposes the only variance of any real significance is the expenditure variance. Since we are dealing with a fixed cost, then the cost will not change simply because we are operating at something other than budgeted output level.

Thus the volume variance is really uncontrollable, and arises due to our failure to operate at the budgeted activity level.

A partial solution

One solution to this criticism is to sub-divide the volume variance into capacity and efficiency. The capacity variance compares actual hours worked with budgeted hours that should have been worked. When actual hours exceed budgeted hours, the capacity variance is favourable, because we are making better use of our facilities than expected. In other words, we have obtained more productive hours worth of output for the same fixed cost.

If the capacity variance is of some use in terms of explaining utilisation of facilities, then how can we use the efficiency variance? The answer is that the fixed overhead efficiency variance is very different from the efficiency variances computed for labour. Efficient use of the latter can reduce actual cost, but fixed overhead cost cannot be affected by efficiency in the short-run. Further, there is little to be gained in terms of information to management since they are already aware of inefficiencies through the variable cost reports.

Test your understanding 1

PD has the following data concerning its fixed production overheads:

Budget cost	£50,000
Budget production	10,000 units
Budget labour hours	20,000
Actual cost	£47,500
Actual production	8,450 units
Actual labour hours	16,600

Calculate the fixed overhead total variance assuming an absorption system based upon labour hours.

Absorption rate = £_____ per std hour

Actual output in standard hours = _____ standard hours

	£
Overhead cost	
Overhead absorbed	
Variance	

Test your understanding 2

A company has budgeted fixed overheads of £40,000 and budgeted output is 20,000 units.

Actual output was 19,000 units and actual overheads were £39,000.

Complete the following table.

			£
Budgeted/Standard fixed cost for actual production			
Variances	F	A	
Fixed overhead expenditure			
Fixed overhead volume			
Total variance			
Actual fixed cost for actual production			

Test your understanding 3

A company has budgeted fixed overheads of £1,250,000 and budgeted output is 25,000 units.

Actual output was 24,100 units and actual overheads were £1,245,000.

Complete the following table.

			£
Budgeted/Standard fixed cost for actual production			
Variances	F	A	
Fixed overhead expenditure			
Fixed overhead volume			
Total variance			
Actual fixed cost for actual production			

Test your understanding 4

From the information below calculate (a) the fixed overhead variance and (b) all the sub-variances, using absorption costing (based on absorbing by unit).

TP has the following data concerning its fixed production overheads:

Budget fixed overhead	£44,000
Budget production	8,000 units
Budget labour hours	16,000
Actual fixed overhead	£47,500
Actual production	8,450 units
Actual labour hours	16,600

Solution

Fixed overhead recovery rate =

Standard hours per unit =

(a) **Fixed overhead total variance**

(b) **Sub-variances**

(i) Fixed overhead expenditure variance:

(ii) Fixed overhead volume variance:

Test your understanding 5

Malik Brothers run a taxi and courier service both locally and a specific service to Manchester Airport for holiday makers and business personnel.

On the Manchester Airport run the 'round trip' is benchmarked as 5 standard hours. In the quarter ended 31 March 20X2, 184 trips are planned. (Overheads are recovered based on hours.)

The fixed costs incurred by the business, including the drivers' salary, are budgeted to be £11,638 for the period.

The actual fixed costs for the period were £12,400 and 176 standard trips were made. The actual hours worked were 940.

Task

Calculate:

(a)   The standard hours in the budget.

(b)   The fixed overhead recovery rate per trip.

(c)   The fixed overhead total variance.

(d)   The fixed overhead expenditure variance.

(e)   The fixed overhead volume variance.

Solution

(a)   Standard hours in the budget

(b)   Fixed overhead recovery rate per trip

       = £   per trip

(c)   Fixed overhead total variance

(d)   Fixed overhead expenditure variance

(e)   Fixed overhead volume variance

 Test your understanding 6

You are employed as a financial analyst at Drampton plc, a computer retailer.

The company sells two types of computer; desktop computers for individual use and mainframe computers for large organisations. Desktop computers are sold by advertising in newspapers. Customers telephone Drampton to place an order and the telephone call is answered by trained operators. Drampton pays the cost of the telephone call. The total standard cost of one telephone call is shown below.

STANDARD COST OF ONE CALL			
Expense	*Quantity*	*Cost*	*Cost per call*
Operators' wages	6 minutes	£3.50 per hour	£0.35
Fixed overheads[1]	6 minutes	£6.50 per hour	£0.65
Standard cost of one telephone call			£1.00

[1] Fixed overheads are based on budgeted number of calls.

Drampton's finance director gives you the following information for the three months ended 31 May 20X2.

- Budgeted number of calls   900,000 calls
- Actual number of calls   1,000,000 calls
- Actual expenses   *Quantity*   *Cost*
- Operators' wages   114,000 hours   £478,800
- Fixed overheads   £540,400

Actual cost of actual operations   £1,019,200

Task

Calculate the following information:

(i)	Labour rate variance:		
(ii)	Labour efficiency variance:		
(iii)	Fixed overhead expenditure variance:		
(iv)	Fixed overhead volume variance:		

Test your understanding 7

You are a newly appointed trainee accounting technician with Primary Chemicals plc. One of your responsibilities is to prepare and monitor standard costing variances for the distillation department. The distillation department prepares barrels of a refined chemical using a continuous process.

Fixed overheads are charged to production on the basis of machine hours. This is because the machine hours required determines the speed of production.

The budgeted and actual results of the distillation department for the week ended 30 November 20X2 are shown below.

Distillation Department – Operating results week ended 30 November 20X2				
Production	Budget 2,500 barrels		Actual 2,400 barrels	
	Standard cost		Actual cost	
Material	12,500 litres	£106,250	11,520 litres	£99,072
Labour	10,000 labour hrs	£60,000	10,080 labour hrs	£61,488
Fixed overheads	20,000 machine hrs	£200,000	18,960 machine hrs	£185,808
Total cost		£366,250		£346,368

Task

(a)   Calculate the following variances:

(i)	Material price variance	
		————
		————
(ii)	Material usage variance	
		————
		————

(iii)	Labour rate variance	
		———
		———
(iv)	Labour efficiency variance	
		———
		———
(v)	Fixed overhead expenditure variance	
		———
		———
(vi)	Fixed overhead volume variance	
		———
		———

Test your understanding 8

You are an accounting technician employed by Garforth Cookridge and Co, a firm of accountants and registered auditors. A new client is Econair Ltd. Econair is a small airline that operates two routes from its home airport.

One of your tasks is to prepare standard costing variances for Econair. To help you, the airline provides you with the following information for the 28 days ended 30 November 20X3 for the route between the home airport and Alpha City.

Budgeted and actual operating results 28 days ended 30 November 20X3

	Budget		Actual	
	Quantity	*£*	*Quantity*	*£*
Operating data				
Number of flights		168		160
Number of flying hours		672		768
Expenses	*Quantity*	*£*	*Quantity*	*£*
Fuel	33,600 gallons	50,400	38,400 gallons	61,440
Pilots' remuneration	1,344 pilot hours	67,200	1,536 pilot hours	79,872
Aircraft fixed overheads	672 flying hours	75,600	768 flying hours	76,200
Cost of operations		193,200		217,512

Other information

- Pilot hours are the same as labour hours for a manufacturer.

- Flying hours are the same as machine hours for a manufacturer.

- The number of flights is the same as production volume for a manufacturer.

- Fuel and pilots' remuneration are treated as variable costs.

- Fixed overheads are charged to operations on the basis of flying hours.

Task

Calculate the following variances:

(i)	Fuel price variance:	
(ii)	Fuel usage variance:	
(iii)	Rate variance for pilots:	
(iv)	Efficiency variance for pilots:	
(v)	Fixed overhead expenditure variance:	
(vi)	Fixed overhead volume variance:	

Test your understanding 9

Brown Ltd manufactures and sells office furniture. The company operates an integrated standard cost system in which:

purchases of materials are recorded at standard cost

finished goods are recorded at standard cost

direct materials and direct labour costs are both variable costs

fixed production overheads are absorbed using direct labour hours.

You are an accounting technician at Brown Ltd. You report to Sam Thomas, the Finance Director.

The company's most popular product is an executive desk. Its standard cost is as follows:

Product: Executive desk

Inputs	Quantity	Unit price £	Total cost £
Direct materials	30 kgs	5.00	150.00
Direct labour	5 hours	6.00	30.00
Fixed production overheads	5 hours	4.00	20.00
Standard cost			200.00

Actual and budgeted data for the manufacture of executive desks for May 20X4 are shown below:

- 27,500 kg of direct materials were purchased for £143,000.

- Issues from stores to production totalled 27,500 kg.

- The actual output for the month was 900 desks.

- The budgeted output for the month was 1,000 desks.

- 4,200 direct labour hours were worked at a cost of £26,040.

- Actual fixed production overheads were £23,000.

Task

Calculate the following variances for the production of executive desks for May:

(i)	Material price variance	
(ii)	Material usage variance	

(iii)	Labour rate variance	
(iv)	Labour efficiency variance	
(v)	Fixed overhead expenditure variance	
(vi)	Fixed overhead volume variance	

2 Summary

In this chapter we have focussed in on the various fixed overhead variances a company may calculate and that must be mastered to pass the Decision and Control exam.

We have also incorporated some full assessment style questions covering all the variances studied so far.

Test your understanding answers

Test your understanding 1

Absorption rate $= \dfrac{\text{Budgeted cost}}{\text{Budgeted hours}} = \dfrac{£50,000}{20,000} = £2.50/\text{std hour}$

Actual output in standard hours $= 8,450 \times \dfrac{20,000}{10,000} = 16,900$ std hrs

Actual overheads	£47,500
Amount absorbed = 16,900 × £2.50 =	£42,250
Variance – under-recovery	£5,250 A

Test your understanding 2

Actual fixed overheads = £39,000

Expenditure variance = £1,000 F

Budgeted fixed overheads = £40,000

Volume variance = £2,000 A

SQ × SR
19,000 × £2 = £38,000

			£
Budgeted/Standard fixed cost for actual production			38,000
Variances	F	A	
Fixed overhead expenditure	1,000		
Fixed overhead volume		2,000	
Total variance	1,000	2,000	1,000
Actual cost for production			39,000

Test your understanding 3

Actual fixed overheads = £1,245,000

                Expenditure variance = £5,000 F

Budgeted fixed overheads = £1,250,000

            Volume variance = £45,000 A

SQ × SR

24,100 × £50 = £1,205,000

			£
Budgeted/Standard fixed cost for actual production			1,205,000
Variances	F	A	
Fixed overhead expenditure	5,000		
Fixed overhead volume		45,000	
Total variance	5,000	45,000	40,000
Actual fixed cost for actual production			1,245,000

 Test your understanding 4

Fixed overhead recovery rate $\dfrac{\text{Budget overhead}}{\text{Budget hours}} = \dfrac{£44,000}{16,000} = £2.75/\text{hr}$

Standard hours per unit $= \dfrac{16,000}{8,000} = 2$ hrs per unit

(a) **Fixed overhead variance**

Fixed overhead recovered in production achieved

= 8,450 × 2 = 16,900 hours

                                         £

Fixed overhead recovered = 16,900 × £2.75/hr =   46,475

Actual fixed overhead incurred =   47,500

Variance (under-recovered)   1,025 (A)

(b) **Sub-variances**

    (i)   Fixed overhead expenditure variance:

	£
Actual cost	47,500
Budgeted overhead	44,000
	£3,500 A

        £3,500 adverse, represents an overspend

    (ii)   Fixed overhead volume variance:

	£
Budget overhead	44,000
Actual production 16,900 × £2.75	46,475
Over-recovery	£2,475 F

Test your understanding 5

(a) **Standard hours in the budget**

184 trips × 5 standard hours

=   920 standard hours

(b) **Fixed overhead recovery rate per trip**

£11,638/184 = £63.25 per trip

(c) **Fixed overhead total variance**

	£
Actual fixed cost	12,400
The actual number of trips multiplied by FORR per trip 176 × 63.25	11,132
	1,268 Adverse

(d) **Fixed overhead expenditure variance**

	£
Actual fixed costs	12,400
Budgeted fixed costs	11,638
	£762 Adverse

(e) **Fixed overhead volume variance**

	£
Budgeted OH cost	11,638
Actual trips × FORR per trip	
176 × £63.25	11,132
	£506 Adverse

Test your understanding 6

(i)   Labour rate variance:

114,000 × £4.20   =   £79,800 (A)

114,000 × £3.50

(ii)   Labour efficiency variance:

114,000 × £3.50   =   £49,000 (A)

100,000 × £3.50

(iii)   Fixed overhead expenditure variance:

£540,400 – £585,000   =   £44,600 (F)

(iv)   Fixed overhead volume variance:

90,000 × £6.50   =   £65,000 (F)

100,000 × £6.50

KAPLAN PUBLISHING

Test your understanding 7

(i)	Material price variance	
	Actual price × actual quantity (given)	£99,072
	Standard price × actual quantity (£8.50 ×11,520)	£97,920
		£1,152 (A)

(ii)	Material usage variance	
	Standard price × actual quantity (£8.50 × 11,520)	£97,920
	Standard price × standard quantity (£8.50 × 5 litres × 2,400)	£102,000
		£4,080 (F)

(iii)	Labour rate variance	
	Actual rate × actual hours (given)	£61,488
	Standard rate × actual hours (£6.00 × 10,080)	£60,480
		£1,008 (A)

(iv)	Labour efficiency variance	
	Standard rate × actual hours (£6.00 × 10,080)	£60,480
	Standard rate × standard hours (£6.00 × 4 × 2,400)	£57,600
		£2,880 (A)

(v)	Fixed overhead expenditure variance	
	Actual fixed overheads	£185,808
	Budgeted fixed overheads	£200,000
		£14,192 (F)

(vi)   Fixed overhead volume variance
Standard rate × budgeted machine hours
(£10.00 × 8 × 2,500)   £200,000
Std rate × actual machine hours produced
(£10.00 × 8 × 2,400)   £192,000

                          £8,000 (A)

Test your understanding 8

(i)   Fuel price variance:
£61,440
38,400 × £1.50   £3,840 (A)

(ii)   Fuel usage variance:
38,400 × £1.50
32,000 × £1.50   £9,600 (A)

(iii)   Rate variance for pilots:
£79,872
1,536 × £50.00   £3,072 (A)

(iv)   Efficiency variance for pilots:
1,536 × £50.00
1,280 × £50.00   £12,800 (A)

(v)   Fixed overhead expenditure variance:
£76,200 – £75,600   £600 (A)

(vi)   Fixed overhead volume variance:
£75,600
640 × £112.50   £3,600 (A)

Test your understanding 9

(i)	The material price variance	
	Actual price paid for 27,500 kg	£143,000
	Standard price 27,500 kg × £5	£137,500
	Variance	£5,500 (A)
(ii)	The material usage variance	
	Actual material used for 900 desks = 27,500 kg × £5	£137,500
	Standard usage for 900 desks = 900 × 30 = 27,000 kg × £5	£135,000
	Variance	£2,500 (A)
(iii)	The labour rate variance	
	Actual price paid for 4,200 hours	£26,040
	Standard price for 4,200 hours × £6	£25,200
	Variance	840 (A)
(iv)	The labour efficiency variance	
	Actual hours producing 900 desks	4,200 hours × £6
	Standard hours = 900 × 5 hours	4,500 hours × £6
	Variance	£1,800 (F)

(v) The fixed overhead expenditure variance

£23,000 – £20,000 = £3,000 (A)

(vi) The fixed overhead volume variance

5,000 × £4 compared to 4,500 × £4 = £2,000 (A)

Operating statements and backwards variances

Introduction

In this chapter we shall start by revising the variances we calculated in the previous chapters. We shall then concentrate on the ways in which management use these variances. The main focus will be on the way in which the calculations are laid out in the reports to management. We will also look at how we can work backwards from a known variance to identify the figures input.

ASSESSMENT CRITERIA	CONTENTS
Actual and standard costs derived from variances (backwards variances) (2.3)	1 Operating statements
	2 Using variances backwards
Prepare a standard costing operating statement reconciling budgeted cost with actual cost of actual production (2.4)	
Explain the differences between marginal costing and absorption costing operating statements (2.4)	
Reconcile the difference between the operating statement under marginal costing and absorption costing (2.4)	

1 Operating statements

1.1 Introduction

Having computed all of the variances, we can now reconcile the budgeted and actual cost.

1.2 Absorption costing operating statements

Katzman Ltd produces soap in bulk.

The standard cost per drum of soap is made up as follows:

Raw materials	100 kg costing £2 per kg
Labour	12 hours costing £3 per hour
Variable overheads	12 hours costing £2 per hour

Fixed production costs per month are budgeted at £90,000. For April 20X8, budgeted production was 7,500 drums.

Fixed overheads are absorbed on a unit basis.

The actual costs incurred in the month were:

Raw materials (900,000 kg purchased)	£1,755,000
Labour (110,000 hours worked and paid)	£341,000
Variable production overheads	£176,500
	£2,272,500
Fixed production costs	£86,000
	£2,358,500

During April 7,800 drums of soap were actually produced. There were no raw materials in stock at the start or end of the period.

In Chapter 12, variances were calculated as follows:

Materials price £45,000 F

Materials usage £240,000 A

Labour rate £11,000 A

Labour efficiency £49,200 A

Variable overhead expenditure £43,500 F

Variable overhead efficiency £32,800 A

Fixed overhead expenditure £4,000 F

Fixed overhead volume £3,600 F

The absorption costing profit statement would look like this:

		£	£	£
Flexed budgeted/standard absorption cost of actual production (7,800 units × £272)				2,121,600
Cost variances		*Adverse*	*Favourable*	
Materials	price		45,000	
	usage	240,000		
Labour	rate of pay	11,000		
	efficiency	49,200		
Variable overheads	expenditure		43,500	
	efficiency	32,800		
Fixed overheads variance	expenditure		4,000	
	volume		3,600	
Total variances		333,000	96,100	236,900 A
Actual cost (per question)				2,358,500

The flexed budgeted cost is at the top of the operating statement, the actual cost is at the bottom, and the variances are listed out in between. If all calculations are correct, the statement should add down.

1.3 Marginal costing operating statements

So far we have dealt exclusively with the calculations for absorption costing. We shall now look at the calculations for marginal costing.

There is only one very important difference between the two. As we have seen, with absorption costing we absorb the fixed overheads into the units produced at a standard absorption rate based on labour hours.

With marginal costing, we don't attempt to absorb the fixed overheads into the units produced.

Using the example from earlier, the standard cost card will look as follows:

Standard cost card – marginal costing	
	£
Raw material: 100 kg × £2	200.00
Labour: 12 hours × £3 per hour	36.00
Variable overheads: 12 hours × £2 per hour	24.00
	_____
Total standard cost	260.00
	_____

You can see that the standard costs for direct material, labour and variable overheads are calculated exactly as before. The only difference is that there is no standard amount for fixed overheads absorbed into the units.

Having mastered the sometimes tricky calculations in the previous chapters, you will be delighted to know that the calculations of the material, labour and variable overhead variances are exactly the same as before (and so we don't calculate them again here). Even better, if you struggled a little with the fixed overhead variances, the calculation of the fixed overhead variance in marginal costing is very easy.

Taking the same example as before, the fixed overhead variance is simply the expenditure variance (the difference between the budgeted fixed cost and the actual fixed cost incurred). There is no volume or other variance because we are not attempting to absorb the fixed overheads into the units – hence no volume variance can arise.

Actual fixed cost	£86,000
Budgeted fixed cost	£90,000
	_____
Fixed cost expenditure variance	£4,000
	_____

Having computed all of the variances, we can now reconcile the budgeted and actual cost. Remember that we are dealing here with marginal costing.

		£	£	£
Budgeted marginal cost (7,800 × £260)				2,028,000
Add budgeted fixed overhead				90,000
Cost variances		*Adverse*	*Favourable*	
Materials	price		45,000	
	usage	240,000		
Labour	rate of pay	11,000		
	efficiency	49,200		
Variable overheads	expenditure		43,500	
	efficiency	32,800		
		333,000	88,500	244,500
				2,362,500
Fixed overheads variance	expenditure		4,000	(4,000)
Actual cost (per question)				2,358,500

 Test your understanding 1

The following budgetary control report has been provided for Drug Limited:

	Budget		Actual	
Production		14,700		13,500
Direct material	4,140 kgs	£20,520	3,750 kgs	£20,000
Direct labour	920 hrs	£4,238	890 hrs	£3,971
Fixed overheads		£10,250		£9,600
Total cost		£35,008		£33,571

The following variances have been calculated:

Direct material price	1,413 A
Direct material usage	258 F
Direct labour rate	129 F
Direct labour efficiency	208 A
Fixed overhead expenditure	650 F
Fixed overhead volume	837 A

Produce an operating statement under absorption costing.

Flexed budgeted/standard absorption cost for actual production			
Variances	F	A	
Direct materials price			
Direct materials usage			
Direct labour rate			
Direct labour efficiency			
Fixed overhead expenditure			
Fixed overhead volume			
Total variance			
Actual cost of actual production			

Produce an operating statement under marginal costing.

	F	A	
Budgeted/standard marginal cost for actual production			
Budgeted fixed costs			
Variances	F	A	
Direct materials price			
Direct materials usage			
Direct labour rate			
Direct labour efficiency			
Fixed overhead expenditure			
Total variance			
Actual cost of actual production			

Test your understanding 2

The following budgetary control report has been provided for Plug Limited:

	Budget		Actual	
Production		10,000		12,500
Direct material	50,000 kgs	£400,000	68,750 kgs	£536,250
Direct labour	40,000 hrs	£480,000	47,500 hrs	£579,500
Fixed overheads		£350,000		£340,000
Total cost		£1,230,000		£1,455,750

Some of the variance calculations have been done:

	£	Favourable/Adverse
Direct material price	13,750	
Direct material usage	50,000	A
Direct labour rate		A
Direct labour efficiency	30,000	
Fixed overhead expenditure	10,000	F
Fixed overhead volume		F

Complete the operating statement under absorption costing.

			£
Flexed budgeted/standard absorption cost for actual production			
Variances	Favourable/ Adverse		
Direct materials price			
Direct materials usage			
Direct labour rate			
Direct labour efficiency			
Fixed overhead expenditure			
Fixed overhead volume			
Actual cost of actual production			

Note: the different presentation is deliberately done as the AAT will expect a candidate to be comfortable with the process however the statement is presented.

2 Using variances backwards

2.1 Introduction

So far, variance calculations have started with standard and actual costs given in the question and you have been required to calculate the variances.

The assessor may also set questions where the question will, for example, give the standard and the variance and ask you to calculate the actual.

Example

A Ltd purchases 1,000 kg of material at a cost of £550.

The adverse material price variance is £50. What was the standard cost of 1 kg of material?

Solution

	£
Actual cost of 1,000 kg	550
Adverse variance	(50) (A)
Therefore, standard cost of 1,000 kg	500
Therefore, standard cost of 1 kg	0.50

 Example

Alternatively, you could be given data on the standard cost and variance and be asked to calculate the actual cost paid.

For example, B Ltd purchases 200 litres of oil which should have cost £1 per litre at standard. The adverse material price variance is £0.10 per litre. Calculate the actual cost of the 200 litres purchased.

Solution

	£
200 litres should have cost 200 × £1	200
Price variance = 200 × £0.10	20 (A)
Therefore, 200 litres did cost	£220

Example

An added complication could involve a change in inventory, for example.

C Ltd produces 600 widgets in March.

The standard cost card for a widget shows the following:

	Standard cost per unit £
Material – 3 kg at £2 per kg	6.00

There was no materials usage variance.

There was no opening inventory but closing inventory of material was 200 kg.

There was a £200 adverse price variance.

Calculate the actual amount paid for materials purchased in March.

Solution

	Kg
Standard amount of material used (600 × 3 kg)	1,800
	———
No usage variance, therefore actual amount used	1,800
Closing inventory	200
	———
Total purchased	2,000
	———

	£
Standard cost of purchases 2,000 × £2	4,000
Price variance	200 (A)
	———
Actual cost	4,200
	———

Test your understanding 3

The standard labour cost for one unit was £24, and the budgeted labour cost to produce 250 units was therefore £6,000.

In a period 300 units were produced and the total direct labour variance was £60 favourable.

420 hours were worked and the standard labour time per unit was 1.5 hours.

Complete the below table:

	£
Actual labour cost	
Labour rate variance	
Labour efficiency variance	
Standard labour cost of production	

3 Summary

In this chapter we have looked at the way in which management might structure the variance reports. The investigation of variances is a part of the control process and it is important that you understand the layout of the reports before we look at causes of variances and their typical remedies.

We also looked at the use of backwards variances, a favourite with examiners to test deeper understanding of the variance calculations.

Test your understanding answers

Test your understanding 1

Budgeted/standard cost for actual production (W1)			32,150
Variances	**F**	**A**	
Direct material price		1,413	
Direct material usage	258		
Direct labour rate	129		
Direct labour efficiency		208	
Fixed overhead expenditure	650		
Fixed overhead volume		837	
Total variance	1,037	2,458	1,421
Actual cost of actual production			33,571

(W1) £35,008 × 13,500/14,700 = £32,150

	F	A	
Budgeted/standard variable cost for actual production (W2)			22,737
Budgeted fixed costs			10,250
Variances	**F**	**A**	
Direct material price		1,413	
Direct material usage	258		
Direct labour rate	129		
Direct labour efficiency		208	
Fixed overhead expenditure	650		
Total variance	1,037	1,621	584
Actual cost of actual production			33,571

(W2) £20,520 + £4,238 = £24,758 × 13,500/14,700 = £22,737

Test your understanding 2

			£
Flexed budgeted/standard absorption cost for actual production (W1)			1,537,500
Variances	**Favourable/adverse**		
Direct materials price (W2)	Favourable		13,750
Direct materials usage	Adverse		50,000
Direct labour rate (W3)	Adverse		9,500
Direct labour efficiency (W3)	Favourable		30,000
Fixed overhead expenditure	Favourable		10,000
Fixed overhead volume (W4)	Favourable		87,500
Actual cost of actual production			1,455,750

(W1)   £1,230,000/10,000 × 12,500 = £1,537,500

(W2)   AQ × AP

                                  536,250

        AQ × Std P   13,750 **F**

        68,750 × £8   550,000

(W3)   AH × AR

                                    579,500

        AH × Std R   **9,500 A**

        47,500 × 12   570,000

        SH × AP × Std R   30,000 **F**

        4 × 12,500 × 12   600,000

(W4)   Budget   350,000

        Actual Production × OAR   **87,500 F**

        12,500 × (350,000/10,000)   437,500

Test your understanding 3

Using the information we know the standard cost per hour must be £24/1.5 hrs = £16 per hour.

AH × AR

420 hrs × ? =   ?

              Rate variance

AH × Std R

420 hrs × £16 =   £6,720

              Efficiency variance

Std H × AProd × Std R

1.5 hours × 300 × £16 = £7,200

              Total variance   £60 favourable

The total variance is £60 favourable and the standard labour cost of production is £7,200.

That means the actual labour cost of production must be £60 less than that.

Actual labour cost is £7,140

Rate variance: £7,140 – (420 hrs × £16) = £420 adverse

Efficiency variance: (420 hrs × £16) – £7,200 = £480 favourable

Solution

	£
Actual labour cost	7,140
Labour rate variance	420 A
Labour efficiency variance	480 F
Standard labour cost of production	7,200

Nature of variances

Introduction

In this chapter we shall look at how we can separate out the variances we have calculated previously into two parts, one that a manager or employee can influence and the other that a manger or employee cannot influence.

ASSESSMENT CRITERIA	CONTENTS
Identify the nature of variances. (2.5) Identify elements of a variance that are controllable and non-controllable (2.5)	1 Controllable and uncontrollable variances

1 Controllable and uncontrollable variances

1.1 What can we control?

Budgets are often set too far in advance to take into account any changes to the budgetary period. For example, after the budget is set, but before the budgetary period, a material price may rise due to inflation. Rather than revising the budget, which may be a significant task, we may calculate the variances and then split them into the controllable part (that which is due to managers' actions) and the uncontrollable part (that which might be due to inflation or some other change which is outside of the managers' control).

1.2 Material price variance and price changes

In some assessment tasks you may be given information about specific price indices that have affected the materials prices during the period. In these circumstances it is possible to split the materials price variance into that element which relates to the price increase and any other factors.

 Example

The standard material cost for a business' single product is 4 kg at a price of £12.00 per kg. The standard price was set when the index for this material price stood at 120. During August, 10,000 units of the product were made using 42,000 kgs at a total cost of £525,000. The August price index for this material is 122.

What is the total material price variance, the element relating to the price increase and the element relating to other causes?

Solution

Total material price variance		£
Actual cost		525,000
Standard cost of actual material	42,000 × £12.00	504,000
		21,000 Adverse

This adverse variance of £21,000 can then be split into the element relating to the price increase and the element relating to other factors:

Variance relating to other factors

		£
Actual cost		525,000
Revised price for actual material	42,000 × (£12.00 × 122/120)	512,400
		————
		12,600 Adverse

This part of the variance is controllable and should be investigated.

Variance relating to price increase

		£
Revised price for actual material	42,000 × (£12.00 × 122/120)	512,400
Standard cost of actual material	42,000 × £12.00	504,000
		————
		8,400 Adverse

This part of the variance is uncontrollable by the managers since they cannot dictate inflation levels.

Variances can be broken down like this for many reasons, not just because of price changes. Any decision that has been taken and needs to be isolated should be calculated in this way.

 Test your understanding 1

A company produces and sells a single product.

One product should use 2.5 kg of materials. The quantity index was set when the index was 100.

The material has a standard cost of £5 per kg (set when the price index was 100).

During July, the standard material price per kg was revised due to the price index rising to 105. Its standard material usage was also revised as the quantity index had risen to 110.

Actual results were:

Production: 1,000 units

Direct materials: 2,550 kg purchased and used at a cost of £12,000.

Solution

The controllable material price variance is £

The uncontrollable material price variance is £

The controllable material usage variance is £

The uncontrollable material usage variance is £

(Answers should be to 2 decimal places.)

2 Summary

In this chapter we have examined how some aspects of work are controllable and some are uncontrollable. It is important to understand the portion of variances we can control and we must judge people on things we can do something about. If people are judged on things they can't control it can have an adverse effect on motivation and productivity.

Test your understanding answers

Test your understanding 1

Revised price = £5 × 105/100 = £5.25

Revised quantity = 2.5 kg × 110/100 = 2.75 kg

AQ × AP

2,550 kg × £? = £12,000

AQ × RP

2,550 × £5.25 = £13,387.50

Controllable price variance = £1,387.50 F

AQ × RP

2,550 × £5.25 = £13,387.50

AQ × SP

2,550 × £5 = £12,750

Uncontrollable price variance = £637.50 A

AQ × SP

2,550 × £5 = £12,750

RQ × SP

1,000 × 2.75 kg × £5 = £13,750

Controllable usage variance = £1,000.00 F

RQ × SP

1,000 × 2.75 kg × £5 = £13,750

SQ × SP

1,000 × 2.5 kg × £5 = £12,500

Uncontrollable usage variance = £1,250.00 A

Interpreting variances

Introduction

In this chapter we shall concentrate on the ways in which management use these variances. This will include investigating the causes of the variances, seeking ways to control the variances and ways in which the variances can be reported.

ASSESSMENT CRITERIA	CONTENTS
How the type of standard can impact on variance (2.1)	1 Measuring the significance of variances
How variances may interrelate (2.5)	
Identify what causes standard costing variances such as wastage, economies of scale, learning effect, inflation and skills mix (2.5)	2 Investigation of variances
Identify possible action that can be taken to reduce adverse variances and increase favourable variances (2.5)	3 Responsibility accounting and the interdependence of variances
Effectively communicate what the standard costing variance means in report format (2.5)	

1 Measuring the significance of variances

1.1 Introduction

As we have seen, the key tool for management control within a costing system is some form of variance analysis report or budgetary control statement. The aim is to prepare a report to management on a routine basis in which variances are clearly identified and can be acted upon as appropriate.

In exercising control, it is generally impracticable to review every variance in detail at each accounting period and attention will usually be concentrated on those variances which have the greatest impact on the achievement of the budget plan.

1.2 Identifying significant variances

One method of identifying significant variances is to express each variance as a percentage of the related budget allowance or standard value. Those showing the highest percentage deviation would then be given the most urgent attention.

This method, however, could result in lack of attention to variances which, although representing a small percentage of the standard value, nevertheless involve significant sums of money. Both percentages and absolute values should be looked at in deciding where the priorities for control actually lie.

In practice, management will review the variance report presented to them and decide which variances should be investigated on the basis of whether the costs of investigation are outweighed by the benefits (called a cost-benefit analysis).

Management will often request a more detailed analysis and explanation of specific variances to be produced as the decision as to whether or not a variance merits action may need more information than is provided in the original variance report.

1.3 Fluctuating variances – looking at trends

The variances of a particular period may not be representative of a general trend. Items like stationery costs can fluctuate widely from month to month, dependent on the amount of stationery that has been invoiced.

Sometimes, the accountant will make estimated adjustments to either the budget or the actual figures in an attempt to give a better picture of the underlying trend but this is not a completely satisfactory way of dealing with the matter.

The simplest way of getting the month's figures into context is to show also the accumulated cost for the year to date. High cost and low cost periods will then be revealed but will balance out in the cumulative figures.

A development of the above idea is also to report each period the manager's latest forecast compared with the annual budget. It will then be possible to see whether variances from budget currently being reported are likely to continue to accumulate during the remainder of the year, or whether they will be offset by later variances.

Although this technique of forecasting is dependent on managers' subjective assessments, it is a good way of ensuring that the correct control action gets taken on the current figures.

1.4 Comparing against forecasts

Some large organisations in the UK have taken the idea of comparing against forecasts a step further. Many companies employ the following comparisons.

	Comparison	Information
1	Budget v actual	What progress have we made towards achieving objectives?
2	Budget v forecast	Will we continue to progress towards achievement of objectives?
3	Budget v revised forecast	Will suggested corrective actions lead us back to achievement of objectives?
4	Latest forecast v previous	Why are the forecasts different and are circumstances getting better or worse?
5	Actual v past forecast	Why were forecasts incorrect and can they be improved?

It may not be necessary to perform each of these control comparisons every month or quarter. The actual versus past forecast may only be necessary annually or less frequently.

It must be remembered that managers will need to be motivated to produce these forecasts and use them. They must be educated to recognise why and how they can use them to enable them to do a better job and not feel that they are just another means for higher level management to check on them and apply pressure.

Finally, this year's results are sometimes compared with those for the corresponding period last year. In some cases this may be helpful in establishing a trend, but it must never be forgotten that the budget is this year's plan, and it is against that plan that performance must be controlled.

2 Investigation of variances

2.1 Introduction

Variance analysis, if properly carried out, can be a useful cost-controlling and cost-saving tool. However, the type of variance analysis seen so far is only a step towards the final goal of controlling and saving costs.

2.2 Generalised reasons for variances

The causes of variances can be classified under four headings:

- Planning errors

- Measurement errors

- Random factors

- Operational factors.

Planning errors lead to the setting of inappropriate standards or budgets. This may be due to carelessness on the part of the standard setter (not taking account of known changes in the production process or expected price rises, for example) or due to unexpected external changes (a market shortage of a resource leading to increased price. These need to be isolated from hindsight information and a revision of the standard considered for future budgets. It could even be a conscious decision by the company to use a particular type of standard. An ideal standard would make a favourable variance almost impossible to achieve, or a historic standard is likely to lead to favourable usage/efficiency variances due to learning.

Measurement errors include errors caused by inaccurate completion of timesheets or job cards and inaccurate measurement of quantities issued from stores. The rectification of such errors, or errors caused by random factors, will probably not give rise to any cost savings (though this is a generalisation).

Random factors are by definition uncontrollable, although they need careful monitoring to ensure that they are not, in fact, one of the other types of variance.

2.3 Operational causes of variances

Examples of some possible reasons for individual variances are shown below.

Variance		Possible causes
Materials:	Price	Bulk discounts (economies of scale)
		Different suppliers/ different materials
		Unexpected delivery costs
		Different buying procedures
		Inflation
	Usage	Different quality material
		Theft, obsolescence, deterioration
		Different quality of staff
		Different mix of material
		Different batch sizes and trim loss
Labour:	Rate	Different class of labour
		Excessive overtime
		Productivity bonuses
		National wage negotiations
		Union action
		Inflation
	Efficiency	Different levels of skill
		Different working conditions
		The learning effect
		Lack of supervision
		Works to rule
		Machine breakdowns

Lack of material
Lack of orders
Strikes (if paid)
Too long over coffee breaks

Overhead:	Expenditure	Change in nature of overhead
		Unforeseen price changes
	Volume	Excessive idle time
		Increase in workforce

It will nearly always be useful to consult staff working in operational departments to resolve any queries as they will have 'local' knowledge of the day-to-day operations.

Example

An adverse materials usage variance of £50,000 arose in a month as follows:

Standard cost per kg	£10
Actual cost per kg	£12
Units produced	2,000
Standard quantity per unit	25 kg
Actual quantity used	55,000 kg

	£
Standard cost of actual usage (55,000 kg × £10)	550,000
Standard cost of standard usage (2,000 × 25 kg × £10)	500,000
Adverse usage variance	50,000

On further investigation, the following is ascertained:

1 The actual quantity used was based on estimated stock figures. A stock take showed that 53,000 kg were in fact used.

2 3,000 kg is the best estimate for what might politely be called the monthly 'shrinkage' but, in less polite circles, theft.

3 2,000 kg of stock were damaged by vandals who broke into the stores.

4 The supervisor feels that existing machinery is outmoded and more efficient machinery could save 1,000 kg a month.

Additional considerations

1   A security guard would cost £9,000 a year to employ and would stop 20% of all theft. Resultant dissatisfaction amongst works staff might cost £20,000 per annum.

2   Given the easy access to stores, vandals might be expected to break in every other month; £10,000 would make the stores vandal-proof.

3   New machinery would cost £720,000.

Required:

Analyse the usage variance in the light of this information and comment on your results.

Solution

The original £50,000 usage variance could be analysed as follows:

		Favourable/(Adverse) variance £
(a)	Bad measurement (53,000 – 55,000) × £10	(20,000)
(b)	Theft (3,000 × £10)	(30,000)
(c)	Damage (2,000 × £10)	(20,000)
(d)	Obsolete machinery (1,000 × £10)	(10,000)
(e)	Other operational factors (balance)	30,000
		(50,000)

In each case, the variances should be studied and compared with the cost of rectification.

(a)   **Bad measurement** – Assuming no costly decisions were made, or are likely to be made in the future, such as over-stocking, the component is of no future consequence.

(b)   **Theft** – Annual cost due to theft is 12 × £30,000 or £360,000; 20% of this saved would amount to £72,000 at a cost of £9,000 + £20,000, thus the security guard is worth employing.

(c) **Damage** – Annual cost due to vandalism is 6 × £20,000 or £120,000; this would presumably be avoided by spending £10,000 now; again worthwhile.

(d) **Obsolete machinery** – Annual cost of using old machines is 12 × £10,000 or £120,000; the cost of making this saving (the saving would increase as purchase prices increased or if production increased) is £720,000; the decision over this investment would require further analysis using discounted cash flow.

(e) **Other factors** – We now see a favourable usage variance once all known factors above have been accounted for. This may need further investigation, particularly if it affects the quality of goods produced.

Test your understanding 1

An adverse materials price variance might mean that _____ (BETTER / WORSE) quality material was bought than standard. This changed the way the employees used it, given the different quality, so worked _____ (MORE / LESS) efficiently than standard.

(Insert the correct word in each case.)

Test your understanding 2

If better quality material was bought than had been allowed for in the standard, which four of the following variances are most likely to result?

Favourable material price	
Adverse material price	
Favourable material usage	
Adverse material usage	
Favourable labour efficiency	
Adverse labour efficiency	
Favourable labour rate	
Adverse labour rate	
Favourable variable overhead efficiency	
Adverse variable overhead efficiency	

2.4 Possible action on variances

Having calculated the variance and ascertained the reason for the variance, the next step would be to take some action either to:

(i) Reinforce a favourable variance

(ii) Reduce an adverse variance.

Reinforcing a favourable variance could be achieved by something as simple as recognising the good work of a team or individual.

Reducing an adverse variance would usually involve some kind of control process, for example additional supervision.

Here are some other actions that could be taken on variances.

Controlling efficiency and idle time

Efficiency and idle time can be prevented or reduced considerably by:

(a) Proper maintenance of tools & machinery

(b) Advanced production planning

(c) Timely procurement of stores

(d) Assurance of supply of power

(e) Advance planning for machine utilisation.

Material waste

Material waste may also be a normal part of a process and could be caused by:

- evaporation

- scrapping

- testing.

Waste would affect the material usage variance.

The purchasing of materials is a highly specialised function that can control waste by:

(a) Ordering the right quantity and quality of materials at the most favourable price

(b) Ensuring the material arrives at the right time in the production process

(c) Take active measures against theft, deterioration, breakage and additional storage costs.

2.5 The cost of variance analysis

The provision of any information incurs the costs of collecting the basic data, processing it, and reporting the results. Variance analysis is no exception and, as with other forms of management information, the benefits to which it gives rise must be commensurate with the costs incurred.

(a) Variance analysis allows 'management by exception' and it is for this purpose that standard costing system has been introduced.

(b) When variances are known to exist, failure to make adequate investigations will weaken the control system and thus the motivation of managers.

(c) The amount of analysis required can sometimes be reduced by defining levels of significance below which detailed investigation is not required.

(d) The costs of clerical work can be over-estimated. In most working days there will be some spare capacity that can be utilised without extra cost.

What has to be considered, therefore, is the amount of detail that can be incorporated usefully in variance analysis. This will fall into two categories:

(a) **Including more detailed codings** in source documents indicating causes and responsibilities. Such coding is likely to involve people outside the accounts department, who may be unwilling to give time to the task. How useful the analysis will be, will depend on whether or not it is practicable to identify causes and responsibilities at the time the document is initiated.

(b) **Investigation and re-analysis of variances after the event**. The process of investigation may be more useful for the management of the business than any quantity of formal variance calculations.

3 Responsibility accounting and the interdependence of variances

3.1 Introduction

Actions and their consequences should be traced to the person responsible. This may give the impression of 'laying the blame', but it is equally possible to award praise (and remunerate accordingly).

Responsibility accounting is a system which recognises various decision centres within a business and traces costs (and possibly revenues) to the individual managers who are primarily responsible for making decisions about the items in question.

Example

An opportunity arises for a buying department to obtain a consignment of a particular material at an exceptionally low price. The purchase is made; a favourable price variance is recorded and the buying department is duly praised.

Subsequently, when products are being manufactured using this type of material, significant adverse material usage variances and labour efficiency variances are recorded, and are initially regarded as the responsibility of the department where the work is done.

Is it fair to blame the adverse variances on the operational departments?

Solution

Investigations may reveal a number of relevant facts, for example:

- The 'cheap' material was of poor quality, and in consequence much of it was wasted in the process of machining. The resultant material usage and labour efficiency variances should presumably be regarded as the responsibility of the buying department, to offset the favourable price variance.

- Due to an employee leaving it had been necessary to use an operator who was not familiar with the job. At least part of the excess usage of materials could be attributed to this cause; but whether it should be regarded as the responsibility of the operating department or of the personnel department (for failing to recruit a replacement) is still open to question. If the employee who left had been highly paid, his removal might cause a favourable wage rate variance in the period under review – an offset to the adverse efficiency variance.

- The tools used had been badly worn, thus causing excessive time on the job. It would be necessary to consider whether this condition was attributable to the operating department (failing to sharpen tools or to requisition replacements) or to the tools store-keeper or to the buying department (for failing to buy on time or for buying poor quality items again).

The important points to bear in mind are as follows:

- Different types of variance can be inter-linked by a common cause.

- In many cases, the responsibility for variances cannot be identified merely by reference to the cost centre where the variance has been reported. Responsibility may be shared by several managers or may lie completely outside the cost centre in which the variance has arisen.

- In some instances, after questioning the managers as to the cause of a variance an independent assessment needs to take place. For example, the production manager may say that the quality of raw materials, the old machinery or the unskilled staff may have caused the adverse material usage variance, when the material price variance was also adverse. However, it could be that the buyer bought an inferior material but still paid more than the standard. An independent assessment of the material quality might need to take place.

Test your understanding 3

WH Limited uses a standard costing system which produces monthly control statements to manufacture product M, a perishable, high quality raw material which is carefully weighed by direct employees. Some wastage and quality control rejects occur at this stage. The employees then compress the material to change its shape and create product M.

All direct employees are paid a basic hourly rate appropriate to their individual skill level and a bonus scheme is in operation. Bonuses are paid according to the daily rate of output achieved by each individual.

A standard allowance for all of the above operational factors is included in the standard cost of product M. Standard cost data for one unit of product M is as follows:

		Standard cost £ per unit
Direct material X:	4.5 kg × £4.90 per kg	22.05
Direct labour:	10.3 hours × £3.50 per hour	36.05
Standard direct cost		58.10

The production manager has approached you for further explanations concerning the standard costing control system. He is particularly interested in understanding how the standard price is set per kg of material used.

Task 1

Write a memo to the production manager, explaining the following:

(a)   what information would be needed to determine the standard price per kg of material X

(b)   the possible sources from which this information might be obtained.

During November, the following costs were incurred producing 400 units of product M:

		Actual costs £
Direct material X:	2,100 kg @ £4.60 per kg	9,660
Direct labour:	4,000 hrs @ £4.00 per hr	16,000
Actual direct cost		25,660

Task 2

(a) Calculate the following direct cost variances for product M for November:

   (i)   direct material price

   (ii)   direct material usage

   (iii) direct labour rate

   (iv) direct labour utilisation or efficiency.

(b) Present the variances in a statement which reconciles the total standard direct cost of production with the actual direct cost for product M in November.

The production manager receives a copy of the standard costing control statement for product M every month. However, he has recently confessed to you that he does not really have a clear understanding of the meaning of the variances.

He has also been baffled by the following statement made by the finance director at a recent meeting of senior managers: 'Assigning responsibility for variances can be complicated if the variances are interdependent, for example if an adverse variance in one part of the organisation is caused by a favourable variance elsewhere.'

Task 3

As assistant accountant for WH Limited, you are asked to write a memo to the production manager which explains the following:

(a) the meaning of each of the direct cost variances calculated for product M

(b) two possible causes of each of the variances which you have calculated for product M for November

(c) two examples of interdependence which may be present in the variances which you have calculated for product M for November. Explain clearly why the variances may be interdependent, so that the manager can better understand the meaning of the finance director's statement.

Solution

Task 1

WH Limited

MEMORANDUM

To: Production Manager

From: Assistant Accountant

Date: 12 December 20X4

Subject: Determining the standard price per kg of material X

As requested I detail below the information which would be needed to determine the standard price of material X and possible sources of the information.

(a) *The information which is needed*   (b) *Possible sources*

Task 2

(a) (i)   Direct material price variance   =

(ii)   Direct material usage variance   =

(iii)   Direct labour rate variance   =

(iv)   Direct labour efficiency variance =

(b)   Reconciliation of standard direct cost of production with actual direct cost for November:

		£	£
Standard direct cost of production			
Direct cost variances:	*F*	*A*	
Material – price			
– usage			
Labour – rate			
– efficiency			
Total variance			
			———
Actual direct cost of production			
			———

Note: A = adverse variance; F = favourable variance

Task 3

WH Limited

MEMORANDUM

To:

From:

Date:

Subject:

As requested I detail below explanations of the direct cost variances and possible suggestions as to their causes in November.

(a)   **The meaning of the variances**

Direct material price variance

Direct material usage variance

Direct labour rate variance

Direct labour efficiency variance

(b) **Possible causes of the variances**
Favourable direct material price variance

Adverse direct material usage variance

Adverse direct labour rate variance

Favourable direct labour efficiency variance

(c)   Two examples of interdependence, where one variance can be related to others, could include the following.

Test your understanding 4

You are employed as a trainee Accounting Technician with Gransden, Yelling and Co, a firm of accountants and registered auditors. One of your clients is CD Products Ltd.

CD Products uses expensive equipment to make compact discs for customers in other companies. It has two manufacturing departments: the CD pressing department and the finishing department. The CD pressing department uses one machine to write digital data from a master disc to blank discs. The finishing department then prints information on the front of the discs, packages them and sends the completed discs to the customers.

KAPLAN PUBLISHING

CD Products uses standard costs to help prepare quotations for customers but does not yet use them for reporting purposes. Details of the standard costs used in the pressing department are shown below.

STANDARD COST PER MACHINE HOUR – CD PRESSING DEPARTMENT	
Blank compact discs: 800 × £0.20 each	£160.00
Labour: 8 labour hours × £7.00	£56.00
Fixed overheads	£200.00
Standard cost of pressing 800 compact discs per machine hour	£416.00

CD Products has prepared the following financial and operating information for the week ended 30 November 20X1.

CD Pressing Department information:

- Budgeted labour hours — 880 hours
- Actual number of compact discs manufactured — 96,000 CDs
- Actual cost of blank compact discs issued to production — £20,790
- Actual price paid for each blank compact disc — £0.21
- Actual labour hours worked — 980 hours
- Actual cost of labour — £7,252
  Factory information:
- Budgeted total factory fixed costs — £33,000
- Actual total factory fixed costs — £34,500
- Budgeted total factory labour hours — 1,320 hours
- Both budgeted and actual fixed overheads are apportioned between the pressing and finishing departments on the basis of budgeted labour hours.

The Chief Executive of CD Products is Jamil Baharundin. He tells you that the weekly financial and operating information does not help him manage the business. You suggest a standard costing statement might be more helpful. Jamil asks you to prepare a standard costing statement for the CD Pressing Department, using the information for the week ended 30 November 20X1.

Task

(a)   Calculate the following variances for the CD Pressing Department:

(i)	Material price variance:	
(ii)	Material usage variance:	
(iii)	Labour rate variance:	
(iv)	Labour efficiency variance:	
(v)	Fixed overhead expenditure variance:	
(vi)	Fixed overhead volume variance:	

KAPLAN PUBLISHING

(b) Prepare a statement for the CD Pressing Department reconciling the standard absorption cost of actual production to the actual absorption cost of actual production.

Standard costing reconciliation statement – week ended 30 November 20X1

			£
Standard cost of actual production			
Summary of variances:	Fav	Adv	
Material price			
Material usage			
Labour rate			
Labour efficiency			
Fixed overhead expenditure			
Fixed overhead volume			
	——	——	
Total variances			
			——
Actual cost of actual production			
			——

In a letter to you, Jamil tells you that your standard costing statement helped explain why CD Products' profits have recently been falling. He plans to use similar statements in the future but, before doing so, he raises the following issues:

*   He is not certain if all variances should be investigated. As an example, he explains that for every 100 fault-free compact discs produced in the week ended 30 November 20X1, two had to be scrapped. As the unit cost of a blank CD is so small, he feels it is not worth investigating the other reasons for the material usage variance.

- The standard costs for quotation purposes assumed customers would want their discs to be both pressed and finished. The demand for disc pressing is so high that it exceeds the capacity of the CD Pressing Department but most customers then take the pressed compact discs elsewhere for finishing.

- The CD Pressing Department requires a dust-free, air-conditioned environment using an expensive machine but the Finishing Department does not use any expensive resources.

An analysis of the budgeted factory fixed overheads showing their usage by department was included in the letter and is reproduced below.

	CD Pressing	Finishing	Total
Rent, rates and insurance	£8,600	£1,300	£9,900
Air conditioning, heat, light and power	£9,600	£900	£10,500
Depreciation and maintenance	£12,600		£12,600
	£30,800	£2,200	£33,000

Task

Write a letter to Jamil Baharundin. In your letter you should:

(a) Identify FOUR issues to consider before deciding to investigate a variance.

(b) Sub-divide the material usage variance into that part due to discs being scrapped and that part due to other reasons.

(c) *Briefly* explain, with reasons, why there might be excess demand for the CD Pressing Department but much less demand for the Finishing Department.

Gransden, Yelling and Co
Accountants and Registered Auditors

Today

Jamil Baharundin
CD Products Ltd
Anytown

Dear Mr Baharundin

Thank you for your letter and observations regarding the introduction of the new reporting format based on the standing costing technique.

I list my response to your questions below:

(a) **Issues to consider before investigating a variance**

(b) **Sub-division of the material usage variance**

(c)   **Demand for pressing and finishing**

Yours sincerely
AAT Student

 Test your understanding 5

You are employed as a management accountant in the head office of Travel Holdings plc. Travel Holdings owns a number of transport businesses. One of them is Travel Ferries Ltd. Travel Ferries operates ferries which carry passengers and vehicles across a large river. Each year, standard costs are used to develop the budget for Travel Ferries Ltd. The latest budgeted and actual operating results are shown below.

Travel Ferries Ltd

Budgeted and actual operating results for the year to 30 November 20X0

Operating data:	Budget		Actual	
Number of ferry crossings		6,480		5,760
Operating hours of ferries		7,776		7,488
		£		£
Cost data:				
Fuel	1,244,160 litres	497,664	1,232,800 litres	567,088
Labour	93,312 hours	466,560	89,856 hours	471,744
Fixed overheads		466,560		472,440
		——————		——————
Cost of operations		1,430,784		1,511,272

Other accounting information:

Fuel and labour are variable costs.

Fixed overheads are absorbed on the basis of standard operating hours.

One of your duties is to prepare costing information and a standard costing reconciliation statement for the Chief Executive of Travel Holdings.

Task

(a) Calculate the following variances:

	(i)	Material price variance:		
			=	
	(ii)	Material usage variance:		
			=	
	(iii)	Labour rate variance:		
			=	
	(iv)	Labour efficiency variance:		
			=	
	(v)	Fixed overhead expenditure variance:		
			=	
	(vi)	Fixed overhead volume variance:		
			=	

(b) Prepare a statement reconciling the actual cost of operations to the standard cost of operations for the year to 30 November 20X0.

Travel Ferries Ltd – **Reconciliation statement for the year ended 30 November 20X0**			
			£
Standard cost of actual operations			
Summary of variances:	Fav	Adv	
Material price			
Material usage			
Labour rate			
Labour efficiency			
Fixed overhead expenditure			
Fixed overhead volume			
	———	———	
Total variances			
			———
Actual cost			
			———

Task

Since the budgeted fuel price was set market fuel prices have risen by 20% due to inflation.

Write a memo to the Chief Executive. Your memo should:

Sub-divide the material price variance into:

(i)   that part arising from the standard price being different from the actual market price of fuel, and

(ii)   that part due to other reasons.

MEMO

To:

From:

Date:

Subject:

I refer to the concern you have expressed recently regarding the adverse variances in the report on Travel Ferries' operations for the year ended 30 November.

In reply to your comments, I wish to make the following observations concerning further analysis of the material price variance.

Test your understanding 6

NGJ Ltd is a furniture manufacturer. It makes 3 products: the Basic, the Grand and the Super. You are the management accountant reporting to the product line manager for the Basic. Reproduced below is NGJ's unit standard material and labour cost data and budgeted production for the year to 31 May 20X0 together with details of the budgeted and actual factory fixed overheads for the year.

Unit standard material and labour cost data by product for the year to 31 May 20X0			
Product	*Basic*	*Grand*	*Super*
Material at £12 per metre	6 metres	8 metres	10 metres
Labour at £5.00 per hour	6 hours	1 hour	1 hour
Budgeted production	10,000 units	70,000 units	70,000 units

Total budgeted and actual factory fixed overheads for the year to 31 May 20X0		
	Budgeted	*Actual*
	£	£
Rent and rates	100,000	100,000
Depreciation	200,000	200,000
Light, heat and power	60,000	70,000
Indirect labour	240,000	260,000
Total factory fixed overheads	600,000	630,000

Apportionment policy:

As all products are made in the same factory, budgeted and actual total factory fixed overheads are apportioned to each product on the basis of budgeted total labour hours per product.

During the year 11,500 *Basics* were made. The actual amount of material used, labour hours worked and costs incurred were as follows:

Actual material and labour cost of producing 11,500 Basics for the year to 31 May 20X0		
	Units	*Total cost*
Material	69,230 metres	£872,298
Labour	70,150 hours	£343,735

Task

(a) Calculate the following variances for *Basic* production:

(i)	Material price variance		
		=	

(ii)	Material usage variance:		
		=	

(iii)	Labour rate variance:		
		=	

(iv)	Labour efficiency variance:		
		=	

(v)	Fixed overhead expenditure variance:		
		=	

(vi)	Fixed overhead volume variance:		
		=	

(b) Prepare a statement reconciling the actual absorption cost of actual *Basic* production with the standard absorption cost of actual *Basic* production.

Standard costing reconciliation statement – year ended 31 May 20X0			
			£
Standard cost of actual production			
Summary of variances:	Fav	Adv	
Material price			
Material usage			
Labour rate			
Labour efficiency			
Fixed overhead expenditure			
Fixed overhead volume			
	———	———	
Total variance			
			———
Actual cost of actual production			
			———

The product line manager for the *Basic is* of the opinion that the standard costs and variances do not fairly reflect the effort put in by staff. The manager made the following points:

*   Because of a shortage of materials for the Basic, the purchasing manager had entered into a contract for the year with a single supplier in order to guarantee supplies.

*   The actual price paid for the material per metre was 10% less than the market price throughout the year.

- The *Basic is* a hand-made product made in a small, separate part of the factory and uses none of the expensive machines shared by the *Grand* and the *Super.*

- *Grand* and *Super* production uses the same highly mechanised manufacturing facilities and only one of those products can be made at any one time. A change in production from one product to another involves halting production in order to set up the necessary tools and production line.

In response to a request from the Basic product line manager, a colleague has re-analysed the budgeted and actual factory fixed overheads by function. The revised analysis is reproduced below.

Functional analysis of factory fixed overheads for the year ended 31 May 20X0

	Budget £	Actual £
Setting up of tools and production lines	202,000	228,000
Depreciation attributable to production	170,000	170,000
Stores	60,000	59,000
Maintenance	40,000	48,000
Light, heat and power directly attributable to production	48,000	45,000
Rent and rates directly attributable to production	80,000	80,000
Total factory fixed overheads	600,000	630,000

Task

Write a memo to the *Basic* product line manager. Your memo should:

(a) Identify the market price of the material used in the *Basic.*

(b) Sub-divide the material price variance into that part due to the contracted price being different from the market price and that due to other reasons.

(c) Identify ONE benefit to NGJ Ltd, which is not reflected in the variances, arising from the purchasing manager's decision to enter into a contract for the supply of materials.

MEMO

To:

From:

Date:

Subject:

Further to your comments on the variances relating to Basic production, I wish to make the following observations.

(a)

(b)

(c)

4 Summary

In this chapter we have examined ways of measuring the significance of variances and the way in which management might introduce controls based on the variance reports provided to them. The investigation of variances is a part of this process and it is important that you understand the causes of variances and their typical remedies.

We then considered responsibility accounting and the possible interaction of variances. This is a very important area in the context of management appraisal. As we have seen, purchasing of cheap materials may cause a knock-on effect into the working of those materials thereby giving the impression that the workforce (and by implication the managers of the workforce) are inefficient. This may not be the case as the problems may be caused by poor purchasing of materials rather than inefficient labour.

Answers to chapter test your understandings

Test your understanding 1

An adverse material price variance might mean that BETTER quality material was bought than standard. This changed the way the employees used it, given the different quality, so worked MORE efficiently than standard.

Test your understanding 2

Adverse material price

Favourable material usage

Favourable labour efficiency

Favourable variable overhead efficiency

Test your understanding 3

Task 1

WH Limited

MEMORANDUM

To: Production Manager

From: Assistant Accountant

Date: Today

Subject: Determining the standard price per kg of material X

As requested I detail below the information which would be needed to determine the standard price of material X and possible sources of the information.

(a) *The information which is needed*	(b) *Possible sources*
• Type and quality of material	Technical specification
• Quantity and timing of purchases, for determining any bulk discounts	Production and purchasing schedules
• Past trend in prices	Historical records in company
	Supplier price lists
	Government statistics
	Trade association statistics
	Movements in price indexes
• Future trend in prices	Discussions/negotiations with suppliers
	Trade association forecasts
	Financial press forecasts
	Government forecasts of key indices

•	Carriage costs to be added	Historical records in company
		Supplier records
•	Type of standard to be set, e.g. average for year, or increasing with inflation	Company policy on standard setting

Task 2

(a) (i) Direct material price variance

2,100 × £4.60

2,100 × £4.90

= £630 F

(ii) Direct material usage variance

2,100 × £4.90

400 × 4.5 × £4.90

= £1,470 A

(iii) Direct labour rate variance

4,000 × £4.00

4,000 × £3.50

= £2,000 A

(iv) Direct labour efficiency variance

4,000 × £3.50

400 × 10.3 × £3.50

= £420 F

(b)   Reconciliation of standard direct cost of production with actual direct cost for November:

	£	£
Standard direct cost of production		
(400 × £58.10)		23,240
Direct cost variances:		
Direct material – price	630 (F)	
– usage	1,470 (A)	
	———	
		840 (A)
Direct labour – rate	2,000 (A)	
– efficiency	420 (F)	
	———	
		1,580 (A)
		———
Actual direct cost of production		25,660
		———

Note that adverse variances are added to the standard cost to give the actual cost.

Note: A = adverse variance; F = favourable variance

Task 3

WH Limited

MEMORANDUM

To: Production Manager

From: Assistant Accountant

Date: Today

Subject: Direct cost variances for November

As requested I detail below explanations of the direct cost variances and possible suggestions as to their cause in November. Page 1 of 3

(a)   **The meaning of the variances**

Direct material price variance

This variance shows the saving or overspending which resulted from paying a lower or higher price than standard for the direct material used in the period. The favourable variance indicates that a lower than standard price was paid.

Direct material usage variance

This variance shows the saving or overspending, at standard prices, which resulted from using less or more material than standard to manufacture the production for the period. The adverse variance indicates that more material was used than standard.

Direct labour rate variance

This variance shows the saving or overspending which resulted from paying a lower or higher hourly rate than standard for the hours worked in the period. The adverse variance indicates that a higher than standard hourly rate was paid.

Direct labour efficiency variance

This variance shows the saving or overspending, at standard rates, which resulted from working less or more hours than standard to manufacture the production for the period. The favourable variance indicates that fewer hours were worked than standard.

(b) **Possible causes of the variances**

Favourable direct material price variance

Bulk discounts were received which were not allowed for in the standard.

The standard price of material was set too high.

A lower quality material was purchased, at a lower price than standard.

Effective negotiations by the buyer secured a price lower than the standard.

Adverse direct material usage variance

Material wastage was higher than allowed in the standard.

The standard usage was set too low.

There was a higher than standard level of rejects.

Theft of material.

Adverse direct labour rate variance

High levels of overtime were paid for compared with the standard allowance.

The standard wage rate was set too low.

A higher grade of labour was used.

Bonus payments were higher than standard.

Favourable direct labour efficiency variance

Employees were working faster than standard.

More skilled employees were used.

There were savings through the learning effect.

The standard labour time was set too high.

The material was easy to process, leading to savings against the standard time.

(c) Two examples of interdependence, where one variance can be related to others, could include the following.

The savings made on material price (favourable material price variance) may indicate that poor quality material was purchased, leading to high wastage, rejects and an adverse usage variance.

Bulk discounts may have resulted in the saving on material price. However, the consequent excessive stocks may have led to deterioration and write-offs, hence the adverse usage variance.

Direct workers may have been of a higher grade than standard, resulting in higher hourly rates and the adverse rate variance. However, the higher skill level may have led to time savings and the favourable efficiency variance.

Higher than standard bonus payments may have caused the adverse labour rate variance, but the bonuses may have resulted from faster working and hence the favourable efficiency variance.

Faster working resulted in the favourable efficiency variance, but less care may have been taken over weighing and handling the material, hence the adverse material usage variance.

Test your understanding 4

(a) (i)   Material price variance:
          99,000 × £0.21
          99,000 × £0.20   £990 A
    (ii) Material usage variance:
          99,000 × £0.20
          96,000 × £0.20   £600 A
    (iii) Labour rate variance:
          980 × £7.40
          980 × £7.00   £392 A
    (iv) Labour efficiency variance:
          960 × £7.00   £140 A
          980 × £7.00

	(v) Fixed overhead expenditure variance:	£
	Actual fixed cost	23,000
	Budgeted fixed cost	22,000
		£1,000 A

    (vi) Fixed overhead volume variance:
          880 × £25
          960 × £25   £2,000 F

(b)

			£
Standard cost of actual production			49,920

Summary of variances:	Fav	Adv	
Material price		990	
Material usage		600	
Labour rate		392	
Labour efficiency		140	
Fixed overhead expenditure		1,000	
Fixed overhead volume	2,000		
	2,000	3,122	(1,122)
Actual cost of production			51,042

Gransden, Yelling and Co
Accountants and Registered Auditors

Today

Jamil Baharundin
CD Products Ltd
Anytown

Dear Mr Baharundin

Thank you for your letter and observations regarding the introduction of the new reporting format based on the standing costing technique.

I list my response to your questions below:

(a) **Issues to consider before investigating a variance**

There are two principal factors to consider here:

Cost v benefit.

Is the variance a 'one off' or an early warning of a longer term problem?

A variance may thus be investigated if it:

- exceeds a minimum absolute amount
- exceeds a minimum percentage amount constitutes an element of a continuing trend is totally unexpected
- is considered to be a sign of a longer term problem.

You may decide not to investigate a variance if:

- the cause is already known and considered out of management's span of control
- it is considered as 'one off' and will correct itself in the short-run.

(b) **Sub-division of the material usage variance**

For the week ended 30 November 20X1, 96,000 CDs were pressed although 99,000 blank CDs were used. Of the 3,000 difference, 1,920 (96,000 × 2%) could be accounted for as scrapped production, leaving 1,080 unaccounted for. The sub-division of the material usage variance is:

Variance arising from scrapped discs (1,920 × £0.20)	£384 A
Variance arising from other reasons (1,080 × £0.20)	£216 A
Material usage variance	£600 A

(c) **Demand for pressing and finishing**

Fixed overheads have simply been apportioned to cost centres on the basis of labour hours and a recovery rate based on labour hours has been pre-determined.

An analysis of the activities reveals that a large proportion of the fixed costs relate to the CD Pressing Department.

As a result the standard costs of the pressing activity have been understated while finishing costs are overstated. If this has been built into selling prices for these activities then it may explain why there is excess demand in the CD Pressing Department.

Budgeted fixed overheads of £30,800 are attributable to pressing and thus the fixed overhead recovery rate for this activity should be £35 (£30,800 ÷ 880) per labour hour and not £25 as the 'blanket rate' suggests.

Yours sincerely
AAT Student

Test your understanding 5

(a) (i) Material price variance:

        1,232,800 × £0.40   £(73,968) A

(ii) Material usage variance:

        1,105,920 × £0.40   £(50,752) A

(iii) Labour rate variance:

        89,856 × £5.00   £(22,464) A

(iv) Labour efficiency variance:

        82,944 × £5.00   £(34,560)

(v) A Fixed overhead expenditure variance:

	£
Actual fixed overhead	472,440
Budgeted fixed overhead	466,560
Variance	(5,880) A

(vi) Fixed overhead volume variance:

        6,912 × £60   £(51,840) A

(b) **Travel Ferries Ltd – Reconciliation statement for the year ended 30 November 20X0**

Fav = Favourable

Adv = Adverse

			£
Standard cost of actual operations (W)			1,271,808

Summary of variances:	Fav	Adv	
Material price		(73,968)	
Material usage		(50,752)	
Labour rate		(22,464)	
Labour efficiency		(34,560)	
Fixed overhead expenditure		(5,880)	
Fixed overhead volume		(51,840)	
	0	(239,464)	(239,464)
Actual cost			1,511,272

Working:

£1,430,784 × 5,760/6,480 = £1,271,808

MEMO

To: Chief Executive

From: Management Accountant

Date: Today

Subject: Explanation of variances

I refer to the concern you have expressed recently regarding the adverse variances in the report on Travel Ferries' operations for the year ended 30 November.

In reply to your comments, I wish to make the following observations concerning further analysis of the material price variance.

Material price variance (fuel)

Actual market price was £0.40 × 1.2 = £0.48 per litre.

Actual price paid was £0.46 per litre.

Variance due to other reasons:

1,232,800 litres × £0.46	=	£24,656 F
1,232,800 litres × £0.48		

The variance due to an invalid standard was:

1,232,800 litres × £0.48	=	£(98,624) A
1,232,800 litres × £0.40		

Price variance reported	£(73,968) A

Test your understanding 6

(a)	(i)	Material price variance:		
		69,230 × £12.00		£(41,538) A
	(ii)	Material usage variance:		
		69,000 × £12.00		£(2,760) A
	(iii)	Labour rate variance:		
		70,150 × £5.00		£7,015 F
	(iv)	Labour efficiency variance:		
		69,000 × £5.00		£(5,750) A
	(v)	Fixed overhead expenditure variance:		£
		Actual fixed cost		189,000
		Budgeted fixed cost 60,000 × £3		180,000
		Variance		£(9,000) A
	(vi)	Fixed overhead volume variance:		
		69,000 × £3		£27,000 F

(b) **Standard costing reconciliation statement – year ended 31 May 20X0**

	Fav	Adv	£
Standard cost of actual production			1,380,000
Summary of variances:	Fav	Adv	
Material price		(41,538)	
Material usage		(2,760)	
Labour rate	7,015		
Labour efficiency		(5,750)	
Fixed overhead expenditure		(9,000)	
Fixed overhead volume	27,000		
	34,015	(59,048)	(25,033)
Actual cost of production			1,405,033

Fav = Favourable
Adv = Adverse

MEMO

To: Basic Product Line Manager

From: Management Accountant

Date: Today

Subject: Variances

Further to your comments on the variances relating to Basic production, I wish to make the following observations.

(a) Market price of material per metre during the year was: £12.60 × (100/90) = £14.00

(b) The sub-division of the price variance on further analysis shows a variance arising due to the contracted price being different from the actual price, amounting to: (£14.00 – £12.60) × 69,230

$$= £96,922 \text{ F}$$

Variance arising from other reasons:
(£12.00 – £14.00) × 69,230   £(138,460) A

£(41,538) A

(c) A value adding benefit from the purchasing manager's action not shown in the variances is the continuous supply of material supporting production as a result of the contract.

Performance indicators

Introduction

Cost variances, covered earlier, give one type of performance indicator – how individual operational managers perform against pre-set budget and standard cost targets. Here we continue this theme, but look at measures for productivity and efficiency; ratios that assist in assessment of resource utilisation; and overall profitability measures that may be applied to operating divisions and the business as a whole. We also look at the particular performance evaluation aspects of service industries, in particular the measurement of quality of service. The objective will always be to highlight activities, processes, products and business units that need some attention in order to enhance their value to the business.

ASSESSMENT CRITERIA	CONTENTS
Identify a range of and select key performance indicators (4.1)	1 Types of performance indicator
Calculate key performance indicators and manipulate them (4.1)	2 Ratio analysis
What the performance indicator means (4.2)	3 Profitability
How the various elements of the indicator affect its calculation (4.2)	4 Liquidity
The impact of various factors on performance indicators including learning effect and economies of scale (4.2)	5 Gearing
	6 Manufacturing industries
How some performance indicators interrelate with each other (4.2)	7 Service departments
How proposed actions may affect the indicator (4.2)	8 Service sectors
	9 Total quality management (TQM)
What actions could be taken to improve the indicator (4.2)	10 The balanced scorecard
	11 Other considerations

1 Types of performance indicator

1.1 Introduction

Performance indicators may be categorised as quantitative or qualitative.

1.2 Quantitative performance indicators

Quantitative measures are expressed in numerical terms which include the following:

(a) variances

(b) profit, sales, costs

(c) ratios and percentages

(d) indices.

1.3 Qualitative performance indicators

Qualitative indicators are far more subjective and cannot be expressed as an objective, numerical measure. Examples relevant to business and managerial performance would include the following:

(a) level of customer satisfaction: expressed as a subjective level 'very satisfied' ... to ...'not at all satisfied'

(b) staff performance grades: 'excellent', 'average', 'poor'

(c) company performance: 'steady', 'volatile results', 'disappointing'.

1.4 Efficiency

Performance indicators can be used to measure the efficiency of organisations.

 Definition

Efficiency can be defined as the relationship between inputs and outputs achieved. The fewer the inputs used by an organisation to achieve any given output, the more efficient is that organisation. In commercial organisations, efficiency is usually measured in terms of profitability, often in relation to assets employed.

2 Ratio analysis

2.1 Introduction

Ratio analysis is one of the main tools utilised in appraising the performance of a company, the main advantage being that the magnitude of the individual figures is eliminated, allowing the appraiser to concentrate on relative movements.

Ratio analysis is generally utilised in two ways as follows:

(a) comparison of performance year to year

(b) comparison with other companies.

It is important that you can calculate and interpret appropriate ratios.

2.2 Types of ratio

The main types of ratio used are:

(a) profitability ratios

(b) liquidity ratios

(c) gearing ratios

(d) investment ratios.

Of these, profitability and liquidity ratios are of the greatest significance to the management accountant.

Example

In order to illustrate the most common ratios, let's look at some calculations based on the summarised accounts of Knotty plc. The information from Knotty plc's financial statements will be used in the following sections.

Statement of profit or loss and other comprehensive income for the year ended 31 July 20X9

	Notes	20X9		20X8	
		£000	£000	£000	£000
Revenue			37,589		30,209
Cost of sales			(28,380)		(22,808)
			————		————
Gross profit			9,209		7,401
Distribution costs		(3,755)		(3,098)	
Administrative expenses		(2,291)		(2,030)	
		————		————	
			(6,046)		(5,128)
			————		————
Profit from operations			3,163		2,273
Other operating income			108		0,279
			————		————
Operating profit			3,271		2,552
Interest receivable			7		28
			————		————
			3,278		2,580
Finance costs			(442)		(471)
			————		————
Profit before taxation			2,836		2,109
Tax			(1,038)		(650)
			————		————
Profit for the period from continuing operations			1,798		1,459
			————		————

Statement of financial position as at 31 July 20X9

	Notes	20X9		20X8	
		£000	£000	£000	£000
ASSETS					
Non-current assets					
Tangible assets			8,687		5,669
Investments			15		15
			8,702		5,684
Current assets					
Inventories		8,486		6,519	
Receivables	1	8,836		6,261	
Cash and cash equivalents		479		250	
			17,801		13,030
Total assets			26,503		18,714
EQUITY AND LIABILITIES					
Called up share capital					
Ordinary shares of	2				
20p each			2,003		1,762
4.2% cumulative preference					
shares of £1 each			150		150
			2,153		1,912
Share premium account			123		123
Other reserves			2,576		–
Retained earnings			8,704		6,670
			13,556		8,705
Non-current liabilities					
Debentures			2,840		2,853
Current liabilities					
Bank loans and overdrafts		929		511	
Other amounts falling					
due within one year		9,178		6,645	
			10,107		7,156
Total equity and liabilities			26,503		18,714

Notes:

1   Receivables at 31 July 20X9 include trade receivables of £8,233,000 (20X8 £5,735,000).

2   The number of ordinary shares in issue at 31 July 20X9 was 10,014,514 (20X8: 8,808,214).

3 Profitability

3.1 Return on capital employed (ROCE)

Return on capital employed (ROCE) expresses profit as a percentage of the assets in use (the capital employed in the business) and can be further subdivided into profit margin and asset turnover (use of assets):

Profit margin × Asset turnover = Return on capital employed (ROCE)

$$\frac{\text{Profit}}{\text{Turnover}} \times \frac{\text{Turnover}}{\text{Assets}} = \frac{\text{Profit}}{\text{Assets}}$$

The equation helps to demonstrate how management can influence the rate of return on capital employed:

(a) By increasing profit margins:

    (i)   increase sales prices

    (ii)   reduce costs.

(b) By increasing asset turnover (use of assets):

    (i)   increase revenues

    (ii)   reduce assets (capital employed).

3.2 Year-end or average capital employed

Ideally, the profits for the year ended 31 July 20X9 should be related to the assets in use throughout the year (the average capital employed). In practice, the ratio is usually computed using the assets at the year-end (the year-end capital employed). Using year-end figures of capital employed can distort trends and inter-company comparison; if new investment has been undertaken near to the year-end and financed (for example) by the issue of new shares, the capital employed will have risen by the total finance raised, whereas the profits will only have a month or two of the new investment's contribution.

A range of different acceptable measures of the assets in use is available; the matter of principle should be that the profit figure which is related to the capital employed should include all types of return on those assets.

Solution

For Knotty plc, a suitable calculation would be as follows.

	20X9 £000	20X8 £000
Equity	13,556	8,705
Add: Debentures	2,840	2,853
Year-end capital employed	16,396	11,558

	20X9 £000	20X8 £000
Operating profit	3,271	2,552
Interest receivable	7	28
Profit before finance costs and tax	3,278	2,580

So the return on capital employed is calculated as:

$$\frac{\text{Profit before finance costs and tax}}{\text{Equity and long-term debt}} \times 100\%$$

20X9 $\qquad \frac{3,278}{16,396} \times 100 = 20.0\%$

20X8 $\qquad \frac{2,580}{11,558} \times 100 = 22.3\%$

The capital employed figure includes the long-term debt, the debentures. Therefore, the profit used must be that available to these providers of capital, the profit before finance costs.

The rate of return on year-end capital employed has fallen in 20X9 compared with 20X8 and might indicate less effective management. To comment further, we need to sub-analyse the ratio into profit margin and asset turnover.

We also need to understand that the way in which business managers are assessed can have a great influence on the decisions that they make. The use of ratios such as ROCE can lead to a lack of goal congruence where managers improve the performance of certain ratios but this may not be in the best interests of the organisation as a whole.

For example, a manager may not be prepared to invest in new machinery if the increase in the net asset position will reduce the ROCE. (Despite the investment reducing other costs, leading to zero defects or an increase in customer satisfaction.)

3.3 Profit margin

If the profitability ratios are to interlock perfectly, the profit margin will be calculated expressing the same profit before interest payable and tax as a percentage of revenue:

$$\frac{\text{Profit before finance costs and tax}}{\text{Revenue}} \times 100\%$$

A small problem with the approach in this example is that the profit includes interest receivable which is not represented in revenue; however, as the amount is small, this can be ignored.

In order that the profit can be related more fairly to revenue, profit margin is sometimes calculated using operating profit.

> **Solution**
>
> For Knotty plc: 20X9 $\frac{3,271}{37,589} \times 100 = 8.7\%$
>
> 20X8 $\frac{2,552}{30,209} \times 100 = 8.4\%$
>
> Operating profit margins have improved slightly over the last year, possibly due to better cost control.

Low margins within a sector may arise from a policy designed to increase market share by cutting selling prices, or may be due to high development costs associated with new products, both of which may be positive factors for the future. However, low margins are often associated with inefficiency and poor quality management.

Conversely, high margins relative to competitors, or improving margins, are usually taken as indicators of efficiency and good management. High margins achieved by dominating a particular market may, however, attract competitors into that market and imply lower margins in the longer term.

3.4 Costs as a % of revenue

The calculation of any type of cost as a percentage of revenue is simply performed using the formula:

$$\frac{\text{Cost}}{\text{Revenue}} \times 100\%$$

Solution

For the distribution costs in our example:

Distribution cost as a % of revenue = $\dfrac{\text{Distribution cost}}{\text{Revenue}} \times 100\%$

20X9 $\dfrac{3,755}{37,589} \times 100\% = 9.99\%$ 20X8 $\dfrac{3,098}{30,209} \times 100\% = 10.26\%$

Distribution costs as a percentage of revenue are falling which will improve profit.

3.5 Asset turnover

Another aspect of efficient management is to 'make the assets work'. This may involve disposing of those 'underperforming' assets which cannot be made to generate revenue, as well as developing and marketing the company's products or services.

Solution

Once again, the simplest method of computing the ratio is to relate revenue to the same figure of year-end capital employed used in calculating return on capital employed:

Asset turnover = $\dfrac{\text{Revenue}}{\text{Capital employed}}$

20X9 $\dfrac{37,589}{16,396} = 2.3$ times   20X8 $\dfrac{30,209}{11,558} = 2.6$ times

Asset turnover has fallen which is bad for the business at this time. Revenue has not increased in line with investment. However this may improve in the future. The business has invested in assets which may not be generating increased turnover quite yet. Hopefully this will happen soon and the asset turnover ratio will improve.

However, as with profit margins, certain assets represented by capital employed have no turnover implications. One method of avoiding this illogicality is to exclude long and short-term investments from capital employed. For companies with substantial investments this will make a considerable difference.

Asset turnover will tend to be lower in capital-intensive manufacturing industries, which carry substantial tangible non-current assets, inventories and trade receivables, than in service industries where the principal resource is people rather than plant and machinery, and where inventories are low.

There are often trade-offs between asset turnover and profit margins in different sectors. For example, food retailers have relatively low profit margins compared to electronic equipment manufacturers, but asset turnover is higher. Typical numbers might be:

	Profit margin %	×	Asset turnover	=	ROCE %
Food retailer	3.7	×	6.7	=	24.8
Electronic equipment manufacturer	10.3	×	2.3	=	23.7

3.6 Gross profit margin

The profit margin given above used a profit figure that included non-productive overheads and sundry items of income. The gross profit margin looks at the profitability of the pure trading activities of the business:

$$\frac{\text{Gross profit}}{\text{Revenue}} \times 100\%$$

Solution

For Knotty plc: 20X9 $\frac{9,209}{37,589} \times 100 = 24.5\%$

20X8 $\frac{7,401}{30,209} \times 100 = 24.5\%$

The company has maintained its gross profit margin; thus the slight rise in operating profit margin must be due to overhead costs being better controlled.

KAPLAN PUBLISHING

3.7   Return on net assets

Return on net assets (RONA) is very similar to return on capital employed, except that the denominator is net assets (non-current assets plus current assets less current liabilities and long term liabilities).

$$\frac{\text{Profit before finance costs and tax}}{\text{Net assets}} \times 100\%$$

Solution

For Knotty plc: 20X9 $\dfrac{3,278}{13,556}$ × 100 = 24.2%

20X8 $\dfrac{2,580}{8,705}$ × 100 = 29.6%

The RONA has fallen over the year due to the increased investment in non-current assets. These new assets should generate increased profits in the future and therefore the profit figure should increase. This should increase the RONA back to where it was in 20X8 or better (hence the reason for the investment) .i.e. this is simply a timing difference.

 Test your understanding 1

WH Limited is a member of a trade association which operates an inter-company comparison scheme. The scheme is designed to help its member companies to monitor their own performance against that of other companies in the same industry.

At the end of each year, the member companies submit detailed annual accounts to the scheme organisers. The results are processed and a number of accounting ratios are published and circulated to members. The ratios indicate the average results for all member companies.

Your manager has given you the following extract, which shows the average profitability and asset turnover ratios for the latest year. For comparison purposes, WH Limited's accounts analyst has added the ratios for your company.

	Results for year 4	
	Trade association average	*WH Limited*
Return on capital employed	20.5%	18.4%
Net (operating) profit margin	5.4%	6.8%
Asset turnover	3.8 times	2.7 times
Gross margin	14.2%	12.9%

Required:

As assistant accountant for WH Limited, your manager has asked you to prepare a report for the senior management committee. The report should cover the following points:

(a)   an explanation of what each ratio is designed to show

(b)   an interpretation of WH Limited's profitability and asset turnover compared with the trade association average

(c)   comments on any limitations of these ratios and of comparisons made on this basis.

Solution

WH Limited

REPORT

To:

From:

Date:

Subject:

We have received the Trade Association results for year 4 and this report looks in detail at the profitability and asset turnover ratios.

(a)   **What each ratio is designed to show**

    (i)   Return on capital employed (ROCE)

    (ii)   Net operating profit margin

    (iii)   Asset turnover

(iv)   Gross margin

(b)   **WH Limited's profitability and asset turnover**

(c)   **Limitations of the ratios and of inter-company comparisons**

4 Liquidity

4.1 Current ratio and quick ratio

When analysing a company's balance sheet without access to management information, it is customary to calculate two ratios as indicators of the company's ability to pay its way:

Current ratio $\quad\quad\quad\quad\quad\quad\quad = \dfrac{\text{Current assets}}{\text{Current liabilities}}$

Quick ratio (or acid test ratio) $\quad = \dfrac{\text{Current assets less inventories}}{\text{Current liabilities}}$

Solution

For Knotty plc:

		20X9		20X8	
(a)	Current ratio	$\dfrac{17,801}{10,107}$	= 1.76	$\dfrac{13,030}{7,156}$	= 1.82
(b)	Quick ratio	$\dfrac{9,315}{10,107}$	= 0.92	$\dfrac{6,511}{7,156}$	= 0.91

The current assets (with or without inventory) cover the current liabilities should they become due. This means that the business is 'liquid' and shouldn't have any immediate cashflow problems when paying its suppliers.

4.2 Cash and funds flow analysis

Although current and quick ratios are used to measure liquidity, they are limited insofar as they concentrate on only one area of the statement of financial position. If the company needs adequate cash to meet its obligations, there are sources other than the sale of inventories and the collection of amounts owed by receivables.

Analysis of cash flows is a more comprehensive method of assessing liquidity, although significant variations in the liquidity ratios may indicate important changes.

4.3 Other working capital ratios

An analysis of the movement in the elements of working capital can be made with the help of the following ratios.

4.4 Inventory holding period (inventory days)

Inventory holding periods can be calculated using:

$$\frac{\text{Inventories}}{\text{Cost of sales}} \times 365 \text{ days}$$

Solution

20X9 $\dfrac{8,486}{28,380} \times 365 = 109$ days

20X8 $\dfrac{6,519}{22,808} \times 365 = 104$ days

There has been a slight increase in the holding period, indicating inventory is taking longer to sell. A review of inventories may be necessary to determine whether levels of obsolete or damaged inventories are increasing. There may be a deliberate policy to increase inventories prior to a promotion or in response to a specific order.

4.5 Trade receivables collection period (trade receivable days)

This calculation is always made using revenue since trade receivables includes the profit element:

$$\frac{\text{Trade receivables}}{\text{Revenue}} \times 365 \text{ days}$$

Solution

20X9 $\dfrac{8,233}{37,589} \times 365 = 80$ days

20X8 $\dfrac{5,735}{30,209} \times 365 = 69$ days

The company is taking approximately 11 days longer, on average, to collect its debts.

As the year-end figures may be unrepresentative (due perhaps to seasonality of revenues), an average receivables figure for the year might be used if this were available.

4.6   Trade payables payment period (trade payable days)

A similar calculation can be made to determine the trade payables payment (settlement) period:

$$\frac{\text{Trade payables}}{\text{Purchases}} \times 365 \text{ days}$$

If purchases is not given, an acceptable approximation to purchases would be cost of sales.

✏ Test your understanding 2

Two working capital ratios are:

Inventory turnover	☐
Receivables days	☐
Return on capital employed	☐
Gearing	☐

✏ Test your understanding 3

Stately Hotels plc is considering making an offer to buy a small privately owned chain of hotels, Homely Limited. In order to carry out an initial appraisal, you have been provided with an abbreviated set of their accounts for 20X4.

Homely Limited – Statement of profit or loss for the year ended 31 December 20X4 (extract)

	£000
Revenue	820
Operating costs	754
	―――
Operating profit	66
Finance costs	4
	―――
Profit before tax	62
Taxation	18
	―――
Profit after tax	44
Dividends	22
	―――
Profit for the year	22
	―――

Homely Limited – Statement of financial position as at 31 December 20X4 (extract)

	£000
Non-current assets at carrying amount	230
Net current assets	70
	───
Total assets less current liabilities	300
Long-term loans	50
	───
Equity	250
	───
Number of employees (full-time equivalents)	20
Number of rooms, each available for 365 nights	18
Number of room nights achieved in 20X4	5,900

Stately Hotels plc uses a number of key accounting ratios to monitor the performance of the group of hotels and of individual hotels in the chain. An extract from the target ratios for 20X4 is as follows:

Stately Hotels plc – target ratios for 20X4 (extract)

(i)   Return on capital employed, based on profit before finance costs and tax — 26%

(ii) Operating profit percentage — 13%

(iii) Asset turnover — 2 times

(iv) Working capital period = $\dfrac{\text{Working capital}}{\text{Operating costs}} \times 365$ — 20 days

(v)   Percentage room occupancy = $\dfrac{\text{Number of room nights let}}{\text{Number of room nights available}} \times 100\%$ — 85%

(vi) Revenue per employee (full-time equivalent) — £30,000

Required:

(a)   Calculate the six target ratios above based on Homely Limited's accounts and present them in a table which enables easy comparison with Stately Hotels' target ratios for 20X4.

(b) Prepare a memorandum for the management accountant of Stately Hotels plc, giving your initial assessment of Homely Limited based on a comparison of these ratios with Stately Hotels' target ratios. Your memorandum should provide the following information for each of the six ratios.

(i) Comments on the performance of Homely Limited and suggestions about the management action which might be necessary to correct any apparent adverse performance.

(ii) A discussion of any limitations in the use of the ratio for this performance comparison.

Solution

Homely Limited

(a) **Target ratios**

Return on capital employed   =

Operating profit percentage   =

Asset turnover   =

Working capital period   =

Percentage room occupancy   =

Revenue per employee   =

Key ratios for 20X4

	Stately Hotels plc target	*Homely Limited actual*
Return on capital employed	26%	
Operating profit percentage	13%	
Asset turnover	2.0 times	
Working capital period	20 days	
Percentage room occupancy	85%	
Revenue per employee	£30,000	

MEMORANDUM

To:

From:

Date:

Subject:

I have carried out an initial assessment of Homely Limited, based on an extract from their accounts for 20X4. I have calculated their key accounting ratios and compared them with our company's target ratios and my conclusions and recommendations are as follows.

Return on capital employed (ROCE)

Operating profit percentage

Asset turnover

Working capital period

Percentage room occupancy

Revenue per employee

4.7 Comparing entities using performance indicators

Comparing an entity with a similar one may come up as a very practical task in an examination. The likely situation is where you have two firms in competition with each other, and one of them sets itself a performance indicator as a target to help it achieve a competitive advantage. The other firm must try to match or better that target.

4.8 What if? analysis

'What if? analysis' is a technique used to test the effect on a set of figures of altering one of the variables that produced those figures. Flexible budgeting is a form of what if? analysis – what if we produce 20,000 units rather than 15,000, say?

With 'what if? analysis' we need to understand that elements of the income statement and statement of financial position are linked. For example, a 10% increase in sales volume will lead to a 10% increase in variable costs as more units are produced but no increase in fixed costs, assuming that capacity exists. A 10% increase in sales price, however, will not lead to any changes in costs. The increase in costs (caused by volume change) will change the profit and, if no dividends are paid, this will increase the net assets of the business. The change will therefore affect several ratios.

 Example

Theo has cost of sales of £250,000 and Inventories of £45,000.

Calculate Theo's inventory days.

$$\frac{45,000}{250,000} \times 365 = 65.7 \text{ days}$$

Theo would like to improve on his inventory days by setting a target of only 60 days.

If Theo intends to achieve this by lowering his inventory holding, inventory would need to be:

$$\frac{x}{250,000} \times 365 = 60 \text{ days}$$

x = £41,096

If Theo intends to achieve this by altering his cost of sales, cost of sales would need to be:

$$\frac{45,000}{x} \times 365 = 60 \text{ days}$$

x = £273,750

Test your understanding 4

Diamond Limited is a retail jeweller operating 30 branches in similar localities. Common accounting policies operate throughout all branches, including a policy of using straight-line depreciation for non-current assets.

All branches use rented premises. These are accounted for under 'other costs' in the operating statement. Non-current assets are predominantly fixtures and fittings.

Each branch is individually responsible for ordering inventory, the authorising of payments to trade payables and the control of trade receivables. Cash management, however, is managed by Diamond's head office with any cash received by a branch being paid into a head office bank account twice daily.

You are employed in the head office of Diamond Limited as a financial analyst monitoring the performance of all 30 branches. This involves calculating performance indicators for each branch and comparing each branch's performance with company standards. Financial data relating to Branch 24 is reproduced below.

Diamond Limited – Branch 24 – Year ended 31 December 20X9

Operating statement	£000	£000	Operating net assets at year end	£000	£000
Revenue		720.0	Non-current assets		
Opening inventory	80.0		Cost		225.0
Purchases	340.0		Accumulated depreciation		(90.0)
Closing inventory	(60.0)				
		360.0	Carrying amount		135.0
Gross profit		360.0	Working capital		
Wages and salaries	220.6		Inventories	60.0	
Depreciation	45.0		Receivables	96.0	
Other costs	36.8		Payables	(51.0)	
					105.0
		302.4	Net assets		240.0
Operating profit		57.6			

Task 1

Prepare a statement showing the following performance indicators for Branch 24:

(a) the return on capital employed

(b) the gross profit margin as a percentage

(c) the asset turnover

(d) the revenue (or net profit) margin as a percentage

(e) the average age of receivables in months

(f) the average age of payables in months

(g) the average age of the closing inventory in months.

The financial director of Diamond Limited is Charles Walden. He is concerned that Branch 24 is not performing as well as the other branches. All other branches are able to meet or exceed most of the performance standards laid down by the company.

Charles is particularly concerned the branches should achieve the standards for return on capital employed and for asset turnover. He also feels that managers should try to achieve the standards laid down for working capital management.

The relevant standards are:

Return on capital employed	40%
Asset turnover	4 times per annum
Average age of receivables	0.5 months
Average age of payables	3 months
Average age of closing inventory	1 month

Charles Walden has recently attended a course on financial modelling and scenario planning. Charles explains that scenario planning shows the likely performance of a business under different assumed circumstances. It requires an understanding of the relationship between the different elements within the financial statements and how these change as the circumstances being modelled change. As an example, he tells you that if the volume of branch revenue was to increase then the cost of sales would also increase but that all other expenses would remain the same as they are fixed costs.

He believes scenario planning would be particularly helpful to the manager of Branch 24, Angela Newton. Charles had previously discussed the performance of the branch with Angela and emphasised the importance of improving the asset turnover and maintaining control of working capital. However, Angela raised the following objections:

- Turning over assets is not important; making profit should be the main objective.

- Branch 24 has been in existence for two years less than all the other branches.

Task 2

Show the return on capital employed that Branch 24 would have achieved had it been able to achieve the company's asset turnover during the year to 31 December 20X9 while maintaining prices and the existing capital employed.

Solution

Task 1

**Diamond Ltd
Performance report – Branch 24
Year ended 31 December 20X9**

(a)	Return on capital employed	
(b)	Gross profit margin	
(c)	Asset turnover	
(d)	Revenue margin	
(e)	Average age of receivables	
(f)	Average age of payables	
(g)	Average age of inventory	

Task 2

	£
Revised revenue	
Cost of sales = 50%	
	———
Gross profit	
Fixed costs	
	———
Operating profit	
	———
Revised return on capital employed	

Example

Break even analysis and the make or buy decision

X Ltd is considering the outsourcing of the production of P to a third party who would supply ready-made P's for £35 per unit. P currently has a production cost of:

	£
Material	20
Labour	15
Variable overhead	5
Fixed overhead	8

The expected production level or purchasing requirement for next year is 1,000 units. P sell for £50 per unit.

If X does decide to outsource production the total fixed overhead is expected to increase by £2,000, and the capital employed will decrease from £40,000 to £30,000 due to the sale of some obsolete machinery.

Required:

(a) Calculate the contribution per unit of P when it is made by X and when it is purchased.

(b) Calculate the total profit when P is made by X and when it is purchased.

(c) Calculate the net profit margin and the return on capital employed under both options.

(d) Calculate the breakeven point and margin of safety under both options.

(e) Explain whether production should be outsourced.

Solution

(a)

		Make	Buy
		£	£
Selling price		50	50
Material		20	35
Labour		15	–
Variable overhead		5	–
Contribution		10	15

(b)

		Make	Buy
		£	£
Contribution per unit		10	15
Units		1,000	1,000
Total contribution		10,000	15,000
Fixed overheads		8,000	10,000
Profit		2,000	5,000

(c)

		Make	Buy
Profit margin		$\dfrac{2,000}{50,000} \times 100\%$	$\dfrac{5,000}{50,000} \times 100\%$
		= 4%	= 10%
Return on capital employed		$\dfrac{2,000}{40,000} \times 100\%$	$\dfrac{5,000}{30,000} \times 100\%$
		= 5%	= 16.67%

(d)

		Make	Buy
BEP (units)		$\dfrac{8,000}{10}$	$\dfrac{10,000}{15}$
		= 800	= 667
Margin of safety		1,000 – 800	1,000 – 667
		= 200 units	= 333 units

(e) Production should be outsourced. Even though fixed costs will rise, the contribution per unit and total profit is higher when outsourced.

The profit margin and the return on capital employed are improved by outsourcing.

When outsourced, the breakeven point is lower which is good, and the margin of safety is greater which will make managers more comfortable.

 Example

M Ltd has made losses for the past two years and the management has now decided that in order to cut costs and return to profit they must either transfer production overseas where the labour costs are lower and rents are cheaper, or mechanise their factory which would also lower the labour cost but require huge investment.

Current total costs and sales price at a production level of 10,000 units are:

		£
Sales price per unit		30
Total costs:		
Materials		100,000
Labour		75,000
Variable overhead		50,000
Fixed overhead		100,000

If production is transferred overseas, labour costs and variable overhead would fall by 40% and rent of £50,000 (a fixed cost) would fall by 50%.

If the factory is mechanised the new machinery would cost £200,000, depreciation (a fixed cost) would be 25% per annum, and the labour cost would fall by 80%.

Required:

(a)   Should the company stay as they are, transfer overseas or mechanise?

(b)   Calculate the break-even point in the three scenarios.

Solution

(a)	Current	O/S	Overseas	Mech	Mechanise
	£		£		£
Revenues	300,000		300,000		300,000
Materials	(100,000)		(100,000)		(100,000)
Labour	(75,000)	60%	(45,000)	20%	(15,000)
Variable overhead	(50,000)	60%	(30,000)	20%	(50,000)
Contribution	75,000		125,000		135,000
Fixed overhead	(100,000)	Less rent	(75,000)	Plus dep'n	(150,000)
Profit/(loss)	(25,000)		50,000		(15,000)

Therefore M Ltd should transfer production overseas in order to improve their profit.

(b)	£	£	£
Contribution	75,000	125,000	135,000
Per unit	7.50	12.50	13.50
Fixed costs	100,000	75,000	150,000
BEP (units)	$\frac{100,000}{7.50} = 13,334$	$\frac{75,000}{12.50} = 6,000$	$\frac{150,000}{13.50} = 11,112$

5 Gearing

5.1 Calculating gearing

There are two ways to calculate the levels of debt versus equity in a company:

$$\frac{\text{Debt}}{\text{Equity}} \quad \text{or} \quad \frac{\text{Debt}}{\text{Debt} + \text{Equity}}$$

Total debt consists of all interest bearing debt and does not include current liabilities.

If a company has a high gearing level then it is potentially more risky than a low geared company. This is because when interest rates rise the interest paid on the debt may rise and will place a strain on the profits generated by the company.

However, certain industries are more accepting than others of high gearing, so any gearing level calculated must be compared against similar companies in order to ascertain whether the company is at risk or not.

Solution

For Knotty plc:

		20X9	20X8
(a)	$\dfrac{\text{Debt}}{\text{Equity}}$	$\dfrac{2{,}840}{13{,}556} = 0.21$	$\dfrac{2{,}853}{8{,}705} = 0.33$
(b)	$\dfrac{\text{Debt}}{\text{Debt} + \text{Equity}}$	$\dfrac{2{,}840}{2{,}840 + 13{,}556} = 0.17$	$\dfrac{2{,}853}{2{,}853 + 8{,}705} = 0.25$

(**Note:** Preference shares are often deemed to be debt finance. However the examiner has never gone into this level of detail so they have been included as equity to keep this example simple.)

---

6 Manufacturing industries

6.1 Introduction

The performance of a manufacturing business and its constituent activities will commonly be measured in quantitative terms, mainly monetary. However, we shall also consider relevant non-monetary and qualitative factors that can be useful.

6.2 Productivity

Productivity is a measure of the efficiency of resource usage and expresses the rate of output in relation to resource used, often in non-financial terms.

Examples include the following:

(a) units produced per labour or machine hour

(b) productive hours to total hours paid

(c) actual output to full capacity output

(d) number of operations undertaken per day

(e) number of passengers transported per month

(f) number of vehicles manufactured per week

(g) units produced per worker per day

(h) rooms cleaned per hour

(i) meals served per sitting.

Productivity is closely linked with resource utilisation (which is considered later).

6.3 Value added

Definition

Value added is the pool of wealth created, out of which a business provides for:

- payment of wages, salaries and other employee benefits
- reward for providers of capital, in the form of interest and dividends
- payment of government taxation
- maintenance and expansion of assets.

It is also defined as:

- the value of revenue less the cost of bought in materials and services.

Example

Value added statement

	£m
Revenue	1.35
Bought in materials and services	0.55
Value added	0.80

Number of employees = 20

- Value added per employee

$$\frac{£0.80}{20} = £0.04m \text{ or } £40,000$$

Test your understanding 5

Task

(a) From the following information, draft the value added statement for the years 20X2 and 20X3.

Sandsend Engineering Ltd

Extract from Statements of profit or loss for the years ended 31 December 20X2 and 20X3

	20X2 £m	20X3 £m
Revenue	6.1	6.5
*Costs	4.2	4.5
Operating profit	1.9	2.0
Finance costs	0.6	0.6
	1.3	1.4
Taxation	0.3	0.3
Profit	1.0	1.1

*Costs comprise:

	£m	£m
Wages and salaries	1.8	1.9
Depreciation	0.4	0.5
Other bought in items	2.0	2.1
Other information: Dividends	0.2	0.2

	20X2 £m	20X3 £m
Revenue		
Less bought in materials and services		
	—	—
Value added		
	—	—

(b)   Calculate for both years the value added per '£' of employee costs, and state why this measure is considered an indicator of labour productivity.

	20X2	20X3
	£m	£m
Value added		
Employee costs		
	——	——
Value added per '£' of employee costs		
	——	——

Why value added is considered to be a measure of productivity:

6.4   Unit costs

Unit costs are the actual average cost of production of each unit of product in the period. Management will attempt to drive down unit costs over time.

6.5   Resource utilisation

This is a measure of the extent to which resources were used in relation to maximum capacity. Examples of utilisation and related measures for different resources include the following:

Machines   –   utilisation (hours used : potential hours)
           –   down time (machine down hours : total hours)

Materials   –   wastage (normal/abnormal loss percentage)
           –   inventory turnover (linked to levels of slow-moving inventory)

Labour   –   utilisation (productive : total hours)
         –   absenteeism, lateness
         –   mix variances (where different grades are used)
         –   idle time (non-productive hours : total hours)
         –   labour turnover (leavers replaced : total employed)

6.6 Quality of service

For a manufacturing business, this can be categorised into quality of service to customers and quality of service from service departments. The latter is covered in the section on the service departments.

Quality of service to customers is essentially a subjective, qualitative measure, although some quantitative measures can be used in connection with it – for example, ratios such as customer returns to total sales and customer complaints per units sold. Speed of service can be measured in retail outlets by numbers of customers waiting at each checkout in a supermarket.

The main source of measure of customer satisfaction will generally be through some sort of questionnaire. This is all considered in more detail later in this chapter.

6.7 Other non-monetary measures

Quality is a particular area in which such indicators are required; two others that have recently been identified as important attributes of world-class manufacturing are innovation and flexibility.

6.8 Innovation

Innovation is concerned with the business's ability to beat their competitors in developing new products, improvements to existing ones or additional customer services.

Measurement of innovation must concentrate on its effectiveness as well as its existence – counting the number of new products developed is of little help without knowing the extent to which they have been accepted by the market. Possible measures include the following:

(a) research and development expenditure related to new revenues;

(b) viable new products to existing products;

(c) percentage of total profits relating to new products/ improvements.

6.9 Flexibility

Flexibility is concerned with the business's ability to respond to customers' needs, in terms of speed of delivery of existing products, speed of reaction to changes in demand patterns and ability to respond to particular customer requests or specifications.

In a manufacturing context, it is often the case that flexibility is connected with the amounts of products using common parts. If demand for one type of product falls, it is easier to switch stock and processing to another if there is a common base between them.

7 Service departments

7.1 Introduction

Many of the measures discussed above will be relevant in the assessment of the performance of service departments within a business. Unless an internal charge-out system operates (for example, the charging of user departments per hour of computer department time spent on their work), the emphasis will be on costs rather than profits.

7.2 Types of performance indicator

As well as the normal cost variances (with activity levels based on the departments' own cost unit, e.g. maintenance hours, meals served, data processing hours), other cost ratios will be appropriate, for example:

(a) meal cost per employee per period (canteen);

(b) running costs per van-mile (deliveries);

(c) cost per call-out (maintenance department).

 Example

Consider a transport/distribution department. What type of cost performance indicators might be appropriate?

Solution

(a) **Standing costs** (ascertained as a rate per day), including:

   (i) Road tax

   (ii) Insurance

   (iii) Garage and administration costs

   (iv) Drivers' wages

   (v) Depreciation

(b) **Running costs** (ascertained as a rate per ton/mile), including:

    (i) Fuel and lubricants

    (ii) Tyres

    (iii) Repairs

    (iv) Maintenance

Standing costs will be incurred for vehicles owned whether or not they are in use and are in the nature of stepped fixed costs. Fixed because, for each vehicle, they do not vary in amount and 'stepped' because for each additional vehicle required, costs, on a graph, will rise by a further step and remain fixed for a further range of activity until another vehicle is required.

8 Service sectors

8.1 Introduction

Service organisations include the following:

(a) **Professional services**, such as firms of accountants, architects, surveyors, solicitors, whose main assets will be their employees and who provide individual, personalised services to their customers.

(b) **Mass services**, such as transport, which are highly capital asset based and provide a standard range of services to a wide range of customers.

(c) **Public sector services**, such as health, education and local authorities.

8.2 Types of performance indicator

Service sector measures can be considered under very similar headings as those for manufacturing organisations, although there will be a different emphasis on their relative importance.

The main difference between the two types of organisation is the nature of their output.

Output from manufacturing businesses comprises tangible, clearly identifiable products, usually of a standard design and quality which can be rejected by a customer if not required or unsuitable, and produced in advance of demand and stored until needed.

Think about a service provided to you – can it be said to have any of these characteristics? This leads to a different approach needed for performance measurement where costs per product or units per hour are of little relevance or meaning. However, in earlier chapters, we have seen that cost units do not have to be in terms of products and that measures may be activity rather than product based.

So, using similar headings as before, particular areas to be considered about the performance indicators of service organisations are productivity, unit costs, resource utilisation, profitability and quality of service.

In assessments the tasks will ask for performance indicators which are tailored to the scenario set. Make sure that you read the scenario information carefully and actually calculate the indicators that are asked for.

8.3 Productivity

Productivity can be difficult to measure, because services rarely have a standard unit of output. For example, it would be meaningless to measure a conveyancing solicitor's productivity on the basis of 'property purchase completions per month', as each will have a different degree of complexity and value to the business. Similarly, it would be inappropriate to assess a bus line on the basis of 'journeys per day', as the contribution to the company's profits would depend upon the number of people carried at each stage of the journey and how many buses were operating on the line.

Meaningful measures of productivity or efficiency for a service depend upon a clearly defined measure of activity and resources.

So, for example, the measure of activity for the bus line might be 'passenger miles' and of the resource might be 'driver hours'.

Professional firms, such as accountants and solicitors, will generally use 'chargeable hours' as a measure of activity and employees' productivity will be judged by 'chargeable hours per employee'.

8.4 Unit costs

Again, the difficulty here is in defining an appropriate unit for the activity being measured. Once this has been established, appropriate costs need to be attributed to it. So the cost of a professional chargeable hour would mainly consist of employee costs (salaries, NICs, benefits, etc.) but will also include a recovery of general overheads.

The cost of a 'passenger mile' for a transport company will include driver costs, vehicle running costs and overheads.

8.5 Resource utilisation

Resource utilisation is the extent to which available resources are used for productive service. Examples of suitable measures for various types of service businesses are illustrated by the following ratios:

Professional	Chargeable hours : Total hours available
Transport	Passenger miles : Total train miles available
Hotel	Rooms occupied : Rooms available
Car hire	Car-days hired : Car-days available

8.6 Profitability

Clearly, for the service business overall, the usual measures can apply – ROCE, profit margins, etc. Unit profitability measures will again depend upon the clear definition of the cost unit or unit of activity. The profit can then be determined by comparison of the cost per unit (as discussed above) with the income generated (e.g. the charge-out rate for a professional chargeable hour or the average fare per mile on a bus/train route).

 Test your understanding 6

A transport company is reviewing the way in which it reports vehicle operating costs to the company management. In particular, it is interested in the use of performance ratios which will help to assess the efficiency and effectiveness of the use of its vehicles.

Information on the following items is available for each vehicle for the period as follows:

Costs

Variable costs

Fuel	Tyres
Oil	Other parts
Hydraulic fluid	Repairs and maintenance

Fixed costs

Road fund licence	Cleaning
Insurance	Depreciation
Drivers' wages	

Activity measures

Miles driven	Number of days available for use
Tonnes carried	Number of days vehicle actually used
Journeys made	

Required:

You are asked to indicate six suitable performance ratios which could be used to monitor the effectiveness and efficiency of the usage of each vehicle.

Three of your ratios should relate to the efficient control of costs and three should relate to the effective usage of vehicles.

Solution

Transport company

Performance ratios

(i)   **Costs**

(ii)   **Usage**

8.7 Quality of service

This has more significance in the service sector than in the manufacturing sector. Customers will make their buying decisions in the service sector on the basis of how well they expect the service to be provided.

The factors contributing to quality of service will vary according to the nature of the business. As an illustration, consider the service provided to trainee accountancy students by a private college. Possible factors that would influence a potential student in their choice of college and the ways in which these might be measured are as follows:

Factor	Possible measures
Technical expertise	Pass rates
Communication	Clarity of lectures, study material and administrative information
Access	Staff/student ratios Availability of tutorial help outside lecture hours Ease of finding department/member of staff required Location of college
Friendliness	Approachability of staff
Flexibility	Ability to tailor service to individual student's needs
Facilities	Availability and standard of canteen, library, phones
Aesthetics	Appearance of college Staff presentation
Comfort	Roominess of classrooms Heating/air-conditioning Comfort of seats, size of desks

You can no doubt think of some more factors and different ways in which those given could be measured. For example, it is perhaps a little glib to use pass rates as a measure of the college's technical expertise, as these are also likely to be significantly influenced by the abilities and commitment of the students themselves.

8.8 Quantitative and qualitative performance indicators

Having identified what needs to be measured, how can this be achieved? Some are a matter of fact or record – like pass rates or the existence of facilities; most of the rest are qualitative judgement and would need to be measured by the use of questionnaires completed by students.

An overall measure of the quality of service provided by the college could be the trend in the number of students enrolling for courses, although again this can be affected by other factors, such as the location of the college and students, the policy of the students' employers and the size of the market for trainee accountants.

9 Total quality management (TQM)

 Definition

Total quality management (TQM) can be defined as 'a continuous improvement in quality, efficiency and effectiveness'.

There are several requirements and aims of TQM:

- It aims towards an environment of zero defects at a minimum cost – the principle of 'get it right first time'.

- It requires awareness by all personnel of the quality requirements with supplying the customer with products of the agreed design specification.

- It aims towards the elimination of waste where waste is defined as anything other than the minimum essential amount of equipment, materials, space and workers' time.

- It must embrace all aspects of operations from pre-production to post-production stages in the business cycle.

Total quality management will, therefore, seek method changes which will help in achieving such objectives. Examples include the use of Just-in-time (JIT) production procedures whereby each component or product is produced or purchased only when needed by production or by a customer, rather than for inventory.

9.1 Quality circles

An important element of TQM is that every employee is involved and anyone with an idea about how to improve quality should be heard. This is done by forming groups of employees known as quality circles. These groups normally consist of about 10 employees of differing levels of seniority and with different skills who meet regularly to discuss quality problems and put forward ideas.

9.2 Indicators measuring quality and the cost of quality

Indicators to measure quality of service may include:

* The number of defects
* Units returned
* Warranty claims
* Customer complaints
* The cost of inspection
* Repairs
* Reworking.

Traditionally failure rates, scrap and reworking were subsumed within the costs of production while other aspects of poor quality were accounted for in either production or marketing overheads. TQM does not accept the cost of poor quality as inevitable and requires that the cost of quality is highlighted in management reports. This enables alternative approaches (such as built-in quality at the design stage) to be developed.

Quality-related costs are the expenditure incurred in defect prevention and appraisal activities and the losses due to internal and external failure of a product or service through failure to meet agreed specifications.

9.3 Types of quality-related cost

Quality-related costs may be classified as follows:

(a) **Failure costs** (or non-conformance costs) are the costs required to evaluate, dispose of, and either correct or replace a defective or deficient product.

    (i) **Internal failure costs** are costs incurred before the product is delivered to the customer. Examples include the following:

        * Rework costs
        * Net cost of scrap
        * Disposal of defective products
        * Downtime due to quality problems.

(ii)   **External failure costs** are costs incurred after the product is delivered to customers. Examples include the following:

- Complaint investigation and processing
- Warranty claims
- Cost of lost sales
- Product recalls.

(b)   **Conformance costs** are further divided into prevention costs and appraisal costs.

(i)   **Appraisal costs** are costs of monitoring and inspecting products in terms of specified standards before the products are released to the customer. Examples include the following:

- Measurement equipment
- Inspection and tests
- Product quality audits
- Process control monitoring
- Test equipment expense.

(ii)   **Prevention costs** are designed to reduce the level of failure costs. Examples include the following:

- Quality education and training programmes
- Regular equipment maintenance
- Supplier reviews
- Investment in improved production equipment
- Quality circles.

 Example

Carlton Limited makes and sells a single product.

The following information relates to its costs and revenues.

1   5% of incoming material from suppliers is scrapped due to poor receipt and storage organisation.

2   4% of material X input to the machine process is wasted due to processing problems.

3   Inspection of the storage facilities for material X costs 10 pence per square metre purchased.

4   Inspection during the production cycle, calibration checks on inspection equipment and other checks cost £25,000 per period.

5   Production quantity is increased to allow for the downgrading of 12.5% of product units at the final inspection stage. Downgraded units are sold as 'second quality' units at a discount of 30% on the standard selling price.

6   Production quantity is increased to allow for returns from customers which are replaced free of charge. Returns are due to specification failure and account for 5% of units initially delivered to customers. Replacement units incur a delivery cost of £8 per unit. 80% of the returns from customers are rectified using 0.2 hours of machine running time per unit and are re-sold as 'third quality' products at a discount of 50% on the standard selling price. The remaining returned units are sold as scrap for £5 per unit.

7   Product liability and other claims by customers are estimated at 3% of sales revenue from standard product sales.

8   Machine idle time is 20% of gross machine hours used (i.e. running hours = 80% of gross hours).

9   Sundry costs of administration, selling and distribution total £60,000 per period.

10   Carlton Limited is aware of the problem of excess costs and currently spends £20,000 per period on training staff in efforts to prevent a number of such problems from occurring.

Give examples of internal and external failure costs, appraisal costs and prevention costs borne by Carlton Limited.

Solution

Internal failure costs. The machine processing losses, downgrading of products, and materials which are scrapped due to poor receipt and storage.

External failure costs. Product liability claims and the costs of making free replacements, including delivery costs.

Appraisal costs. Inspection during the production process, inspection of materials in storage and calibration checks.

Prevention costs. Training costs.

It is generally accepted that an increased investment in prevention and appraisal is likely to result in a significant reduction in failure costs. As a result of the trade-off, there may be an optimum operating level in which the combined costs are at a minimum. In short, an investment in "prevention" inevitably results in a saving on total quality costs.

📝 Test your understanding 7

An example of an external failure cost is:

A   Customer survey

B   Product recalls

C   Inspection

D   Rework

9.4   Successful implementation of TQM

An organisation should undertake to achieve each of the following to ensure TQM is successful:

- Total commitment throughout the organisation.

- Get close to their customers to fully understand their needs and expectations.

- Plan to do all jobs right first time.

- Agree expected performance standards with each employee and customer.

- Implement a company-wide improvement process.

- Continually measure performance levels achieved.

- Measure the cost of quality mismanagement and the level of firefighting.

- Demand continuous improvement in everything you and your employees do.

- Recognise achievements.

- Make quality a way of life.

10 The balanced scorecard

10.1 Introduction

The balanced scorecard approach to performance indicators recognises that historically too much emphasis has been placed on financial ratios in assessing an entity's performance. A successful business will only succeed in the long-term if it keeps its customers happy as well as making profits. The approach therefore combines financial measures with operational, organisational innovation and customer service measures. All of these perspectives must be managed by managers if the business is to prosper in the long-term.

The balanced scorecard becomes the manager's instrument panel for managing the complexity of the organisation within a dynamic external environment.

10.2 Four perspectives of the balanced scorecard

The table below is an example of a balanced scorecard performance management system which demonstrates the role of critical success factors (CSFs) and key performance indicators (KPIs) in this process.

The balanced scorecard

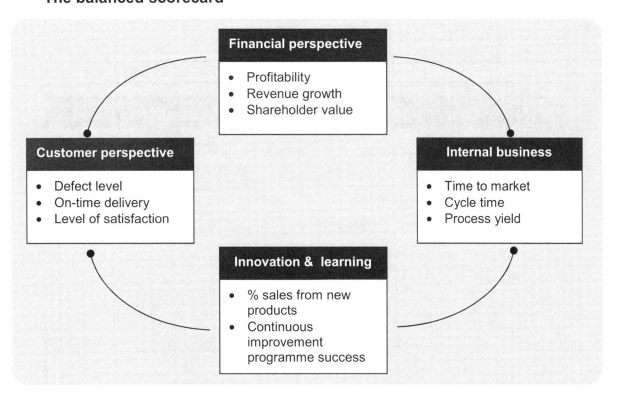

10.3 Key performance indicators

Typical key performance indicators for the balanced scorecard approach are illustrated below.

	Financial perspective	*Customer perspective*	*Internal business process perspective*	*Innovation and learning perspective*
Strategic objective	Shareholder satisfaction	Customer satisfaction	Manufacturing excellence	New product innovation
Critical success factor	Grow shareholder wealth	Achieve preferred supplier status	State-of-the-art process plant	Successful new product development
Key performance indicators	ROCE	Number of new customers	Cycle times Unit cost % yield	% of revenue represented by new products

 Test your understanding 8

The four perspectives of the balanced scorecard include:

A Competitor

B Financial

C Economic

D Political

 Test your understanding 9

Kaplan and Norton's concept of the 'balanced scorecard' is a way of viewing performance from four perspectives, namely:

• the financial perspective

• the customer perspective

• the internal business process perspective

• the innovation and learning perspective.

Task

(a)   Explain what is meant by each of these perspectives.

The financial perspective

The customer perspective

The internal business process perspective

The innovation and learning perspective

(b) You work as an accounting technician in the business planning unit of a large company which has a number of subsidiaries. You use the balanced scorecard concept in appraising performance.

The following information relates to subsidiary A for the year ended 31 December 20X3.

	£m
Revenue	6.85
Cost of sales	5.71
Operating profit	1.14
Number of employees	75

Cost of sales includes training costs of £40,000 and quality assurance costs of £350,000. Assets employed by the subsidiary total £6.30m.

Analysis of revenue by products:

	£m
Existing products	4.85
New products	2.00

Analysis of revenue by customer:

	£m
Existing established customers	4.90
New customers	1.95

Task

Identify a performance indicator for each of the four perspectives for subsidiary A for the year ended 31 December 20X3.

Financial perspective:

Customer perspective:

Internal business process perspective:

Innovation and learning perspective:

11 Other considerations

11.1 How to change a ratio

In the exam there may be questions about how a proposal may affect a performance indicator, so it is important to be comfortable with both the mechanics of the indicator, but also the impact of a proposal.

In terms of the mechanics, most ratios involve some kind of division, for example gross profit margin equals gross profit **divided** by revenue multiplied by 100 to give a percentage.

To improve this ratio, the end percentage needs to be higher. To make the end percentage higher, either increase the number on the top of the division (the numerator) in this case gross profit or reduce the number on the bottom of the division (the denominator), in this case revenue.

For something like gearing, the ratio is debt **divided** by equity (or debt plus equity) multiplied by 100. If gearing is very high then reducing it is an improvement. To reduce it either debt (the numerator) needs to be lower or equity (the denominator) needs to be increased.

11.2 Working backwards

The examiners like to test that a formula has been learnt, but more importantly that it has been understood. The understanding can come from written questions or through working backwards. Similar to backwards variances, there could be questions where you are given the result of a ratio and are required to work back to calculate one of the inputs to that ratio.

Example

Theo has cost of sales of £250,000 and would like his inventory days to be 60.

What does Theo need his inventory balance to be?

Inventory days:

$$\frac{\text{Inventory}}{\text{Cost of sales}} \times 365$$

$$\frac{\text{Inventory}}{250,000} \times 365 = 60 \text{ days}$$

Rearranging:

Inventory = 60/365 × 250,000 = £41,096

Test your understanding 10

What would the revenue need to have been for the asset turnover to be 5 times if the total assets are £50,000?

What would the operating profit need to have been for the ROCE to be 20% if the net assets are £400,000?

What would the gross profit need to have been if sales revenue was £1,000,000 and the gross profit margin was 20%?

┌─────────────┐
│   │
└─────────────┘

What would the inventory value need to be if the current ratio was 2, current liabilities were £200,000, and receivables and cash totalled £120,000?

┌─────────────┐
│   │
└─────────────┘

What would sales revenue need to be (to the nearest £) if receivable days were 80 days and receivables were £400,000?

┌─────────────┐
│   │
└─────────────┘

What would be the 'value added' if sales revenue was £950,000, materials used were £400,000; labour employed was £150,000 and bought in services were £200,000?

┌─────────────┐
│   │
└─────────────┘

What would payables need to be (to the nearest £) if sales were £1,200,000, cost of sales were £700,000 and the payables days were 30 days?

┌─────────────┐
│   │
└─────────────┘

11.3   Influences on performances indicators

Another area to consider is how as a business evolves or as operations change a performance indicator may change.

When a business first sets up, or when it launches a new operation they are unlikely to be very efficient, but a number of factors could lead to efficiency improving and performance indicators improving

(i)   **Economies of scale** – volume could grow which would mean more effective use of fixed costs, as the costs is spread over more units. It may also lead to buying larger quantities from suppliers and being offered a bulk buy discount.

(ii)   **The learning effect** – as workers become more familiar with a process they will work more efficiently reducing the time they take to make a unit and potentially making savings on the amount of material used as less mistakes are made and material wastage reduces.

11.4   What gets measured gets done

In some respects the statement seems obvious – measuring something gives you the information you need in order to make sure you actually achieve what you set out to do. Without a standard, there is no logical basis for making a decision or taking action.

The statement assumes that staff have some motivation to deliver what is measured, whether due to the potential of positive feedback and/or rewards or the consequences of failure. The statement could thus be modified to say "What gets measured and fed back gets done well. What gets rewarded gets repeated."

If managers know they are being appraised on various aspects of performance, they will pay attention to these areas.

Careful attention must be paid to the choice of performance indicators. Selection of the wrong measure, would lead to individuals/departments trying to achieve that measure and it could detrimentally impact the overall business performance. Prioritising personal gains over business objectives is often referred to as dysfunctional behaviour and usually means a lack of goal congruence too.

Example

A salesperson paid a bonus for hitting a target based on number of sales transactions in a month could offer excessive discounts to customers to increase sales or could ask customers to place lots of smaller orders instead of one big order.

The excessive discounts would reduce revenue and margins, the smaller orders would increase administrative work and most likely increase costs.

 Test your understanding 11

You work as an accounting technician for Moran and Geoff, a firm of licensed accounting technicians.

One of your clients, Stonehill Quarries Ltd, has experienced an increase in revenue but a downturn in their overall financial performance in recent times. The company is owner managed by Ernie Heyes and a small management team.

The following is a summary of the Quarrying Trade Association's performance for the sector as a whole for the year 20X3.

Performance indicators

Return on capital employed	24%
Asset turnover	1.6
Net profit before finance costs and tax as a percentage of revenue	15%
Current ratio	1.5 : 1
Quick ratio (acid test)	1.03 : 1
Receivables collection period	60 days
Payables payment period	70 days
Finished goods inventory in days	38 days
Labour costs as % of revenue	18.1%
Operating costs as % of revenue	85.01%
Distribution costs as % of revenue	9.5%
Administrative costs as % of revenue	4.5%
Value added per '£' of employee costs	£1.95

An extract from the company's financial statements for the years 20X2 and 20X3 shows the following:

Income statements

	20X2 £m	20X3 £m
Revenue	5.38	6.68
*Operating costs	4.43	5.82
	0.95	0.86
Finance costs	0.08	0.08
	0.87	0.78
Taxation	0.30	0.27
Profit for the year	0.57	0.51
Dividends	0.16	0.16

*Operating costs comprise:

	£m	£m
Wages, salaries and other employee costs	0.98	1.25
Bought in materials and services	3.21	4.32
Depreciation	0.24	0.25
	4.43	5.82

Operating costs include the following:

	£m	£m
Distribution	0.49	0.61
Administration	0.22	0.27

Statements of financial position

	20X2	20X3
Assets	£m	£m
Non-current assets	3.77	3.88
	——	——
Current assets:		
Inventories Raw materials	0.12	0.15
Finished goods	0.43	0.45
Receivables	0.88	1.19
Cash and cash equivalents	0.04	0.05
	——	——
	1.47	1.84
	——	——
Total assets	5.24	5.72
	——	——
Equity and liabilities		
Equity	3.12	3.47
Non-current liabilities:		
Debentures	1.00	1.00
Current liabilities:		
Trade payables	0.66	0.82
Taxation	0.30	0.27
Dividends	0.16	0.16
	——	——
	5.24	5.72
	——	——

Task

(a) Calculate the ratios listed in the trade association statistics for Stonehill Quarries for the years 20X2 and 20X3.

(b)

20X2	20X3
Return on capital employed	
Asset turnover	
Net profit before finance costs and tax as a % of revenue	
Current ratio	
Acid test	
Receivables collection period	
Payables payment period	

Finished goods inventory days	
Labour cost % of revenue	
Operating costs % of revenue	
Distribution costs % of revenue	
Admin costs % of revenue	
Value added	
Value added per £ of employee costs	

(c)   Comment on the performance of Stonehill Quarries compared with the sector as a whole.

Return on capital employed

Asset turnover

Profit margin

Current ratio and acid test

Receivables collection period

Payables payment period

Finished goods inventory in days

Labour costs % of revenue

Operating costs % of revenue

Distribution and admin costs to revenue

Value added per '£' of employee costs

📝 Test your understanding 12

Smithex Ltd makes a single product, the Alpha, which is sold directly to domestic customers. Smithex is able to sell as many Alphas as it can produce.

Each Alpha contains a specialist part, the A10, which is in short supply. Smithex operates a just-in-time stock policy for the other material plus bought in services but not for the A10.

Smithex does not offer credit facilities to customers or hold any inventory of Alphas. The internal accounts of Smithex for the year to 31 May 20X1 are shown below.

Operating statement for the year ended 31 May 20X1

	Units	£	£
Revenue			6,480,000
Purchases A10	12,000	1,200,000	
Less returns	1,200	120,000	
Net purchases	10,800	1,080,000	
Add opening inventory	1,200	120,000	
Less closing inventory	(1,200)	(120,000)	
A10 issued to production	10,800	1,080,000	
Other material plus bought in services		108,000	
Production wages		1,296,000	
Variable cost of production and sales			2,484,000
Contribution			3,996,000
Production overhead		3,024,000	
Inspection cost of A10 goods received		69,600	
Cost of A10 returns		48,000	
Cost of remedial work		120,000	
Customer support for faulty products		194,400	
Administrative and distribution expenses		216,000	
Total fixed overheads			3,672,000
Net operating profit			324,000

Statement of financial position as at 31 May 20X1

	£	£
Net non-current assets		1,600,000
Inventories	120,000	
Cash	80,000	
Payables	(180,000)	
Net current assets		20,000
Net assets		1,620,000
Financed by:		
Equity		800,000
Loans		820,000
		1,620,000

- Number of production employees 140
- Maximum production capacity per year 12,000
- Closing inventory only consists of units of A10
- Payables only arise from purchases of A10

You are employed by Smithex as its management accountant. One of your duties is to prepare management accounting information for Janet Noble, the Managing Director of Smithex.

Task

Janet Noble asks you to prepare the following performance indicators for Smithex:

(a)	Net operating margin		
(b)	Return on capital employed		
(c)	Asset turnover		

(d)	Average age of inventory			
(e)	Average age of payables			
(f)	Added value per employee			
	Revenue			
	Less: Material A10			
	Less: Other material and bought in services			
	Added value			
	Added value per employee			
(g)	Wages per production employee			
(h)	Contribution per Alpha			

Test your understanding 13

Travel Bus Ltd is a company owned by Travel Holdings plc. It operates in the town of Camford. Camford is an old town with few parking facilities for motorists. Several years ago the Town Council built a car park on the edge of the town and awarded Travel Bus the contract to carry motorists and their passengers between the car park and the centre of the town.

Originally, the Council charged motorists £4.00 per day for the use of the car park but, to encourage motorists not to take their cars into the town centre, parking has been free since 1 December 20X1.

The journey between the car park and the town centre is the only service operated by Travel Bus Ltd in Camford. A summary of the results for the first two years of operations, together with the net assets associated with the route and other operating data, is reproduced below.

Operating statement year ended 30 November

	20X1 £	20X2 £
Revenue	432,000	633,600
Fuel	129,600	185,328
Wages	112,000	142,000
Other variable costs	86,720	84,512
Gross profit	103,680	221,760
Bus road tax and insurance	22,000	24,000
Depreciation of buses	12,000	12,000
Maintenance of buses	32,400	28,512
Fixed garaging costs	29,840	32,140
Administration	42,000	49,076
Net profit/(loss)	(34,560)	76,032

Extract from statement of financial position as at 30 November

	20X1 £	20X2 £
Buses	240,000	240,000
Accumulated depreciation	168,000	180,000
Carrying amount	72,000	60,000
Net current assets	14,400	35,040
	86,400	95,040

Other operating data	20X1	20X2
Fare per passenger per journey	£0.80	£1.00
Miles per year	324,000	356,400
Miles per journey	18.0	18.0
Days per year	360	360
Wages per driver	£14,000	£14,200

Throughout the two years the drivers were paid a basic wage per week, no bonuses were paid and no overtime was incurred.

In two weeks there will be a meeting between officials of the Town Council and the Chief Executive of Travel Holdings to discuss the performance of Travel Bus for the year to 30 November 20X2. The previous year's performance indicators were as follows:

Gross profit margin	24%
Net profit margin	−8%
Return on capital employed	−40%
Asset turnover	5 times
Number of passengers in the year	540,000
Total cost per mile	£1.44
Number of journeys per day	50
Maintenance cost per mile	£0.10
Passengers per day	1,500
Passengers per journey	30
Number of drivers	8

Task

In preparation for the meeting, you have been asked to calculate the following performance indicators for the year to 30 November 20X2:

(a)	Gross profit margin:	
(b)	Net profit margin:	
(c)	Return on capital employed:	
(d)	Asset turnover:	
(e)	Number of passengers in the year:	
(f)	Total cost per mile:	
(g)	Number of journeys per day:	
(h)	Maintenance cost per mile:	
(i)	Passengers per day:	
(j)	Passengers per journey:	
(k)	Number of drivers:	

On receiving your performance indicators, the Chief Executive of Travel Holdings raises the following issues with you:

- The drivers are claiming that the improved profitability of Travel Bus reflects their increased productivity.

- The managers believe that the change in performance is due to improved motivation arising from the introduction of performance related pay for managers during the year to 30 November 20X2.

- The officials from the Town Council are concerned that Travel Bus is paying insufficient attention to satisfying passenger needs and safety.

The Chief Executive asks for your advice.

Task

Write a memo to the Chief Executive of Travel Holdings plc. Where relevant, you should make use of the data and answers to earlier Tasks to:

(a) *Briefly* discuss whether or not increased productivity always leads to increased profitability.

(b) Develop ONE possible measure of driver productivity and suggest whether or not the drivers' claim is valid.

(c) Suggest ONE reason, other than improved motivation, why the profitability of Travel Bus might have improved.

(d) Suggest:

    (i) ONE *existing* performance indicator which might measure the satisfaction of passenger needs; and

    (ii) ONE other possible performance indicator of passenger needs which cannot be measured from the existing performance data collected by Travel Bus.

(e) Suggest:

    (i) ONE *existing* performance indicator which might measure the safety aspect of Travel Bus's operations; and

    (ii) ONE other possible safety performance indicator which cannot be measured from the existing performance data collected by Travel Bus.

MEMO

To:

From:

Date:

Subject:

I refer to your observations relating to the performance of Travel Bus Ltd and detail my comments below.

(a) **Relationship between productivity and profitability**

(b) **Driver productivity**

(c) **Reasons for improved profitability**

(d) **Indicator of passenger satisfaction**

(e)   **Possible safety indicators**

   Test your understanding 14

LandAir and SeaAir are two small airlines operating flights to Waltonville. LandAir operates from an airport based at a town on the same island as Waltonville but SeaAir operates from an airport based on another island. In both cases, the flight to Waltonville is 150 air-miles. Each airline owns a single aircraft, an 80-seat commuter jet and both airlines operate flights for 360 days per year.

You are employed as the management accountant at SeaAir and report to Carol Jones, SeaAir's chief executive. Recently both airlines agreed to share each other's financial and operating data as a way of improving efficiency. The data for the year to 31 May 20X0 for both airlines is reproduced below. The performance indicators for LandAir are reproduced further below.

Operating statement year ended 31 May 20X0

	LandAir	SeaAir
	$000	$000
Revenue	51,840	29,700
Fuel and aircraft maintenance	29,160	14,580
Take-off and landing fees at Waltonville	4,320	2,160
Aircraft parking at Waltonville	720	2,880
Depreciation of aircraft	500	400
Salaries of flight crew	380	380
Home airport costs	15,464	8,112
Net profit	1,296	1,188

Extract from statement of financial position as at 31 May 20X0

	LandAir	SeaAir
	$000	$000
Non-current assets		
Aircraft	10,000	10,000
Accumulated depreciation	2,500	4,000
Carrying amount	7,500	6,000
Net current assets	3,300	5,880
	10,800	11,880

Other operating data

	LandAir	SeaAir
Number of seats on aircraft	80	80
Return flights per day	12	6
Return fare	$200	$275
Air-miles per return flight	300	300

Performance indicators

	LandAir
Return on capital employed	12.00%
Asset turnover per year	4.80
Revenue (or net profit) margin	2.50%
Actual number of return flights per year	4,320
Actual number of return passengers per year	259,200
Average seat occupancy[1]	75.00%
Actual number of passenger-miles[2]	77,760,000
Cost per passenger mile	$0.65

Notes:

[1] Actual number of return passengers ÷ maximum possible number of return passengers from existing flights.

[2] Actual number of passengers carried × number of miles flown.

Task

Carol Jones asks you to prepare the following performance indicators for SeaAir:

(a)	**Return on capital employed:**	
(b)	**Asset turnover:**	
(c)	**Revenue (or net profit) margin:**	
(d)	**Actual number of return flights per year:**	
(e)	**Actual number of return passengers per year:**	
(f)	**Average seat occupancy:**	
(g)	**Actual number of passenger-miles:**	
(h)	**Cost per passenger mile:**	

Carol Jones is concerned that the overall performance of SeaAir is below that of LandAir, despite both airlines operating to the same destination and over a similar distance. She finds it all the more difficult to understand as LandAir has to compete with road and rail transport. Carol Jones has recently attended a seminar on maintaining competitive advantage and is eager to apply the concepts to SeaAir. She explains that there are two ways to gain a competitive advantage:

- by being the lowest cost business; or

- by having a unique aspect to the product or service allowing a higher price to be charged.

This involves managers attempting to eliminate costs which do not enhance value, that is, costs for which customers are not prepared to pay either in the form of a higher price or increased demand.

She makes the following proposals for next year, the year ending 31 May 20X1:

- The number of return flights is increased to 9 per day.

- The estimated average seat occupancy will change to 55%.

- The price of a return fare will remain the same.

As a result of the proposals, there will be some changes in operating costs:

- Fuel and aircraft maintenance, and take-off and landing fees at Waltonville airport, will increase in proportion with the increase in flights.

- Aircraft parking at Waltonville will be halved.

- Aircraft depreciation will increase to $600,000 for the forthcoming year.

- Additional flight crew will cost an extra $58,000.

- There will be no other changes in costs.

Task

Carol Jones is interested in forecasting the performance of SeaAir for next year, the year to 31 May 20X1. Write a memo to Carol Jones. In your memo you should:

(a) Calculate the forecast number of passengers next year for SeaAir.

(b) Calculate SeaAir's forecast net profit for next year.

(c) Show SeaAir's forecast return on capital employed for next year assuming no change in its net assets other than any additional depreciation.

(d) Identify ONE competitive advantage SeaAir has over LandAir.

(e) Identify ONE expense in SeaAir's operating statement which does not add value.

MEMO

To:

From:

Date:

Subject:

I outline below the forecast performance for SeaAir for the year to 31 May 20X1.

(a)	Forecast number of passengers:	
(b)	Forecast net profit for the year to 31 May 20X1:	
		$000
	Revenue:	
		———
	Fuel and aircraft maintenance	
	Take off and landing fees at Waltonville	
	Aircraft parking at Waltonville	
	Depreciation of aircraft	
	Salaries of flight crew	
	Home airport costs	
		———
	Net profit	
		———
(c)	Revised return on capital employed:	

(d)

(e)

 Test your understanding 15

You are employed as a financial analyst with Denton Management Consultants and report to James Alexander, a local partner. Denton Management Consultants has recently been awarded the contract to implement accrual accounting in the St Nicolas Police Force and will shortly have to make a presentation to the Head of the Police Force. The presentation is concerned with showing how performance indicators are developed in 'for profit' organisations and how these can be adapted to help 'not for profit' organisations.

James Alexander has asked for your help in preparing a draft of the presentation that Denton Management Consultants will make to the Head of the Police Force. He suggests that a useful framework would be the balanced scorecard and examples of how this is used by private sector organisations.

The balanced scorecard views performance measurement in a 'for profit' organisation from four perspectives.

The financial perspective

This is concerned with satisfying shareholders and measures used include the return on capital employed and the revenue margin.

The customer perspective

This attempts to measure how customers view the organisation and how they measure customer satisfaction. Examples include the speed of delivery and customer loyalty.

The internal business process perspective

This measures the quality of the organisation's output in terms of technical excellence and consumer needs. An example would be total quality measurement.

The innovation and learning perspective

This emphasises the need for continual improvement of existing products and the ability to develop new products to meet customers' changing needs. In a 'for profit' organisation, this might be measured by the percentage of revenue attributable to new products.

To help you demonstrate how performance indicators are developed in 'for profit' organisations, he gives you the following financial data relating to a manufacturing client of Denton Management Consultants.

Statement of profit or loss for the
12 months ended 30 November 20X0

	£000	£000
Revenue		240.0
Material	18.0	
Labour	26.0	
Production overheads	9.0	
	———	
Cost of production	53.0	
Opening finished inventory	12.0	
Closing finished inventory	(13.0)	
	———	
Cost of sales		52.0
		———
Gross profit		188.0
Research & development	15.9	
Training	5.2	
Administration	118.9	
	———	
		140.0
		———
Net profit		48.0
		———

Extract from statement of financial position at 30 November 20X0

	Opening balance £000	Additions £000	Deletions £000	Closing balance £000
Non-current assets				
Cost	200.0	40.0	10.0	230.0
Depreciation	80.0	8.0	8.0	80.0
Carrying amount				150.0
Net current assets				
Inventory of finished goods			13.0	
Receivables			40.0	
Cash			6.0	
Payables			(9.0)	
				50.0
Net assets				200.0

Task

James Alexander asks you to calculate the following performance indicators and, for each indicator, to identify ONE balanced scorecard perspective being measured:

(a)	Return on capital employed:	
	Scorecard:	
(b)	Revenue margin percentage	
	Scorecard:	
(c)	Asset turnover:	
	Scorecard:	
(d)	Research and development as percentage of production:	
	Scorecard:	

(e)	Training as percentage of labour costs:	
	Scorecard:	
(f)	Average age of finished inventory:	
	Scorecard:	

Test your understanding 16

You are employed by ALV Ltd as an accounting technician. Two companies owned by ALV Ltd are ALV (East) Ltd and ALV (West) Ltd. These two companies are located in the same town and make an identical electrical product which sells for £84.

Financial data relating to the two companies is reproduced below. In addition, performance indicators for ALV (East) Ltd are also enclosed. Both companies use the same straight-line depreciation policy and assume no residual value.

ALV (East) Ltd
Extract from statement of financial position as at 31 May 20X0

	Cost £000	Accumulated depreciation £000	Net book value £000
Non-current assets			
Buildings	1,000	700	300
Plant & machinery	300	240	60
	1,300	940	360
Net current assets			
Inventory		45	
Receivables		30	
Cash		5	
Payables		(40)	40
			400

ALV (East) Ltd
Operating statement – year to 31 May 20X0

	£000
Revenue	840
Material and bought-in services	340
Production labour	180
Other production expenses	52
Depreciation – buildings	20
Dep'n – plant and machinery	30
Admin and other expenses	50
Operating profit	168

Other data

Number of employees	18	Units produced	10,000

Performance indicators for ALV (East) Ltd

Asset turnover	2.1 times	Production labour cost per unit	£18.00
Net profit margin	20.00%	Output per employee	556
Return on capital employed	42.00%	Added value per employee	£27,778
Wages per employee	£10,000	Profit per employee	£9,333

ALV (West) Ltd
Extract from statement of financial position as at 31 May 20X0

	Cost £000	Accumulated depreciation £000	Carrying amount £000
Non-current assets			
Buildings	1,500	120	1,380
Plant & machinery	900	180	720
	2,400	300	2,100
Net current assets			
Inventory		20	
Receivables		30	
Cash		5	
Payables		(55)	Nil
			2,100

ALV (West) Ltd
Operating statement – year to 31 May 20X0

	£000
Revenue	2,520
Material and bought-in services	1,020
Production labour	260
Other production expenses	630
Depreciation – buildings	30
Dep'n – plant and machinery	90
Admin and other expenses	112
Operating profit	378

Other data

Number of employees   20   Units produced   30,000

ALV Ltd is considering closing one of the companies over the next two years. As a first step, the board of directors wish to hold a meeting to consider which is the more efficient and productive company.

Task

In preparation for the board meeting, calculate the following performance indicators for ALV (West) Ltd:

(a)	Asset turnover:	
(b)	Net profit margin:	
(c)	Return on capital employed:	
(d)	Wages per employee:	
(e)	Production labour cost per unit:	

(f)	Output per employee:	
(g)	Added value:	
	Added value per employee:	
(h)	Profit per employee:	

📝 Test your understanding 17

You are the Management Accountant of Care4, a registered charity. You report to Carol Jones, the Chief Executive. Care4 owns Highstone School, a residential school for children with special needs. One of your duties is to prepare performance indicators for Highstone School. The accounts for the year to 31 August 20X2 are shown below.

Operating statement – year to 31 August 20X2

	£	£
Fee income		1,760,000
Teacher salaries	600,000	
Nursing and support staff salaries	480,000	
Administrative expenses	120,000	
Power	128,000	
Housekeeping	160,000	
Depreciation	236,800	
Total expenses		1,724,800
Operating surplus		35,200

Statement of financial position extract at 31 August 20X2

	Land	Buildings and equipment	Total
	£	£	£
Non-current assets			
Cost	4,502,800	11,840,000	16,342,800
Depreciation to date		9,708,800	9,708,800
Carrying amount	4,502,800	2,131,200	6,634,000
Net current assets			
Receivables	440,000		
Cash	62,000		
Payables	(96,000)		406,000
Net assets			7,040,000

Local authorities refer children with special needs to the school and pay the school fees. There is a standard contract that states the number of children per teacher and the number of nursing and support staff required. You are provided with the following additional information:

- The school fee per child for the year ended 31 August 20X2 was £22,000.

- The contracts state there must be:

  - one teacher for every four children (The average salary per teacher is £30,000)

  - one member of the nursing and support staff for every two children. (The average salary per member of the nursing and support staff is £12,000).

- The school can accommodate a maximum of 100 children.

- The buildings and equipment are depreciated by equal amounts each year and are assumed to have no residual value.

- Payables entirely relate to power and housekeeping.

Task

Prepare the following school performance indicators for Carol Jones:

(a)	Operating surplus/fee income	
(b)	Return on net assets	
(c)	Average age of receivables	
(d)	Average age of payables	
(e)	Number of children in school	
(f)	Occupancy rate of school	
(g)	Number of teachers	
(h)	Number of nursing and support staff	
(i)	Total cash-based expenses = total expenses – depreciation	

Test your understanding 18

You are employed as an accounting technician by Aspex Technologies Ltd. One of your duties is to prepare performance indicators and other information for Stuart Morgan, the Financial Director.

Aspex Technologies make a single product, the Zeta. In the year to 30 November 20X3, the company has had problems with the quality of the material used to make Zetas and Stuart would like to know what the cost of quality has been for the year.

The cost of quality is defined as the total of all costs incurred in preventing faults plus those costs involved in correcting faults once they have occurred. It is a single figure measuring all the explicit costs of quality – that is, those costs collected within the accounting system.

Stuart provides you with the following financial statements and data.

Operating statement – year ended 30 November 20X3

	Units	£000	£000
Revenue	360,000		14,400
Purchases	400,000	6,400	
Less returns	(40,000)	(640)	
Net purchases	360,000	5,760	
Add opening inventory	90,000	1,440	
Less closing inventory	(90,000)	(1,440)	
Material issued to production	360,000	5,760	
Production labour		3,600	
Variable cost of production and sales			9,360
Contribution			5,040
Heat, light and power		720	
Depreciation		1,000	
Inspection cost		80	
Production overhead		2,000	
Reworking of faulty production		40	
Customer support		200	
Marketing and administrative expenses		424	
Total fixed overheads			4,464
Operating profit			576

Statement of financial position as at 30 November 20X3

	£000	£000
Non-current assets at cost		8,000
Cumulative depreciation		2,000
		———
Carrying amount		6,000
Inventory	1,440	
Receivables	2,400	
Cash	960	
Payables	(1,200)	
	———	
Net current assets		3,600
		———
		9,600
		———
Financed by		
Debt		6,000
Equity		3,600
		———
		9,600
		———

- The number of production employees in the company is 180.
- Production labour is a variable expense.
- The demand for Zetas in the year to 30 November 20X3 was 390,000 but not all could be produced and sold due to poor quality materials. Any orders not completed this year can be completed next year.
- The only reason for the reworking of faulty production and customer support expenses was the poor quality of the materials.
- Material and heat, light and power are the only bought-in expenses.
- Payables relate entirely to material purchases.
- There are no inventories of finished goods or work in progress.
- Depreciation is based on the straight-line method.

Task

Prepare the following information for Stuart Morgan:

(a)	Selling price per Zeta:	
(b)	Material cost per Zeta:	
(c)	Labour cost per Zeta:	
(d)	Contribution per Zeta:	
(e)	Contribution percentage:	
(f)	Net profit (or revenue) margin:	
(g)	Return on capital employed:	
(h)	Asset turnover:	
(i)	Average age of receivables in months:	
(j)	Average age of inventory in months:	
(k)	Average age of payables in months:	
(l)	Added value per employee	
	Revenue:	
	Material:	
	Heat, light and power:	
	Added value:	
	Added value per employee:	

(m)	**Average delay in completing an order in months**		
	Order volume:		
	Sales volume:		
		———	
	Backlog:		
		———	
	Average delay:		
(n)	**Cost of quality**		
	Inspection:		
	Reworking:		
	Customer support:		

Test your understanding 19

The actual and budgeted operating results for the sale and production of executive desks for the year to May 20X4 are set out below.

	Actual £	Budget £
Revenue	2,750,000	3,000,000
Cost of sales		
Opening finished goods inventory	200,000	200,000
Cost of production	2,329,600	2,400,000
Closing finished goods inventory	(240,000)	(200,000)
Cost of sales	2,289,600	2,400,000
Gross profit	460,400	600,000
Distribution and administration costs	345,000	360,000
Operating profit	115,400	240,000

Other data for the production and sale of executive desks for the year to May 20X4 is as follows:

	Actual	Budget
Number of desks sold	11,000	12,000
Number of desks produced	11,200	12,000
Direct labour hours	58,200	60,000
Net assets employed	£1,075,400	£1,200,000

Task

(a) Calculate the following actual and budgeted performance indicators:

	Actual	Budget
Gross profit margin		
Operating profit margin		
Return on capital employed		
Inventory turnover (in months)		

(b) Write a memo to Sam Thomas. Your memo should include ONE course of action the company could take to improve EACH performance indicator.

MEMO

To:

From:

Date:

Subject:

(i) **Gross profit margin**

(ii)   **Operating profit margin**

(iii) **Return on capital employed**

(iv)   **Inventory turnover**

Sam Thomas has been on a course on product management. He was particularly interested in the concept of value engineering or value analysis. This was explained to be a process which involves different specialists to evaluate a product's design. The objective of the process is to identify how a product may be redesigned to improve its value.

Task

Write a brief memo to Sam Thomas. Your memo should describe how value engineering or value analysis may be used to reduce the production cost of an item such as an executive desk.

MEMO

To:

From:

Date:

Subject:

12 Summary

As you have seen, there are numerous possible performance indicators and their relevance will depend upon the type of organisation and the aspect of performance being assessed.

The most important ratios for you to be able to compute (and interpret) are as follows:

Profitability:	Return on capital employed (ROCE)
	Return on net assets (RONA)
	Gross and net profit margins
Liquidity:	Current ratio
	Quick (acid test) ratio
	Inventory turnover
	Receivables' collection period
	Payables' payment (settlement) period
Investor:	Gearing

Remember that a ratio on its own is not particularly useful information; it needs to be compared, internally or externally.

Many of the ideas covered in earlier chapters will have relevance here (e.g. variance analysis and the use of indices).

Make sure you are quite clear about the necessary attributes of a cost unit (or unit of activity) in order for it to provide a useful basis for measurement. This is particularly important for service activities. Try to think of services you have had experience of yourself and how the various aspects may be measured.

There will rarely be a unique right or wrong answer, so do not be afraid to use your imagination!

Answers to chapter test your understandings

 Test your understanding 1

WH Limited

REPORT

To: Senior Management Committee

From: Assistant Accountant

Date: Today

Subject: Profitability and asset turnover ratios

We have received the Trade Association results for year 4 and this report looks in detail at the profitability and asset turnover ratios.

(a) **What each ratio is designed to show**

   (i) *Return on capital employed (ROCE)*

     This ratio shows the percentage rate of profit which has been earned on the capital invested in the business (i.e. the return on the resources controlled by management). The expected return would vary depending on the type of business and it is usually calculated as follows:

     Return on capital employed =
$$\frac{\text{Profit before finance costs and tax}}{\text{Capital employed}} \times 100\%$$

     Other profit figures can be used, as well as various definitions of capital employed.

   (ii) *Net operating profit margin*

     This ratio shows the operating profit as a percentage of revenue. The operating profit is calculated before finance costs and tax and it is the profit over which operational managers can exercise day to day control. It is the amount of revenue remaining after all direct costs and overheads have been deducted.

     Net operating profit margin = $\dfrac{\text{Operating profit}}{\text{Revenue}} \times 100\%$

(iii) *Asset turnover*

This ratio shows how effectively the assets of a business are being used to generate sales:

$$\text{Asset turnover} = \frac{\text{Revenue}}{\text{Capital employed}}$$

If the same figure for capital employed is used as in ROCE, then ratios (i) to (iii) can be related together as follows.

(i) ROCE = (ii) Net operating profit margin × (iii) Asset turnover

(iv) *Gross margin*

This ratio measures the gross profit compared to revenue:

$$\text{Gross margin} = \frac{\text{Gross profit}}{\text{Revenue}} \times 100\%$$

The gross profit is calculated as the revenue less the cost of goods sold and this ratio therefore focuses on the company's manufacturing and trading activities.

(b) **WH Limited's profitability and asset turnover**

WH Limited's ROCE is lower than the trade association average, indicating either poor profitability (as measured by the net profit margin) or poor asset utilisation (as measured by the asset turnover) or both.

WH Limited's operating profit margin is higher than the trade association average, despite a lower than average gross profit margin. This suggests that overheads are lower relative to revenue in WH Limited.

WH Limited's asset turnover ratio is lower than the trade association average. This may mean that assets are not being used as effectively in our company as they could be.

WH Limited's gross profit margin is lower than the trade association average. This suggests either that WH's direct costs are higher than average, or that selling prices are lower.

(c) **Limitations of the ratios and of inter-company comparisons**

There are a number of limitations of which you should be aware before drawing any firm conclusions from a comparison of these ratios:

(i) The ratios are merely averages, based on year-end balance sheet data, which may not be representative.

(ii) One particular factor which could affect these ratios is if there has been any new investment during the financial year. This investment would increase the value of the assets or capital employed, but the profits from the investment would not yet have accumulated in the income statement. Generally, newer assets tend to depress the asset turnover and hence the ROCE in the short term, as the assets have been purchased at cost and have not been depreciated. It is possible that this is the cause of our company's lower asset turnover and ROCE.

(iii) Although the trade association probably makes some attempt to standardise the data, different member companies may be using different accounting policies, for example in calculating depreciation and valuing inventory.

(iv) Our company's analyst may have used a different formula for calculating any of the ratios. For example, as noted above, there is a variety of ways of calculating capital employed. However, it is likely that the trade association would provide information on the basis of calculation of the ratios.

(v) The member companies will have some activities in common, hence their membership of the trade association. However, some may have a diversified range of activities, which will distort the ratios and make direct comparison difficult.

Test your understanding 2

Two working capital ratios are inventory turnover and receivable days.

Test your understanding 3

(a) **Target ratios**

Return on capital employed $= \dfrac{66}{300} \times 100\%$ = 22%

Operating profit percentage $= \dfrac{66}{820} \times 100\%$ = 8%

Asset turnover $= \dfrac{820}{300}$ = 2.7 times

Working capital period $= \dfrac{70}{754} \times 365$ = 34 days

Percentage room occupancy $= \dfrac{5,900}{18 \times 365} \times 100\%$ = 90%

Revenue per employee $= \dfrac{820,000}{20}$ = £41,000

Key ratios for 20X4

	Stately Hotels plc target	Homely Limited actual
Return on capital employed	26%	22%
Operating profit percentage	13%	8%
Asset turnover	2.0 times	2.7 times
Working capital period	20 days	34 days
Percentage room occupancy	85%	90%
Revenue per employee	£30,000	£41,000

(b)

MEMORANDUM

To: Management Accountant, Stately Hotels plc

From: Assistant to the Management Accountant

Date: Today

Subject: Initial assessment of the performance of Homely Limited

I have carried out an initial assessment of Homely Limited, based on an extract from their accounts for 20X4. I have calculated their key accounting ratios and compared them with our company's target ratios and my conclusions and recommendations are as follows.

Return on capital employed (ROCE)

At 22% the ROCE is below the target which we set for the hotels in our chain. Management action will be necessary to improve the return on capital employed, through improved profitability of operations, increased asset turnover, or both.

The main limitation in the use of this ratio is that the valuation of the capital employed can have a considerable effect on the apparent ROCE. For example, if the capital employed is undervalued, this will artificially inflate the ROCE.

Operating profit percentage

This is considerably below the target ratio set by Stately Hotels plc and it is the cause of the depressed ROCE. Management action will be necessary to improve this, either by increasing prices or by controlling operating costs relative to revenue. Since the former action may depress demand in Homely Limited's market, it is likely that management will need to focus on the control of operating costs.

A limitation in the use of this ratio is that Homely's operations may not be comparable to the average hotel in the Stately group. For example, they may not have conference facilities, which would affect the profile of their costs.

Asset turnover

At 2.7 times this is higher than the target ratio, indicating that, although Homely's operations are not as profitable, they generate more revenue per £ of capital employed. It may be that Homely has a different basis of operating, i.e. charging lower prices, and thus reducing the profitability of revenue, but in the process generating a higher revenue for the level of capital employed.

The main limitation of this ratio stems from the limitation of the ROCE, i.e. its accuracy relies on the correct valuation of capital employed.

Working capital period

This is 34 days of operating costs, almost double the level which we require in our target performance ratios. Working capital levels are probably unacceptably high and need to be reduced. This will require more attention to receivables control, reduction in inventory of, for example, consumable materials and foodstuffs, and an investigation into whether full use is being made of available credit facilities.

A limitation of this ratio is that it relies on the accurate valuation of working capital. For example, although inventories should not account for a high proportion of working capital in a hotel, their valuation can be very subjective.

Another major limitation is that the ratio is based on statement of financial position data, which depicts the working capital level on a single day. This may not be representative of the year as a whole and therefore incorrect conclusions may be drawn from the analysis.

Percentage room occupancy

Homely Limited is achieving a room occupancy rate which is above the level expected in our organisation's target ratios. This is a healthy sign which is encouraging.

Revenue per employee

Homely Limited's revenue per employee is also healthy. However, we must ensure that customer service and quality are not suffering as a result of operating with a lower level of staffing.

Overall, Homely Limited seems to have some strengths which would be worth exploiting. However, their control of operating costs and of working capital needs some attention.

Test your understanding 4

Task 1

Diamond Ltd
Performance report – Branch 24
Year ended 31 December 20X9

(a)	Return on capital employed	57.6/240.0	24%
(b)	Gross profit margin	360.0/720.0	50%
(c)	Asset turnover	720.0/240.0	3 times
(d)	Revenue margin	57.6/720.0	8%
(e)	Average age of receivables	(96.0/720.0) × 12	1.6 months
(f)	Average age of payables	(51.0/340.0) × 12	1.8 months
(g)	Average age of inventory	(60.0/360.0) × 12	2.0 months

Task 2

		£
Revised revenue	£240,000 × 4	960,000
Cost of sales = 50%		480,000
Gross profit		480,000
Fixed costs		302,400
Operating profit		177,600
Revised return on capital employed	£177,600/£240,000	74%

Test your understanding 5

(a) Value added statements

	20X2 £m	20X3 £m
Revenue	6.1	6.5
Less bought in materials and services	2.0	2.1
Value added	4.1	4.4

(b) Value added per £ of employee costs

	20X2 £m	20X3 £m
Value added	4.1	4.4
Employee costs	1.8	1.9
Value added per '£' of employee costs	£2.28	£2.32

Bought in materials and services are consumed by value adding activities which are driven by labour and other resources to produce finished goods or services rendered. These outputs have a value in the form of revenue and when offset by the bought in items create a pool of wealth we know as value added.

Labour is a major resource which contributes to this wealth and therefore we can measure labour's productivity as:

$$\frac{\text{Value added}}{\text{Labour cost}}$$

If the productivity of labour increases then this ratio will increase.

In the case of Sandsend Engineering Ltd above, the ratio has improved from £2.28 to £2.32 – showing an increase in labour productivity.

 Test your understanding 6

Cost control performance ratios

Cost per mile
Cost per tonne carried ⎱
Cost per journey   ⎰ each of these ratios could be calculated
Cost per tonne/mile   for fixed and variable costs separately

Fixed cost per available day
Fixed cost per working day

Usage performance ratios

Tonne/miles per period

Days available as a percentage of total working days

Days used as a percentage of available days

Tonnes carried per available day

Journeys made per available day

Tonnes/miles per journey

 Test your understanding 7

B   External failure costs include the costs of product recalls.

 Test your understanding 8

B   The balanced scorecard includes the financial perspective.

Test your understanding 9

(a) The four perspectives within the 'balanced scorecard' view of performance are:

- *The financial perspective*

  This is concerned with satisfying shareholders and measures used include the return on capital employed and the revenue margin.

- *The customer perspective*

  This attempts to measure how customers view the organisation and how they rate customer satisfaction. Examples include the speed of delivery and customer loyalty.

- *The internal business process perspective*

  This measures the quality of the organisation's output in terms of technical excellence and consumer needs. Examples include unit cost and total quality measurement.

- *The innovation and learning perspective*

  This emphasises the need for continual improvement of existing products and the ability to develop new products to meet customers' changing needs. In a 'for profit' organisation, this might be measured by the percentage of revenue attributable to new products.

(b) **Financial perspective:**

Shareholder satisfaction

Return on capital employed

$$\frac{\text{Operating profit}}{\text{Assets employed}} \times 100\%$$

$$\frac{1.14}{6.30} \times 100\% \qquad = \qquad 18.1\%$$

Customer perspective:

Customer satisfaction

% of revenue to established and existing customers

$$\frac{4.90}{6.85} \times 100\% \qquad = \qquad 71.5\%$$

Internal business process perspective:

Quality assurance costs as a % of total cost

$$\frac{0.35}{5.71} \times 100\% \quad = \quad 6.1\%$$

Innovation and learning perspective:

Revenue generated by new products as a % of total revenue

$$\frac{2.00}{6.85} \times 100\% \quad = \quad 29.2\%$$

📝 Test your understanding 10

$5 \times £50,000 = £250,000$

ROCE = Operating profit/Capital employed × 100%

20% = Operating profit/£400,000

Operating profit = £80,000

Gross profit margin = Gross profit/Sales revenue × 100%

20% = Gross profit × £1,000,000

Gross profit = £200,000

Current ratio = Current assets/Current liabilities

2 = (Inventory + £120,000)/£200,000

Inventory = £280,000

Receivable days = Receivables/Sales revenue × 365

80 = £400,000/Sales revenue × 365

Sales revenue = £1,825,000

Value added = Sales revenue – Cost of materials and bought in services

Value added = £950,000 – £400,000 – £200,000

Value added = £350,000

Payable days = Payables/Cost of sales × 365

30 = Payables/£700,000 × 365

Payables = £57,534

Test your understanding 11

(a) **Return on capital employed**

$$\frac{\text{Net profit before finance costs and tax}}{\text{Total assets} - \text{Current liabilities}} \times 100\%$$

20X2

$$\frac{0.95}{4.12} \times 100\%$$

= 23.06%

20X3

$$\frac{0.86}{4.47} \times 100\%$$

0.92

= 19.24%

Asset turnover

$$\frac{\text{Revenue}}{\text{Total assets} - \text{Current liabilities}}$$

20X2

$$\frac{5.38}{4.12}$$

= 1.31 times

20X3

$$\frac{6.68}{4.47}$$

= 1.49 times

Net profit before finance costs and tax as a % of revenue

$$\frac{\text{Net profit before finance costs and tax}}{\text{Revenue}} \times 100\%$$

20X2

$$\frac{0.95}{5.38} \times 100\%$$

= 17.66%

20X3

$$\frac{0.86}{6.68} \times 100\%$$

= 12.87%

Current ratio

Current assets : Current liabilities

20X2

1.47 : 1.12

= 1.31 : 1

20X3

1.84 : 1.25

= 1.47 : 1

Acid test

(Current assets – Inventories) : Current liabilities

20X2

1.47 – 0.55) : 1.12

= 0.82 : 1

20X3

(1.84 – 0.60) : 1.25

= 0.99 : 1

Receivables collection period

$$\frac{\text{Receivables}}{\text{Revenue}} \times 365 \text{ days}$$

20X2

$$\frac{0.88}{5.38} \times 365 \text{ days}$$

= 60 times

20X3

$$\frac{1.19}{6.68} \times 365 \text{ days}$$

= 65 times

Payables payment period

$$\frac{\text{Trade payables}}{\text{Purchases}}$$

20X2

$$\frac{0.66}{3.21} \times 365 \text{ days}$$

= 75 days

20X3

$$\frac{0.82}{4.32} \times 365 \text{ days}$$

= 69 days

Finished goods inventory days

$$\frac{\text{Inventories (finished goods)}}{\text{Cost of sales}} \times 365 \text{ days}$$

To improve our estimation of Cost of Sales we can add back the distribution and admin expenses to the operating costs.

20X2

$$\frac{0.43}{(4.43 - 0.49 - 0.22)} \times 365 \text{ days}$$

= 42 days

20X3

$$\frac{0.45}{(5.82 - 0.61 - 0.27)} \times 365 \text{ days}$$

= 33 days

Labour cost % of revenue

20X2

$$\frac{0.98}{5.38} \times 100\%$$

= 18.22%

20X3

$$\frac{1.25}{6.68} \times 100\%$$

= 18.71%

Operating costs % of revenue

20X2	20X3
$\frac{4.43}{5.38} \times 100\%$	$\frac{5.82}{6.68} \times 100\%$
= 82.34%	= 87.13%

Distribution costs % of revenue

20X2	20X3
$\frac{0.49}{5.38} \times 100\%$	$\frac{0.61}{6.68} \times 100\%$
= 9.11%	= 9.13%

Admin costs % of revenue

20X2	20X3
$\frac{0.22}{5.38} \times 100\%$	$\frac{0.27}{6.68} \times 100\%$
= 4.09%	= 4.04%

Value added per '£' of employee costs

Value added:

	20X2 £m	20X3 £m
Revenue	5.38	6.68
Bought in materials and services	3.21	4.32
Value added	2.17	2.36

Value added per '£' of employee costs

20X2	20X3
$\frac{2.17}{0.98}$	$\frac{2.36}{1.25}$
= £2.21	= £1.89

(b) **Return on capital employed**

The company has experienced a significant decline in profitability in 20X3 to a level below that for the sector as a whole. However, a return of 19% may be considered a good level of performance but a further decline may be the sign of longer term problems.

Asset turnover

The company has increased its volume of sales to net assets ratio, but is not generating the volume experienced by the sector.

Profit margin

One reason for the reduction in the primary ratio (the ROCE) is highlighted here. There has been a significant fall in the profit margin so, although sales volume has increased, there has been a reduction in the margin.

The return to sales is now approximately 13% compared with 15% for the sector.

Current ratio and acid test

The company's liquidity is still relatively sound, with the acid test only marginally less than the desired level of 1 : 1 and also the average for the sector.

Liquidity has strengthened in 20X3.

Receivables collection period

The receivables day period has increased and is currently 65 days compared with 60 days average for the sector.

Tighter controls are required here and if the trend continues upward the company may be exposing itself to the incidence of bad debts.

Payables payment period

The company's period is typical of the sector as a whole. There has been a fall in payable days as the company has utilised some of its excess cash flow in this area.

Finished goods inventory in days

The company is now holding around one month's supply of finished inventory. It is not sacrificing liquidity by tying up excess working capital in the form of inventory.

The company's inventory management controls are now tighter than those for the sector.

Labour costs % of revenue

There has been a marginal increase here but the ratio is still at an acceptable level of control.

Operating costs % of revenue

There has been a significant increase here which indicates that operating overheads and some other direct costs need tighter controls. It may be that the company has an ageing plant and maintenance charges are on an upward trend.

If these assumptions are not the case, there may have been a significant shift in product mix which can influence product profitability.

An analysis of the above factors needs to be carried out to assess fully the change in this measure of efficiency.

Distribution and admin costs to revenue

These measures are well in line with the sector average and indicate good sound controls in these areas of cost.

Value added per '£' of employee costs

The effectiveness and efficiency of the human asset resource has been offset by the adverse factors highlighted above.

The productivity of labour is now some 3% less than the sector average.

Test your understanding 12

(a) **Net operating margin**
(£324,000/£6,480,000) × 100   5%

(b) **Return on capital employed**
(£324,000/£1,620,000) × 100   20%

(c) **Asset turnover**
(£6,480,000/£1,620,000)   4 times

(d) **Average age of inventory**
(£120,000/£1,080,000) × 12   1.33 months

(e) **Average age of payables**   2 months
(£180,000/£1,080,000) × 12

(f) **Added value per employee**

Revenue	£6,480,000
Less: Material A10	£1,080,000
Less: Other material and bought in services	£108,000
Added value	£5,292,000

Added value per employee (£5,292,000/140)   £37,800

(g) **Wages per production employee**
(£1,296,000/140)   £9,257

(h) **Contribution per Alpha**
Selling price per unit (£6,480,000/10,800) =
Marginal cost per unit (£2,484,000/10,800) =

Contribution per Alpha =   £370

Test your understanding 13

(a) Gross profit margin:

£221,760/£633,600 × 100%   35%

(b) Net profit margin:

£76,032/£633,600 × 100%   12%

(c) Return on capital employed:

£76,032/£95,040 × 100%   80%

(d) Asset turnover:

£633,600/£95,040   6.67 times

(e) Number of passengers in the year:

£633,600/£1   633,600 passengers

(f) Total cost per mile:

(£633,600 – £76,032)/356,400   £1.56

(g) Number of journeys per day:

356,400/(18 miles × 360 days)   55 journeys

(h) Maintenance cost per mile:

£28,512/356,400   £0.08

(i)	Passengers per day:	
	633,600/360	1,760 passengers
(j)	Passengers per journey:	
	1,760/55	32 passengers
(k)	Number of drivers:	
	£142,000/£14,200	10

MEMO

To: Chief Executive

From: Management Accountant

Date: Today

Subject: Performance of Travel Bus Ltd

I refer to your observations relating to the performance of Travel Bus Ltd and detail my comments below.

(a) **Relationship between productivity and profitability**

Productivity is the measure of outputs against inputs and is often a nonfinancial measure.

An example of productivity is output per employee. Increases in productivity do not always lead to an increase in profitability. Profits may fall if finished goods or services rendered are sold at a market price less than previously charged. Cost increases not passed on in increased prices may also adversely affect profitability, even though productivity may have risen.

(b) **Driver productivity**

One measure of driver productivity is miles driven per driver. There has been a reduction in this measure from 40,500 miles per driver in 20X1 to 35,640 in 20X2. These results do not support the drivers' claims.

(**NB:** An alternative measure could have been passengers per driver.)

(c) **Reasons for improved profitability**

Both volume and price have increased, passengers per day and per journey have increased together with fare per passenger journey.

These factors have resulted in fixed costs being recovered faster by an increase in contribution.

Volume has increased and may be the effect of the free parking supported by council policy.

(d) **Indicator of passenger satisfaction**

The number of journeys per day has increased from 50 to 55. This indicates that there was a decrease in waiting time between journeys.

The figures provided do not indicate any measure of the punctuality of the service.

(**NB:** Other comments could include the number of passengers having to stand throughout the journey and the catering for disabled passengers.)

(e) **Possible safety indicators**

Maintenance cost per mile is an indicator of safety issues. The maintenance cost per mile has fallen from £0.10 to £0.08 and as the fleet is a further year older the question of safety needs to be reviewed.

One additional safety indicator is the provision of security facilities at both the car park and the bus terminal.

(**NB:** Accidents per year would also be a useful measure.)

Test your understanding 14

(a)	Return on capital employed:	10.00%
	($1,188,000/$11,880,000) × 100%	
(b)	Asset turnover:	2.50 times
	$29,700,000/$11,880,000	
(c)	Revenue (or net profit) margin:	4.00%
	$1,188,000/$29,700,000 × 100%	
(d)	Actual number of return flights per year:	2,160
	6 × 360	
(e)	Actual number of return passengers per year:	108,000
	$29,700,000/$275	
(f)	Average seat occupancy:	62.50%
	108,000/(2,160 × 80) × 100%	
(g)	Actual number of passenger-miles:	
	108,000 × 300	32,400,000
(h)	Cost per passenger mile:	
	$28,512,000/32,400,000 miles	$0.88

MEMO

To: Carol Jones

From: Management Accountant

Date: Today

Subject: Competitive advantage

I outline below the forecast performance for SeaAir for the year to 31 May 20X1.

(a) Forecast number of passengers:

9 flights × 80 seats × 55.00% occupancy × 360 days = 142,560

(b) Forecast net profit for the year to 31 May 20X1:

	$000
Revenue: 142,560 flights × $275	39,204
Fuel and aircraft maintenance: $14,580,000 × 9/6	21,870
Take-off and landing fees at Waltonville: $2,160,000 × 9/6	3,240
Aircraft parking at Waltonville: $2,880,000 × 50%	1,440
Depreciation of aircraft	600
Salaries of flight crew: $380,000 + $58,000	438
Home airport costs	8,112
Net profit	3,504

(c) Revised return on capital employed:

($3,504,000/$11,280,000) × 100%   31%

(Net assets: $11,880,000 − $600,000 extra depreciation = $11,280,000)

(d) SeaAir has a competitive advantage as its route to Waltonville is over the sea and therefore cannot be threatened by other rail or road transport. This allows SeaAir to charge an economic fare. Also, with a lower seat occupancy, SeaAir customers may have a better choice of flights.

(e) One major expense which does not add value in the eyes of a customer is the cost of aircraft parking at Waltonville.

Test your understanding 15

(a) Return on capital employed:
     ($£48,000 ÷ £200,000$) × 100%   24%
     Scorecard: financial perspective.

(b) Revenue (net profit) margin percentage
     ($£48,000 ÷ £240,000$) × 100%   20%
     Scorecard: financial perspective (and possibly
     internal perspective as partly measuring unit cost).

(c) Asset turnover:
     $£240,000 ÷ £200,000$ 1.2 times
     Scorecard: internal perspective, demonstrating
     intensive use of assets and, hence, unit cost

(d) Research and development as percentage of
     production:
     ($£15,900 ÷ £53,000$) × 100%   30%
     Scorecard: innovation and learning perspective.

(e) Training as percentage of labour costs:
     ($£5,200 ÷ £26,000$) × 100%   20%
     Scorecard: innovation and learning perspective.

(f) Average age of finished inventories:
     ($£13,000 ÷ £52,000$) × 12   3 months
     Scorecard: internal business process perspective
     as the greater the amount of finished inventory, the
     less efficient the business is (working capital is tied
     up).

Test your understanding 16

Performance indicators for ALV (West) Ltd

(a) Asset turnover:
£2,520/£2,100   1.2 times

(b) Net profit margin:
(£378/£2,520) × 100   15%

(c) Return on capital employed:
£378/£2,100 × 100   18%

(d) Wages per employee:
£260,000/20   £13,000

(e) Production labour cost per unit:
£260,000/30,000   £8.67

(f) Output per employee:
30,000/20   1,500 units

(g) Added value:
£2,520,000 – £1,020,000 = £1,500,000
Added value per employee:
£1,500,000/20   £75,000

(h) Profit per employee:
£378,000/20   £18,900

Test your understanding 17

(a)	Operating surplus/fee income	(£35,200/£1,760,000 × 100%)	2%
(b)	Return on net assets	(£35,200/£7,040,000 × 100%)	0.50%
(c)	Average age of receivables	(£440,000/£1,760,000 × 12)	3 months
(d)	Average age of payables	(£96,000/(£128,000 + £160,000) × 12)	4 months
(e)	Number of children in school	(£1,760,000/£22,000)	80
(f)	Occupancy rate of school	(80/100 × 100%)	80%
(g)	Number of teachers	(80 children/4 children per teacher)*	20
(h)	Number of nursing and support staff	(80 children/2 children per member of staff)*	40
(i)	Total cash-based expenses= total expenses – depreciation	= £1,724,800 – £236,800	£1,488,000

*Alternative answers:

Total teachers' salaries/average salary	(£600,000/£30,000)	20
Total nursing and support staff salaries/average salary	(£480,000/£12,000)	40

Test your understanding 18

(a)	Selling price per Zeta: £14,400,000/360,000	£40
(b)	Material cost per Zeta: £5,760,000/360,000	£16
(c)	Labour cost per Zeta: £3,600,000/360,000	£10
(d)	Contribution per Zeta: £5,040,000/360,000	£14
(e)	Contribution percentage: £5,040,000/£14,400,000 × 100%	35%
(f)	Net profit (or Revenue) margin: £576,000/£14,400,000 × 100	4%
(g)	Return on capital employed: £576,000/£9,600,000 × 100	6%
(h)	Asset turnover: £14,400,000/£9,600,000	1.5 times
(i)	Average age of receivables in months: £2,400,000/£14,400,000 × 12	2 months
(j)	Average age of inventory in months: £1,440,000/£5,760,000 × 12	3 months
(k)	Average age of payables in months: £1,200,000/£5,760,000 × 12	2.5 months

(l) Added value per employee

Revenue:	£14,400,000	
Material:	(£5,760,000)	
Heat, light and power:	(£720,000)	
Added value:	£7,920,000	
Added value per employee: £7,920,000/180		£44,000

(m) Average delay in completing an order in months

Order volume:	390,000	
Revenue volume:	360,000	
Backlog:	30,000	
Average delay: 30,000/360,000 × 12		1 month

(n) Cost of quality

Inspection:	£80,000	
Reworking:	£40,000	
Customer support:	£200,000	£320,000

Test your understanding 19

(a)

	Actual	Budget
Gross profit margin (W1)	16.7%	20.0%
Operating profit margin (W2)	4.2%	8.0%
Return on capital employed (W3)	10.7%	20.0%
Inventory turnover (in months) (W4)	1.3	1.0

Workings: Note that the workings only show the calculation of the actual figure. The budget is calculated in the same way.

1    $\dfrac{\text{Gross profit}}{\text{Revenue}} = \dfrac{460,400}{2,750,000}$ = 16.7%

2    $\dfrac{\text{Operating profit}}{\text{Sales}} = \dfrac{115,400}{2,750,000}$ = 0.0419   = 4.2%

3    $\dfrac{\text{Operating profit}}{\text{Net assets}} = \dfrac{115,400}{1,075,400}$ = 0.1073   = 10.7%

4   Inventory turnover (also called 'Inventory holding period')

     $\dfrac{\text{Closing inventory}}{\text{Cost of sales}} \times 12 = \dfrac{240,000}{2,289,600}$ = 1.257   = 1.3

(b)

MEMO

To: Sam Thomas

From: Accounting Technician

Date: Today

Subject: Performance indicators

(i)   **Gross profit margin**

An increase in the selling price or a reduction in the cost of a desk will result in an increase in the gross margin. At present, however, the company is achieving the budgeted price of £250 per desk and it may not be possible to increase the price. If this is the case, efforts should be made to reduce the cost of production.

(ii) **Operating profit margin**

The operating profit margin will increase if the company can reduce its distribution and administration costs. The actual results are £15,000 below budget, so it may be difficult to make further savings in this area.

(iii) **Return on capital employed**

The return on capital employed will improve if operating profits improve with no increase in capital employed. The measures detailed above will, therefore, have the effect of improving the return.

One could also examine whether an asset disposal programme could be implemented and the proceeds distributed to shareholders. This would have the effect of reducing capital employed and improving the return on capital employed.

(iv) **Inventory turnover**

The current Inventory of desks represents 1.2 months' production. An increase in revenue volumes may lead to a reduction in the number of desks held in inventory and will consequently improve this indicator. Alternatively, the company should examine whether inventory levels can be reduced.

MEMO

To: Sam Thomas

From: Accounting Technician

Date: Today

Subject: Value Engineering Production cost of an executive desk

It is clear from the actual results for November that, although the budgeted revenue price has been achieved, the gross margin has not. Value engineering may be employed to examine ways in which production costs may be reduced.

Value engineering is the process of reducing costs by:

- simplifying the product design

- eliminating unnecessary activities in the production process.

Value engineering requires the use of functional analysis which involves the identification of the attributes of the executive desk. Once these are established, a price can be determined for each attribute.

Functional analysis may lead to a change in design and a reduction in the materials required for production. Also, if the product design is simplified, assembly time may be reduced and this will lead to lower labour costs.

Ethics

Introduction

Throughout Management Accounting: Decision and Control we are faced with helping the management make decisions around what is the best course of action for the company. A factor that must always be considered while making any decision is any ethical implication. This chapter explores some of the thought processes that companies may go through.

ASSESSMENT CRITERIA	CONTENTS
How ethical and commercial considerations can affect the behaviour of managers aiming to achieve a target indicator (4.2) How ethical considerations can be included throughout the life of a product (5.5) How ethical considerations can be included in the value analysis/engineering of a product in order to promote good corporate citizenship (5.5)	1 Ethics 2 Personal ethics 3 Business ethics

1 Ethics

1.1 Definition

Ethics are the moral principles governing or influencing conduct which is deemed to be acceptable in the society or context in question.

1.2 Ethics in business

Ethics in business can be seen to occur at 3 levels, these can help frame the possible considerations in the situation presented.

Personal ethics – Relate to the way in which individuals conduct themselves. This may include professional ethics (for a member of the AAT).

Business ethics – The way in which the firm as a whole behaves and whether it lives up to society's expectations.

Corporate responsibility – The belief that a firm owes a responsibility to society and stakeholders.

Given the nature of management accounting decision and control we will focus on the first two.

2 Personal ethics

2.1 Professional ethics

A profession, as opposed to other types of occupation, is characterised by the following factors:

- the mastering of specialised skills during a period of training

- governance by a professional organisation

- compliance with an ethical code

- a process of certification before being allowed to practise.

There are many examples of professions, such as accounting, law, medicine and teaching. A professional accountant (such as an AAT member), for example, fulfils all four of the above criteria.

Professions are distinguished, in part, by having a code of conduct that all members of that profession are required to follow. This ensures that the profession as a whole does not have its reputation damaged by the questionable actions of some of its individual members.

2.2 AAT's Code of Professional Ethics

The AAT's 'Code of Professional Ethics' is based on the IFAC Code and takes a similar conceptual framework approach, listing an identical set of Fundamental Principles that must be followed.

- **Integrity** – This implies fair dealing and truthfulness. Accountants should not be associated with any false, misleading or recklessly provided statements.

- **Objectivity** – Accountants must ensure that their business or professional judgement is not compromised because of bias or conflict of interest.

- **Professional competence and due care** – Accountants are required to have the necessary professional knowledge and skills required to carry out work for clients and must follow all applicable technical and professional standards when carrying out that work.

- **Confidentiality** – Information obtained in a business relationship is not to be disclosed to third parties without specific authority being given to do so, unless there is a legal or professional reason to do so. This information should not be used for the personal advantage of the accountant.

- **Professional behaviour** – Accountants must comply with all relevant laws and regulations and must avoid any actions that would bring the profession into disrepute.

Example

A member of the AAT is a manager and receives a bonus based on net labour variances. The bonus is only paid if the net variance is favourable.

Explain any ethical conflicts or goal congruence issues that may arise.

Solution

Objectivity

The manager's judgement may be compromised by their desire to receive a personal bonus and put their preferences before the business.

Integrity

The manager may not be truthful about why they carried out their actions and may lay off staff and claim that laying off unskilled staff rather than take the time to train them up was the only option.

Professional behaviour

If the manager did lay off staff and their action was discovered to be motivated by personal gain they will have brought the profession into disrepute.

 Test your understanding 1

A worker in the accounts department of a large multinational company receives a bonus if profits for the company are above a certain level. The worker decides to manipulate some of the expenses, artificially increasing the profits and allowing them to get a bonus.

Which of the fundamental principles has the worker NOT breached?

A   Confidentiality

B   Professional behaviour

C   Integrity

D   Objectivity

3 Business ethics

3.1 Introduction

Businesses are part of society. Society expects its individuals to behave properly, and similarly expects companies to operate to certain standards. Business ethics is important to both the organisation and the individual.

3.2 Ethics and performance indicators

When considering performance indicators and ethics it's important to think about how a target will influence the behaviour of an individual or a group. If you assign a measure and a target to a department they will try to achieve it, especially if there is an incentive for achieving that target.

This means that careful consideration of measures should be given to make sure it does not put staff under undue pressure. Any measures used should be controllable.

Example

YGT Inc manufactures and sells cutting edge, high technology gadgets. Peter Jones was appointed a year ago to run the division responsible for gaming products and was told that, if he could significantly improve the bottom line profit, then he would be promoted to the main board. Peter delivered the increase required by a combination of the following:

- outsourcing design and making older design staff redundant

- cutting back on marketing and research costs

- reducing staff training costs.

Peter has not behaved in an ethical manner. He has achieved short term targets at the expense of the division's long term competitive advantage. The negative consequences of the above were not realised within the period Peter was in control but will affect future periods. His successor will be penalised for decisions made by Peter.

3.3 Ethics throughout the life of a product

In terms of product design and packaging, the considerations could link into sustainability and necessity.

 Example

Think about the last time you ordered something to be delivered. When it arrived, how many boxes were used, what sort of packaging was used to stop the item moving around?

The bigger the box, the more air bags, or paper that was used the less environmentally friendly that delivery is.

Being more ethical here could also have a positive business impact as more packaging could cost more to buy and ship.

Most organisations' primary aim is to maximise shareholder wealth. Ethical behaviour often leads to more expense, so some people believe that ethics and business do not always align.

It is possible though, that being ethical can lead to good publicity which could lead to increased sales.

 Example

The Fairtrade mark is a label on consumer products that guarantees that disadvantaged producers in the developing world are getting a fair deal. For example, the majority of coffee around the world is grown by small farmers who sell their produce through a local co-operative. Fairtrade coffee guarantees to pay a price to a producer that covers the cost of sustainable production and also an extra premium that is invested in local development projects.

Consumers in the developed world may be willing to pay a premium price for Fairtrade products, knowing that the products are grown in an ethical and sustainable fashion.

3.4 Ethical considerations in value analysis/engineering

Care must be taken during value analysis/value engineering to make sure that the company is behaving ethically. If a company removes too many features it could adversely affect the end product thus disadvantaging the customer. This could also damage the reputation of the company and hence its long term success.

In attempts to reduce cost a company could put pressure on the suppliers to reduce the price or workers to increase their output. This could be seen as unethical too.

 Test your understanding 2

Consider the following two statements:

(i) Your supervisor at work instructs you to undertake an activity you believe to be illegal. This is an example of an ethical dilemma.

(ii) Adopting a strong ethical code will tend to improve a company's relationship with investors.

Which of these statements is/are correct?

A (i) only

B (ii) only

C Both

D Neither

 Test your understanding 3

Harry is an accountant in a large business. The Finance Director has asked him to lie to the other directors about the profitability of the company.

Which fundamental ethical principle would Harry be breaching if he agreed to the request?

A Objectivity

B Confidentiality

C Integrity

D Professional competence and due care

Test your understanding 4

Nora Ltd is a business which operates several divisions. Each division is judged on a companywide RoCE target of 18%. The bonus system is such that the further above the target the division is, the higher the bonus the manager receives.

The following information relates to division Q:

	£
Profit	90,000
Capital employed	300,000

Give as numeric answers to 1 decimal place.

Calculate the RoCE for division Q:

Sandy, the manager of Division Q, is reviewing a project. The project would costs £100,000 and give annual returns of £20,000.

Complete the below table:

	%
What is the RoCE of the project?	
What will the RoCE of Division Q be if Sandy proceeds with the project?	
	Accept/Reject
What will Sandy do if she is to act in the best interests of the company?	
What will Sandy do if she is to act in the best interests of her bonus?	

Which one of the ethical principles is threatened?

Confidentiality / Professional competence and due care / Objectivity

4 Summary

In this chapter we have revisited basic ethical principles from earlier studies. We've then explored the different ethical dilemmas faced in business and possible responses to these ethical situations.

Answers to chapter test your understandings

 Test your understanding 1

The correct answer is A.

There is no evidence that A has breached confidentiality in this scenario. However, he has produced an inaccurate profit figure, compromising his integrity. He is also breaching objectivity, as he is allowing self-interest to bring bias into his work. His actions, if discovered, would also bring the profession into disrepute, meaning that he is not displaying professional behaviour.

 Test your understanding 2

The correct answer is C.

In an ethical dilemma, you have a morally difficult decision to make, involving judgement of what is the right or wrong thing to do in a given situation. Ethics can improve the relationship between the business and investors, who can be reassured that the company is using their funding fairly.

 Test your understanding 3

The correct answer is C.

Integrity means truthfulness and fair dealing. It states that accountants must not be associated with false or misleading statements.

Test your understanding 4

Calculate the RoCE for division Q:

90,000/300,000 × 100 = **30.0%**

RoCE of the project: 20,000/100,000 × 100 = 20.0%

RoCE of Division Q if Sandy proceeds with the project:
110,000/400,000 = 27.5%

	%
What is the RoCE of the project?	20.0
What will the RoCE of Division Q be if Sandy proceeds with the project?	27.5
	Accept/Reject
What will Sandy do if she is to act in the best interests of the company?	**Accept**
What will Sandy do if she is to act in the best interests of her bonus?	**Reject**

What will Sandy do if she is to act in the best interests of the company? Accept, as the RoCE is above the company target of 18%.

What will Sandy do if she is to act in the best interests of her bonus? Reject, as the RoCE of her division reduces by 2.5% thus reducing the bonus she receives.

Which one of the ethical principles is threatened?

Objectivity, as she stands to benefit personally from the decision she makes, her professional judgement could be affected.

MOCK
ASSESSMENT

1 Mock Assessment Questions

Task 1 (12 marks)

(a) The following information has been calculated for the production of one Oval:

Expense	Units	Unit cost
Direct material	10 litres	£7.50
Direct labour	2 hours	£6.00
Fixed overheads		£8.00

Fixed overheads are absorbed on a labour hour basis.

Complete the standard cost card below by filling in the gaps.

(6 marks)

	Quantity	Unit cost £	Total cost £
Material			
Labour			
Fixed overheads			
Total			

(b) A publisher plans to use 2,500,000 sheets of paper to produce 5,000 books.

The standard number of sheets used in each book is [   ]

(1 mark)

Below is information concerning the factory overheads

Units produced	Total overheads (£)
20,000	300,000
29,000	390,000

Fixed costs increase by £10,000 when more than 32,000 units are produced. Variable costs reduce by £2 per unit for units produced in excess of 30,000 units.

(c)   Calculate the total fixed and variable overheads for the following production levels. Enter your answer to the nearest £. **(4 marks)**

Units	Fixed £	Variable £
25,000		
33,000		

(d)   **Complete the statement below**

A disadvantage of the high low method is that it uses [   ] sets of data.   **(1 mark)**

all / two / seven / no

Task 2   (15 marks)

A company provides you with the following budget and actual information:

Budgeted output   2,400 litres

Standard cost information

Direct material   10 litres @ £7.50 per litre

Direct labour   2 hours @ £6.00 per hour

Fixed overheads   2 hours @ £8.00 per hour

Actual information

Output   2,400 litres

Direct material   24,550 litres

Direct labour   5,040 hours

Fixed overheads   £38,500

Additional information

• Total direct materials variance is £4,616 adverse.

• Total direct labour variance is £1,692 adverse.

• Budgeted fixed overhead for the year is £38,400.

• Overheads are recovered on the basis of direct labour hours.

• Production is anticipated to be evenly spread throughout the year.

(a)   Calculate the following cost variances:

	£	F / A
Direct labour rate variance		
Direct labour efficiency variance		
Direct material price variance		
Direct material usage variance.		
Fixed overhead expenditure variance		
Fixed overhead volume variance		

(12 marks)

(b)   **Answer the following question about variances.   (3 marks)**

Which of the following situations would probably cause an adverse materials usage variance?

better quality materials / higher grade labour / an increase in the minimum quality standards / purchase of new machinery

Which of the following situations would probably cause a favourable labour rate variance?

better quality material / better quality workers / poorer quality materials / decrease in the need for overtime

Which of the following situations would probably cause an adverse fixed overhead capacity variance?

decrease in annual rent / purchase of additional machinery / higher grade labour / strike action by workers

Task 3 (14 marks)

Using the information in Task 2 and 3, prepare a statement reconciling the standard cost of actual production to the actual cost for the period.

	F	A	£
Standard cost of actual production			
Direct labour rate			
Direct labour efficiency			
Direct material price			
Direct material usage			
Fixed overhead expenditure			
Fixed overhead volume			
Total variance			
Actual costs			
Direct material			
Direct labour			
Fixed overhead			
Actual cost of production			

Task 4 (12 marks)

(a) The table below contains the last three months cost per litre for a product.

Jan	Feb	Mar
Actual price was £6.00	Actual price was £6.00	Actual price was £6.30
Seasonal variation was −10p	Seasonal variation was −15p	Seasonal variation was +10p

The trend in prices is an increase of £ [   ] per month.

(2 marks)

(b) **Complete the following sentences:** **(2 marks)**

Seasonal variation is the [   ] data at a point less the trend data at the same point.

actual / budgeted / indexed / forecast

A change in the economy that affects sales of a product is an example of a [   ].

random variation / underlying trend / seasonal variation / cyclical variation

(c) A company has provided the following information:

	Jan	Feb	March
Total cost	£15,000	£20,000	£22,320
Total quantity purchased	2,000 m	2,500 m	2,480 m

The cost index for March, based upon January being the base period with an index of 100, is:

A   120

B   124

C   133

D   149

(2 marks)

(d) **Complete the following sentences:** (2 marks)

To calculate an index number, divide the current period figure by the ☐ figure.

base / future / trend / independent

The RPI can be used to remove distortion in a set of figures to help aid ☐ .

absorption / life cycle costing / comparison / extrapolation

(e) The Production Director has asked for your help. She has been given an equation and information to estimate the cost of asphalt for the coming three months.

The equation is $Y = a + bX$, where

X is the time period in months

The value for X in May 20X1 is 18

Y is the cost of asphalt

Constant 'a' is 100 and constant 'b' is 2.7.

The cost of asphalt is set on the first day of each month and is not changed during the month.

The expected price of asphalt per tonne for June 20X1 is £ ☐ and for July 20X1 is £ ☐

(2 marks)

(f) **Complete the following sentences:** (2 marks)

One of the assumptions of linear regression is that the data used is representative of future ☐

indexes / targets / standards / trends

In the equation $Y = a + bX$, Y is the ☐ variable

independent / index / cyclical / dependent

Task 5   (18 marks)

You are an Accounting Technician reporting to the Finance Director of ABC Ltd. You have just produced the following operating statement:

	Favourable	Adverse	
Budgeted costs for actual production			£386,400
	Favourable	*Adverse*	
Direct material price		£400	
Direct material usage		£1,650	
Direct labour rate	£900		
Direct labour efficiency		£1,200	
Fixed overhead expenditure		£5,000	
Fixed overhead capacity	£10,000		
Fixed overhead efficiency		£6,000	
Total variance	£10,900	£14,250	(£3,350)
Actual cost of actual production			£389,750

The Production Director has given you the following information:

- A pay rise for staff is still outstanding
- Two new operators are being trained
- 3 machines are reaching the end of their operational lives.

Draft a report to the Finance Director giving one reason for each of the following variances:

(i)   direct materials price

(ii)   direct materials usage

(iii) direct labour rate

(iv) direct labour efficiency

(v)   fixed overhead expenditure

(vi) fixed overhead volume.

REPORT

To:

From:

Date:

Subject:

Task 6 (15 marks)

(a) **Complete the statement below.** (1 mark)

An activity where if changed could reduce the cost but also reduce the products value to the customer is a _____ **activity.**

target / life cycle / value added / non value added

(b) **Complete the statement below.** (1 mark)

The accumulation of costs across the entire life of a product is referred to as _____ **.**

target costing / ABC / life cycle costing / absorption costing

(c) Menmuir Ltd has a receivables balance of £200,000, and their receivables collection period is 32 days. They have a gross profit margin of 28% and the split of their cost of sales is 65% variable production costs & 35% fixed production costs. The net profit margin is 8%. The current ratio is 1.64:1, payables payment period is 40 days and the cash balance is £50,000.

Complete the table below using the performance indicators given for Menmuir Ltd.

Enter all figures as positive numbers – do not enter negative figures. (9 marks)

	£
Sales	
Variable production costs	
Fixed production costs	
Cost of sales	
Gross profit	
Net profit	
Payables	
Inventory	

(d) **Complete the statements below by selecting one of the following phrases for each statement:**

financial / customer / internal business / innovation and learning

(4 marks)

Revenue growth would be most likely classified under the [   ] perspective of the balanced scorecard.

Numbers of new products developed would be most likely classified under the [   ] perspective of the balanced scorecard.

The measurement of the time taken to complete the production cycle would be most likely classified under the [   ] perspective of the balanced scorecard.

Profit would be most likely classified under the [   ] perspective of the balanced scorecard.

Task 7   (18 marks)

A company manufactures two products, the Shola and the Sammy. The information below relates to the upcoming reporting period.

Per unit	Shola (£)	Sammy (£)
Direct materials at £8 per kg	12	16
Direct labour at £5 per hour	5	7.5
Variable overheads	2	3
Fixed production overhead	1.50	2.50
Selling price	30	40
	Units	Units
Sales demand	3,000	6,000

As a result of the recent storms and subsequent transportation issues materials are limited to 20,000 kg and labour hours are limited to 9,750 hrs.

(a) **Complete the table below for the upcoming period to calculate the optimal production plan.** **(8 marks)**

	Shola	Sammy
Total materials required (kg)		
Total labour hours required		
Contribution per unit (£)		
Contribution per limiting factor (£) (to TWO decimal places)		
Optimal production (units)		

(b) **What is the maximum extra premium that would be paid for each of the following?** **(2 marks)**

1,500 kg of extra material £ ⬚ .

1,500 hrs of extra labour £ ⬚ .

(c) **Discuss why you have decided on the production plan in (a) and the implications of not using it for this company.** **(5 marks)**

Bonanza Ltd is considering purchasing a new machine to improve efficiency.

	Current performance	New machinery
Direct materials per unit	2 kg at £6	Usage would reduce by 10%
Direct labour per unit	4 hours at £8	Time taken would reduce by 25%
Sales	4,000 units at £100	No change in sales units, but the price would be 1% higher
Fixed costs	£100,000	Increase by 20%

(d) **Calculate the profit figures for the current and proposed situations and indicate whether or not the equipment should be purchased.** **(3 marks)**

	Current situation (£)	Expected situation with new machinery (£)
Profit		

It would/would not be beneficial to purchase the new machinery.

Task 8 (15 marks)

Yarrow Limited manufactures two products, the Marrow and the Barrow.

The overhead activities for these, machine set ups and special parts handling, have budgets of £400,000 and £200,000 respectively.

It takes 2 hours 30 minutes of labour to make a Marrow and 3 hours 30 minutes of labour to make a Barrow.

Other information about the Marrow and Barrow is below.

	Marrow	Barrow
Direct materials – £ per unit	4	6
Direct labour – £ per unit	12.50	17.50
Number of special parts	300	100
Number of machine set ups	150	50
Budgeted production units	10,000	50,000

(a) **Calculate the fixed overheads assuming they are absorbed on a budgeted labour hours basis.** **(2 marks)**

	Marrow (£)	Barrow (£)
Fixed overheads		

(b) **Complete the table below using Activity Based Costing (ABC) principles.** **(6 marks)**

Year	£	Marrow (£)	Barrow (£)
Cost driver rate – special parts handling			
Cost driver rate – machine set ups			
Total special parts			
Total machine set ups			

(c) **Using the information from (a) and (b) calculate the total cost per unit using traditional absorption costing and using ABC. Give you answers to two decimal places.** **(2 marks)**

	Marrow	Barrow
Total unit cost – Absorption costing		
Total unit cost – ABC		

(d) **Discuss the potential issues that Yarrow could have switching from absorption costing to activity based costing.** **(5 marks)**

2 Mock Assessment Answers

Task 1

(a)

	Quantity	Unit cost £	Total cost £
Material	10	7.50	75.00
Labour	2	6.00	12.00
Fixed overheads	2	8.00	16.00
Total			103.00

(b)   2,500,000/5,000 = **500**

(c)   Var cost/unit = (390,000 – 300,000)/(29,000 – 20,000) = £10

Fixed cost = 390,000 – (29,000 × 10) = £100,000

25,000 units: variable = 25,000 × 10 = 250,000

33,000 units: fixed = 100,000 + 10,000 = 110,000

variable = (30,000 × 10) + (3,000 × (10 – 2)) = 324,000

Units	Fixed £	Variable £
25,000	100,000	250,000
33,000	110,000	324,000

(d)   A disadvantage of the high low method is that it uses **two** sets of data.

Task 2

(a) Standard cost of actual production + total variance = actual cost

Actual material cost = (2,400 × 10 × £7.50) + £4,616 adverse = £184,616

Actual labour cost = (2,400 × 2 × £6) + £1,692 adverse = £30,492

	£	F / A
Direct labour rate variance AQ × AP = 5,040 × AP = £30,492 AQ × SP = 5,040 × £6 = £30,240	252	A
Direct labour efficiency variance AQ × SP = 5,040 × £6 = £30,240 SQ × SP = 2,400 × 2 × £6 = £28,200	1,440	A
Direct material price variance AQ × AP = 24,550 × AP = £184,616 AQ × SP = 24,550 × £7.50 = £184,125	491	A
Direct material usage variance. AQ × SP = 24,550 × £7.50 = £184,125 SQ × SP = 2,400 × 10 × £7.50 = £180,000	4,125	A
Fixed overhead expenditure variance Actual = £38,500 Budget = £38,400 (2,400 × 2 × £8)	100	A
Fixed overhead volume variance Budget = £38,400 (4,800 × £8) SH × SR = 2,400 × 2 × £8 = £38,400	nil	nil

(b) Which of the following situations would probably cause an adverse materials usage variance?

an increase in the minimum quality standards

Which of the following situations would probably cause a favourable labour rate variance?

decrease in the need for overtime

Which of the following situations would probably cause an adverse fixed overhead capacity variance?

strike action by workers

Task 3

	F	A	£
Standard cost of actual production (W1)			247,200
Direct labour rate		252	
Direct labour efficiency		1,440	
Direct material price		491	
Direct material usage		4,125	
Fixed overhead expenditure		100	
Fixed overhead volume	NIL	NIL	
Total variance	NIL	6,408	6,408
Actual costs			
Direct material	184,616		
Direct labour	30,492		
Fixed overhead	38,500		
Actual cost of production			253,608

(W1) (£75 + £12 + £16) × 2,400 = £247,200

Task 4

(a)

Jan	Feb	Mar
Actual price was £6.00	Actual price was £6.00	Actual price was £6.30
Seasonal variation was – 10p	Seasonal variation was – 15p	Seasonal variation was 10p
Trend £6.10	Trend £6.15	Trend £6.20

The trend in prices is an increase of **£0.05** per month.

(b) Seasonal variation is the **actual** data at a point less the trend data at the same point.

A change in the economy that affects sales of a product is an example of a **cyclical variation**.

(c) **A**

	Jan	Feb	March
Total cost	£15,000	£20,000	£22,320
Total quantity purchased	2,000 m	2,500 m	2,480 m
Cost per m	£7.50	£8.00	£9.00
Index	100		£9.00/£7.50 × 100 = 120

(d) To calculate an index number, divide the current period figure by the **base** figure.

The RPI can be used to remove distortion in a set of figures to help aid **comparison**.

(e) Y = 100 + (2.7 × 19) = **151.3** (June)

Y = 100 + (2.7 × 20) = **154.0** (July)

(f) One of the assumptions of linear regression is that the data used is representative of future **trends**.

In the equation Y = a + bX, Y is the **dependent** variable.

Task 5

To: Finance Director	Subject: Reason for variances
From: Accounting Technician	Date: Today

(i)   Material price variance – Adverse

The company must have paid a higher price for its materials than it expected, perhaps due to general price increases (inflation), a shortage in supply which can push prices up or rush orders - due to more material being wasted than planned - could increase the price paid.

(ii)   Material usage variance – Adverse

The machines which are reaching the end of their operational life may not be working accurately and causing wastage of the material. Another reason could be that the trainees are making mistakes causing the wastage.

(iii) Direct labour rate variance – Favourable

The actual rate paid to staff must be lower than the standard. This could be due to the standard having been set to take account of the pay rise which has not yet happened. Alternatively, the two new operators may be on lower wages until they are more experienced and they may lower the average wage rate.

(iv)   Direct labour efficiency variance – Adverse

This could be due to the training of the 2 new staff which not only reduces their efficiency but also the efficiency of the other operators training them.

(v)   Fixed overhead expenditure variance – Averse

The actual bills for fixed overheads (such as rent) at the end of the period must total more than the budgeted figure anticipated at the beginning of the period. The increase in bills could be due to additional repairs as the machines come to the end of their useful life.

(vi)   Fixed overhead volume variance – Favourable

The volume variance is the sum of the capacity and efficiency variance i.e. £10,000F + £6,000A = £4,000F. This will have arisen due to the actual number of units produced being greater than the budgeted number. This means that the company has over-absorbed its fixed overhead.

Task 6

(a) An activity where if changed could reduce the cost but also reduce the products value to the customer is a **value added** activity.

(b) The accumulation of costs across the entire life of a product is referred to as **life cycle costing**.

(c) Receivables days = receivables/sales × 365

32 = 200,000/sales × 365

(32/365) × sales = 200,000

Sales = 200,000/(32/365)

Sales = 2,281,250

Gross profit = 2,281,250 × 28% = 638,750

Cost of sales = 2,281,250 – 638,750 = 1,642,500

Var prod cost = 1,642,500 × 65% = 1,067,625

Fix prod cost = 1,642,500 – 1,067,625 = 574,875

Net profit = 2,281,250 × 8% = 182,500

Payables:

Payables day = payables/cost of sales × 365

40 = payables/1,642,500 × 365

40/365 × 1,642,500 = payables

180,000 = payables

Inventory:

Current ratio = (receivables + inventory + cash)/payables

1.64 = (200,000 + inventory + 50,000)/180,000

1.64 × 180,000 = 250,000 + inventory

295,200 – 250,000 = inventory

45,200 = inventory

	£
Sales	2,281,250
Variable production costs	1,067,625
Fixed production costs	574,875
Cost of sales	1,642,500
Gross profit	638,750
Net profit	182,500
Payables	180,000
Inventory	45,200

(d) Revenue growth would be most likely classified under the **financial** perspective of the balanced scorecard.

Numbers of new products developed would be most likely classified under the **innovation and learning** perspective of the balanced scorecard.

The measurement of the time taken to complete the production cycle would be most likely classified under the **internal business** perspective of the balanced scorecard.

Profit would be most likely classified under the **financial** perspective of the balanced scorecard.

Task 7

(a) Material required:

Shola: 12/8 = 1.5 kg per unit, 3,000 × 1.5 =4,500

Sammy: 16/8 = 2 kg per unit, 6,000 × 2 = 12,000

Labour hrs required:

Shola: 5/5 = 1 hr per unit, 3,000 × 1 = 3000

Sammy: 7.5/5 = 1.5 per unit, 6,000 × 1.5 = 9000

Contribution per unit:

Shola = 30 − 12 − 5 − 2 = 11

Sammy = 40 − 16 − 7.5 − 3 = 13.50

Contribution per limiting factor:

The limiting factor is labour hours as 12,000 are needed to meet the demand for both products and only 9,750 are available.

Shola = 11/1 hr per unit = £11 per hr

Sammy = 13.50/1.5 hrs per unit = £9 per hr

Optimum production plan:

As the Shola makes the highest contribution per hour this should be made first.

3000 units, using 1 hour each, which leaves 6750 hours to make Sammy.

6750/1.5 hrs per unit = 4,500 units.

	Shola	Sammy
Total materials required (kg)	4,500	12,000
Total labour hours required	3,000	9,000
Contribution per unit (£)	11	13.50
Contribution per limiting factor (£) (to TWO decimal places)	11	9
Optimal production (units)	3,000	4,500

(b)   1500 kg of extra material £0.

They already have more than enough material to meet the demand, so there would be no benefit in getting any extra.

1500 hrs of extra labour £13,500.

Labour is the limiting factor, so with 1,500 extra hours they could make another 1000 units of the Sammy giving £13.50 each unit. so that is the extra premium they would pay on top of the current costs for it to be financially viable.

(c)   The companies aim is to maximise profits and as fixed costs do not change the aim will be to maximise contribution.

To make the total sales demand they would need 16,500 kgs of material (which they have) and 12,000 labour hours (which they don't have).

As labour hours are the limiting factor they must make best use of these.

Shola is the best use of the labour hours and so they make this first.

The plan recommended will yield the highest contribution, any other option would reduce the overall contribution.

They may consider this if a major customer requested a significant order of Sammy to make sure that longer term they kept the customer happy.

(d)   Current situation:

Sales: 4,000 × 100 = 400,000

Materials: 4,000 × 2 × 6 = 48,000

Labour: 4,000 × 4 × 8 = 128,000

Profit = 400,000 – 48,000 – 128,000 – 100,000 = 124,000

Expected situation:

(400,000 × 1.01) – (48,000 × 0.9) – (128,000 × 0.75) – (100,000 × 1.2) = 144,800

	Current situation (£)	Expected situation with new machinery (£)
Profit	124,000	144,800

It **would** be beneficial to purchase the new machinery.

Task 8

(a)   Labour hours: (10,000 × 2.5) + (50,000 × 3.5) = 200,000

OAR = 600,000/200,000 = £3 per labour hour

Marrow: 25,000 hrs × £3 = £75,000

Barrow: 175,000 hrs × £3 = £525,000

	Marrow (£)	Barrow (£)
Fixed overheads	75,000	525,000

(b)   Cost driver rates:

Special parts = 200,000/(300 + 100) = £500 per special part

Machine set ups = 400,000/(150+50) = £2,000 per set up

Special parts:

Marrow = £500 × 300 = £150,000

Barrow = £500 × 100 = £50,000

Machine set ups:

Marrow = £2,000 × 150 = £300,000

Barrow = £2,000 × 50 = £100,000

Year	£	Marrow (£)	Barrow (£)
Cost driver rate – special parts handling	500		
Cost driver rate – machine set ups	2,000		
Total special parts		150,000	50,000
Total machine set/ ups		300,000	100,000

(c)   Absorption cost per unit:

Marrow = 4 + 12.5 + (75,000/10,000) = 24

Barrow = 6 +17.5 + (525,000/50,000) = 34

ABC cost per unit:

Marrow = 4 + 12.50 + (150,000/10,000) + (300,000/10,000) = 61.50

Barrow = 6 + 17.50 + (50,000/50,000) + (100,000/50,000) = 26.50

	Marrow (£)	Barrow (£)
Total unit cost – Absorption costing	24.00	34.00
Total unit cost – ABC	61.50	26.50

(d)   The problems Yarrow could have all relate to the complexity of activity based costing.

ABC can be time consuming and costly, the benefits obtained from ABC might not justify the costs.

ABC will be of limited benefit if the overhead costs are primarily volume related or if the overhead is a small proportion of the overall cost.

It is impossible to allocate all overhead costs to specific activities.

The choice of both activities and cost drivers might be inappropriate.

Glossary

Term	Description
Absorption costing	Inventory units are valued at variable cost plus fixed production overheads.
Activity based costing	A more accurate method of charging costs to cost units than absorption costing.
Attainable standard	A standard that can be achieved in reasonably good conditions.
Balanced scorecard	An approach to performance measurement that recognises that the business must be successful from several perspectives, not just financially.
Basic standard	A standard that is fixed historically and not changed.
Benchmarking	Comparison of the performance of one's own business with the performance of competitors, in order to identify opportunities for improvement.
Breakeven point	The level of activity required to make no profit and no loss.
Capital expenditure	Expenditure on the purchase or improvement of fixed assets, appearing in the balance sheet.
Contribution	Sales revenue less variable cost of sales.
Cost absorption	The charging of overhead costs to cost units.
Cost accounting	The analysis of costs and revenues to provide useful information to assist the management function.
Cost allocation	The charging of overhead costs to the specific cost centre that incurred them.
Cost apportionment	The splitting of shared overhead costs between relevant cost centres using an appropriate basis.
Cost centre	A location, function, activity or item of equipment in respect of which costs are accumulated.

Term	Description
Cost of quality	The difference between the actual cost of producing, selling and supporting the company's products, and the equivalent cost if there were no failures during production or use.
Cost reduction	A process to drive down the unit cost of products without reducing their suitability for the use intended.
Cost unit	An individual unit of product or service for which costs can be separately ascertained.
Cost-volume-profit (CVP) analysis	Analysis of the effects of changes of volume on contribution and profit.
Depreciation	An annual internal charge to the profit and loss account that spreads the net cost of a fixed asset over the number of years of its useful life.
Direct costs	Costs that can be related directly to a cost unit.
Direct expenses	Expenses that can be related specifically to a cost unit.
Discounted cash flow	An investment appraisal technique which discounts future cash flows to a present value.
Effectiveness	The degree to which an objective or target is met.
Efficiency	The relationship between inputs and the outputs achieved.
Expenses	Items of expenditure that are not labour or materials related.
Financial accounting	The production of an historic record of transactions presented in a standard format for use by parties external to the business.
Fixed costs	Costs that vary with time, not activity level.
Ideal standard	A standard that can only be achieved in perfect conditions.
Idle time	Paid for, but non-productive, hours.

Term	Description
Index numbers	A method of assessing growth by allocating an index number of 100 to a base figure in a series, and converting all other figures in the series to an index number using the formula: $$\text{Index} = \frac{\text{Current year figure}}{\text{Base year figure}} \times 100$$
Indirect cost	Other costs. Also called overheads.
Interdependence of variances	The fact that different variances may be linked by a common cause.
Investigation of variances	Examining the causes of variances with a view to introducing controls.
Key factor analysis	The technique of allocating resources between products according to contribution per unit of resource.
Limiting factor	The resource whose shortage limits the entire capacity of the business operation. Also known as the key factor.
Management accounting	The generation, presentation and interpretation of historic, budgeted and forecast information for management for the purposes of planning, control and decision-making.
Management information system (MIS)	A system providing managers at all levels of a business with the information that they need to carry out their roles.
Marginal costing	Costing system under which stocks are measured at their marginal (Variable) cost only. All fixed costs are written off as incurred.
Margin of safety	The amount by which the level of activity can fall below budget before a loss is made.
Mechanisation	closing down a production department to be replaced by a piece of machinery.
Over/under absorption (recovery)	Where the amount of overhead absorbed into cost units, using the pre-determined absorption rate, is more/less than the overheads actually incurred.
Population	The entire set of data from which a sample is selected.

Term	Description
Present value	The value at today's date of an amount of cash received/paid at some time in the future, taking account of the compound interest earned over the relevant period.
Primary data	Data gathered expressly for the purpose in hand.
Productivity	The efficiency of resource usage (particularly labour) and often measured in non-financial terms.
Random sampling	Sampling method in which every item in the population has an equal chance of being selected.
Revenue expenditure	Expenditure on goods and services that will be charged to the profit and loss account.
Sampling	Investigating less than 100% of the items in a population, in order to draw a conclusion about the population.
Secondary apportionment	The re-apportionment of service cost centres' overhead costs to production cost centres.
Secondary data	Data gathered for a purpose other than the purpose in hand.
Semi-variable costs	Costs with both a fixed and variable element.
Significance of variances	Assessing the importance of variances with a view to investigation, typically by expressing the variance as a percentage of the standard amount.
Standard cost	The planned unit cost of the products, components or services produced in a period.
Time series	A set of values recorded for some variable over a period of time.
Total absorption costing	A costing system under which stocks are measured at their total production cost (including fixed production overheads).
Total absorption costing	A costing system under which stocks are measured at their total production cost (including fixed production overheads).
Trend	The general direction in which a time series is going, once the short-term variations have been eliminated.

Term	Description
Usage	The quantity of items required for production (in the case of components or raw materials) in a given period.
Variable costs	Costs that vary in direct proportion to the level of activity.
Variance	The difference between a planned, budgeted or standard cost/revenue and the actual cost/revenue incurred.

INDEX

A

Absorption, 51, 54

Activity-based costing (ABC), 68

Additive model, 200

Allocation, 50

Apportionment, 50

Appraisal costs, 410

Asset turnover, 375

Automation, 139

Avoidable cost, 126

B

Backwards variances, 307

Balanced scorecard, 413

Basic standards, 8

Batch costs, 20

Benchmarking, 186

Breakeven analysis, 102

Business ethics, 489

C

Capacity variance, 276

Closure, 137

Cluster sampling, 207

Conformance costs, 410

Contribution, 85

Controllable variances, 316

Cost
  accounting, 14
  centres, 21
  classification, 23
  control, 184
  drivers, 68
  pools, 68
  reduction, 184
  units, 18
  variances, 234

Cost-volume-profit (CVP) analysis, 102

Critical success factors (CSFs), 413

Current ratio, 380

Cyclical variations, 193

D

Direct costs, 24

E

Efficiency, 368
  variance, 276

Ethics, 486

F

Failure costs, 409

Fixed costs, 27, 128

Fixed overhead expenditure variance, 275

Fixed overhead volume variance, 275

Flexed budgets, 41

Flexibility, 401

Flexible budgetary control, 41

Further processing, 139

Future incremental cash flow, 126

G

Gearing, 396

Gross profit margin, 376

H

High/low method, 32

I

Ideal standards, 9

Idle time, 254
  ratio, 258

Index numbers, 220

Indirect costs, 25

Innovation, 401

Interdependence of variances, 330

Inventory holding period (inventory days), 381

Investigation of variances, 324

Investment centres, 22

J

Job costs, 20

K

Key performance indicators, 414

L

Labour
    activity ratio, 258
    efficiency ratio, 258
    efficiency variance, 252
    rate variance, 251

Life cycle costing, 149, 162

Limiting factor analysis, 130

Linear regression, 214

Liquidity, 380

M

Make or buy, 135

Margin of safety, 103

Marginal costing, 80, 128

Materials
    price variance, 241
    usage variance, 241

Moving averages, 195

Multiplicative model, 202

Multi-stage sampling, 206

N

Net present cost, 159

Net Present Value (NPV), 152

Net terminal cost, 159

Non relevant costs, 127

Non-conformance costs, 409

Non-random sampling methods, 206

Normal standards, 8

O

Operating statements, 300

Overhead, 49

P

Performance indicator, 368, 402

Prevention costs, 410

Prime cost, 24

Product lifecycle, 167

Productivity, 397, 404

Professional ethics, 486

Profit
    centres, 22
    margin, 374

Profitability, 405

Q

Qualitative performance indicators, 368

Quality circles, 409

Quality of service, 401, 407

Quantitative performance indicators, 368

Quick ratio, 380

Quota sampling, 206

R

Random
    sampling, 205
    variations, 194

Ratio analysis, 369

Relevant costing, 126

Resource utilisation, 400, 405

Responsibility accounting, 330

Return on capital employed (ROCE), 372

S

Scattergraph, 194

Seasonal variations, 193, 200

Semi-variable (mixed) costs, 28

Standard
  cost, 2
  cost card, 237
  costing, 2

Stepped costs, 28

Stratified sampling, 206

Systematic sampling, 206

T

Target costing, 185

Target standards, 8

Time series analysis, 192

Total quality management (TQM), 408

Trade payables payment period (trade payable days), 382

Trade receivables collection period (trade receivable days), 381

Trend, 193

U

Uncontrollable variances, 316

Unit costs, 400, 404

V

Value
  added, 398
  analysis, 185
  engineering, 185
  enhancement, 184, 186

Variable costs, 27, 127

Variance analysis, 237

W

What if? Analysis, 388